How A
HOUSE
WORKS

Designed and edited by Redefinition, Inc.

The credits that appear on page 4 are hereby made a part of this copyright page.

Library of Congress Cataloging in Publication Data

Johnson, Duane.
     How a house works : all the things you need to know about the
inner workings of your home / by Duane Johnson ; [designed and
edited by Redefinition, Inc.].
        p.   cm.
     "Much of the material ... comes from a series of monthly essays
called "How a house works" which I write for The Family handyman
magazine"—Introd.
     Includes index.
     ISBN 0-89577-586-7
     1. Buildings—Mechanical equipment—Amateurs' manuals.
2. Dwellings—Amateurs' manuals. I. Redefinition, Inc. II. Family
handyman.   III. Title
TH6010.J64   1994
696—dc20   94-2333

THE FAMILY
Handyman

How A
HOUSE
WORKS

Duane Johnson

Illustrations by
Don Mannes
and
Ron Chamberlain

READER'S DIGEST ASSOCIATION, INC.
Pleasantville, New York/Montreal

This book was produced by Redefinition, Inc.
for The Reader's Digest Association
in cooperation with The Family Handyman Magazine.

Additional illustrations by
Alec Syme, Del Erickson, and Deborah Hutchinson

Lumber grading stamp on p. 165 used
with permission of Florida Lumber Inspection Service

If you have any questions or comments, feel free to write us at:

The Family Handyman
7900 International Drive
Suite 950
Minneapolis, MN 55425

Foreword

Every house has a life of its own, a notion of independence that my wife, Julia, and I could hardly suspect when we signed the mortgage papers and stood in the empty living room of our house. We were proud of our new domain. We rolled up our sleeves to mold the place to fit

our dreams. We painted the bedrooms, hung curtains, refinished the living and dining room floors, then settled in with a schedule of other improvements soon to follow.

But our house resisted subtly. After the hassle of climbing a ladder to take down the screens and put up the old second floor storm windows, I seriously considered replacing the upstairs sashes with new energy-efficient, double-pane windows. No more ladder climbing. After our first winter, however, we grew to like the wavy imperfections and distortions of the old glass. They were worth preserving. So I repaired the windows and storms and now religiously take out and climb the ladder every spring and fall.

Our house charmed us in other ways, too, and gradually, we began to appreciate its character. Yes, we will continue to make some needed changes, but we realize that what we want is best tempered by understanding and an appreciation of what the house can give— the same elements you find in any good relationship.

My bet is this: the more you understand the house you live in, the more you will appreciate and enjoy it, especially since you will no longer panic when minor disasters strike, such as water dripping in the attic, paint beginning to peel, or lights suddenly going out.

Most of the material for this book comes from a monthly series called "How A House Works" that I write for *The Family Handyman* magazine. These essays take you behind the scenes to examine the materials, building techniques, and design principles that make a house a worthwhile, long-lasting investment and give it a life of its own.

Although your walls cannot speak, I hope this book helps you and your house to become good partners. Not only do I want your family to thrive there, I want your house to thrive as well—to age gracefully, remain in good repair, and serve the next family well when you move on.

—DUANE JOHNSON

Contents

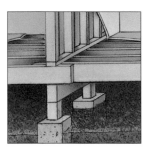

Heating & Cooling

Protecting Your Investment

Sarah's House

How does a house become a home? How does a hollow framework of lumber, drywall, nails, glass, and brick become the place in which you feel settled?

A house casts a spell the day you decide to buy it. Despite all the hard-headed, practical measures that you use to size up a new home, the decision to buy is an emotional one. A sudden spark lets you know when you've found the right house. Sure, the character of the neighborhood, schools, and being a con-

The American foursquare-style house was popular at the beginning of this century until about the 1930s.

venient distance to work, shopping, and local parks all play a role. And so, too, do the basic size and layout of the rooms, the size of the kitchen and garage, and the number of bedrooms and bathrooms.

But there's always a feature that reaches beyond the practical, that stirs the imagination and lets you know that this house is the one you want to live in. The winning feature in my home is the living room. It's unusually large for such a modest-sized house and contains a fireplace, a bay window, and a wide arch that opens to the dining room. Best of all, it has windows on three sides, making it feel bright and airy, even on cloudy days and during the winter when the sun hangs low in the southern sky.

Upon first sight I instantly imagined myself lounging comfortably in the easy chair, a fire crackling in the fireplace, entertaining friends on a cool autumn evening. Despite other drawbacks, this house would do.

For some, spaciousness alone is enough, or dramatic windows and

The Cape Cod-style house is a variation on early Colonial-period houses.

views, or a bright, modern kitchen, or a peaceful setting. No matter what it is about your house that draws the two of you together, you have high expectations that if you put down roots, at least for awhile, this house will fulfill some of your dreams. A partnership has begun.

Making a house your own

Of course, as appealing as you might find a house, it will never feel quite right until you make it yours, until you put up the first picture, paint some walls, hang new curtains, or decorate in some other way. My first move was to tear up the old, yellow shag carpet in the living room and refinish the hardwood floors. Varnished hardwood appeals a whole lot more than yellow shag carpet. Redecorating is the first step that makes a home your own.

Owning a house also becomes more personal when you grapple with some of its character flaws. Every home owner soon finds that no house is perfect, even if you built it yourself. Perhaps the living room feels drafty, the shower flows weakly because of low water pressure, or the kitchen floor has a constant squeak. Maybe the kitchen's too small, the bathrooms are too few, and the basement is too damp. Redecorating won't solve the problems. They're bigger than that. They take you beyond the surface and into the structure and mechanics of the house itself.

Everyone seems to have a "wish list" of projects, awaiting either time or money to do the job. And it's certainly satisfying to complete some of these home improvement projects and enjoy their results.

But judging from the enthusiastic talk about future changes, the planning process itself (and the discussions that surround it) seems to be one of the pleasures of owning a house, too! It's fun to imagine a new set of built-in bookcases, the refinished bathroom, or the new kitchen cabinets when you know it's not just a daydream. In the near future you can make these improvements happen.

Sometimes, though, a house will sucker you into unplanned improvements, for instance, when you fall prey to the "while you're at it" syndrome. It begins with a simple repair like replacing a leaky sink faucet in the bathroom. The new faucet looks great, but it would look a lot nicer on a new sink, so "while you're at it...". Of course, the new sink makes the old floor tile look a bit shabby and out of date. And if you retile the floor, shouldn't you retile the shower to match as well? And while you're tearing out the old shower wall, why not buy a shower faucet to match the sink faucet? And on it goes. Even when you're most vigilant, projects seem to grow!

But through it all you'll discover that your house is an extraordinarily flexible partner. It once reflected the tastes of the builder and the families that lived in it before you (and it probably still will in many subtle ways). Now, as you decorate it, repair its broken parts, and simply enjoy its features, the house begins to reflect your own unique character. It begins to feel like home, a place where you can finally hang your hat, settle in, and feel like you belong.

Sarah's house

Sarah's house is a perfect example. It sits on a corner lot a few blocks from the Mississippi River bluffs that overlook St. Paul, Minnesota.

You can't miss it. It's a massive two-story wood-frame structure with a big front porch, built about 1890.

The size gives the house a touch of grandeur, but that's somewhat misleading. The house is larger because it was built as a duplex—one modestly sized unit on each floor. When Sarah bought it, it housed five apartments. Now it has four, including the one she lives in.

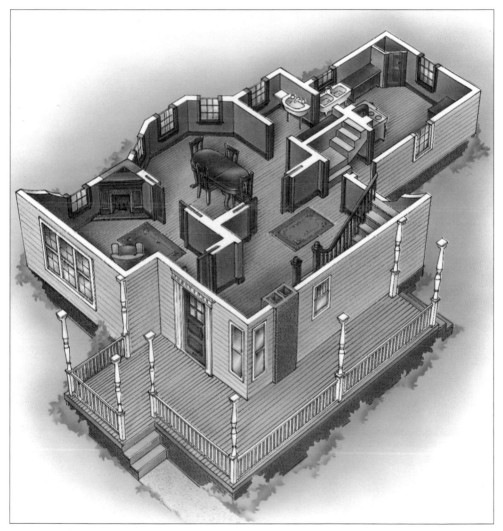

The floor plan of this 1880s house shows the everyday living areas up front and the kitchen and bathroom relegated to the rear of the house.

Old homes are by no means everyone's favorite. This one certainly wouldn't rate high on the typical home buyer's "most wanted" list. When Sarah bought it, it was the perfect picture of shabbiness. Paint was faded and peeling, the porch roof sagged, floor boards had worn bare and cracked, the steps were rickety, the railing was loose, downspouts hung askew, and the front door stuck. A tall, dying American elm still stood along the sidewalk, the last of a half dozen that once towered dramatically over the house and lawn. And all that before you got inside where other problems awaited. Sarah's house would have been a nightmare for most home owners. But Sarah's house fits. She bought it primarily for two reasons, the neighborhood and the front porch.

You rarely buy a house just for the house itself. You may buy into a neighborhood, a place that has the right combination of schools for the kids, a convenient distance to work, safety, yard space, and closeness to any wide variety of local features like parks, shopping, or community character. The character of the community was high on Sarah's list. She enjoys the older homes, as well as the people who own them and happen to share her interest. Her neighborhood is full of both. It's the kind of stable neighborhood where people who move intend to stay.

But the feature that absolutely captivated Sarah was the long, rambling front porch. The front porch spreads across the entire front of the house and around one side as well, since her house occupies a corner lot. It makes the house look dramatic, and it gives her a much wider view.

Traditionally, the front porch was first and foremost a public place, a place to see and be seen, a place to greet those coming down the sidewalk or street and be recognized in return by passersby. It was a place for conversation, news, gossip, bickering, courting, entertaining, and community affairs. In short, it was a place for neighbors to be neighbors.

Sarah loves her front porch because it perfectly reflects her sense of community. She creates an instant neighborhood when she sits out there on a summer evening, greeting folks who are walking by and, likely as not, inviting them to sit down and sip some cool lemonade. She's by no means a restoration buff out to recreate an artifact of the past. She does, however, share some ideals with the past, a perhaps optimistic and romantic notion of how a house can fit within a community.

Why did front porches disappear?

When Sarah was hunting for a house that fit her personality, she didn't have a large inventory to choose from. Homes featuring porches were desirable for less than a period of 50 years, but by about 1920 had begun to decline. And by about 1930 they had all but disappeared from the new house plans. So if you want a front porch, you have to look in older residential sections of a city or town to find that 50-year stretch of residential building history in which they were popular.

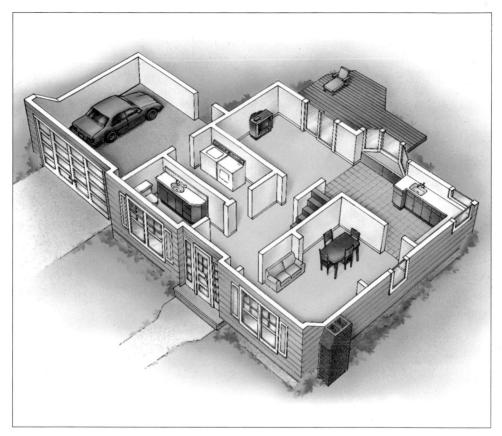

The 1990s suburban floor plan still has a formal room up front, but much of everyday life is spent in the family room at the rear. Notice how the garage and driveway dominate the front of the house.

The decline of porches corresponds almost exactly with the rise of that dominant 20th century feature, the automobile. The auto brought quick and easy mobility and gradually changed the patterns of community life.

Suddenly you could live farther from work and buy a suburban house more distant from the city center. Chances were that you no longer knew your neighbors professionally, since workplace and business acquaintances most likely lived elsewhere.

The automobile also expanded the realm of recreational and social life. You were no longer tied down to the front porch society because you could always jump in the car and visit friends and relax somewhere else (an opportunity that teenagers couldn't refuse). Your community was no longer local. It had expanded beyond the front porch, the street, and the local neighborhood. The front porch was left behind.

These social changes are reflected in home styles since about 1930. As the local neighborhood became less central to social life, houses became plainer. Floor plans were less elaborate, decoration and ornamentation both inside and out diminished, roof detailing was simplified, and popular styles returned to earlier Colonial and English-cottage roots. The front porch, no longer a popular neighborhood meeting place, disappeared.

These changes make sense, not only for the tastes of several generations past, but also for our current generation. The house is no longer the center of community life, so it doesn't have to reflect that same importance with fancier detailing (or as fancy as you could afford in those days).

After 1930, home exteriors looked quieter and more private. Gradually, the garage, which replaced the carriage house out back, moved up alongside and finally was attached to the house, reflecting further the growing importance of the automobile. In fact the trend to feature the automobile in house styling has reached a point where two- and three-car garages now visually dominate the front of a new house, much as the front porch did years ago.

The home was still the center of family life, but that life was more private, too. The old front porch reappeared about 30 years after its demise in back of the house in the form of a deck or screened porch where the family could relax in the privacy of its own back yard. Ex-panded kitchens, the recreation room, and family rooms became the focus of indoor family life, replacing the more formal living room and front parlor of early days. The living room is still there, but it's little used by many families.

Changing popular tastes and lifestyles not only led to new generations of houses, but reduced the demand for homes of the past and their neighborhoods. As house values decreased, upkeep slacked off and many once handsome houses fell into disrepair. Larger ones were divided into small apartments, and many were simply torn down.

But people in some areas resisted. Sarah's neighborhood was one of those. When she bought the old corner house, she wasn't on a crusade to restore the past to some former glory. She, like everyone else, was simply looking for a comfortable place to live, a neighborhood and a house to fit her personality and character.

Making it work

Owning an older home requires a lot of give and take and certainly some tender loving care to make it successful. Sarah got her dramatic front porch, a bay window with fancy glass, and some 10-foot-high ceilings, but she also got a bunch of headaches. The improvement list for an old house is considerably longer than for a new one. That's the curse of an old house, and few home owners are willing to accept the challenge. (And those who do may try it only once!)

Improvements came slowly. Sarah put her house on a "ten" year plan, which means she makes improvements as she finds money to do them. Roof replacement and gutter and downspout repair came first, because failure to divert rainwater will rot the frame and cause the foundation to settle. Both of these are major league problems that you want to avoid at all costs. Then she pulled the rotting and dilapidated porch back into shape because it had suffered years of unuse and neglect. But five years passed before the exterior siding received its much needed coat of paint, a job that restored the luster of the old corner house.

On the inside work began with jacking and bracing a badly sagging floor. This made the doors on the two floors fit better again, but it also cracked the plaster walls. No matter, the plaster already had cracks and wall repair came later anyway. The plumbing fixtures in the bathrooms and kitchens are old and clunky, but they don't leak and will serve for the time being.

Like every other home owner, Sarah has a list of projects that lie ahead. But you never get the impression that the house is unfinished. Whether chatting on the front porch or stepping inside the living room, you immediately sense the comfort, graciousness, and good will.

Sarah's house works. It has come to fit her character and they both make you feel at home.

BUILDING A SOUND HOUSE

As a kid I was fascinated by the house built on the vacant lot down the street. It began as a big hole in the ground. A few days later there was a concrete basement. Over the next couple days carpenters assembled a bewildering array of lumber till the bleak skeleton of the house stood complete, awaiting a skin. Soon wood siding enclosed the exterior and drywall panels divided the inside into a kitchen, living room, bedrooms, and bathrooms. Windows and doors closed it up for good and shut me out. Then a new family moved in. I still watch new homes go up with the boyhood fascination of long ago. I marvel that the pile of lumber, plywood, insulation, concrete, and glass somehow becomes a place to live.

The pros have their own ways of doing it. Through their insights you can understand the materials and building techniques that make a house strong, durable, and stylish. You'll have to wade through some carpentry lingo at first, but then armed with that vocabulary, you can take an historical tour of building techniques up to the present, where change still goes on.

Builders' hands aren't the only things that shape houses. Building codes also play an important role, insuring that our homes are safe, solid, and long-lasting. Engineers get into the act when it comes to figuring out just how strong the parts have to be to withstand the harshest winds and wildest  birthday parties. And architects play an influential role when it comes to shaping homes with wide popularity and appeal.

Finally, a sound house depends upon the proper utilization of good materials, like the concrete foundation that most homes rest upon and quality components like doors and windows. All these elements work together to make a house durable and trouble-free.

The Basic Frame House

Anatomy of a house

My first days as a rookie carpenter were intimidating. I stood chatting with carpentry pros, barely understanding a word they said but pretending that I knew the difference between wood that went by the names of *plates, sills,* and *studs.* Good grief, these pieces of lumber all looked like 2x4s to me, but what was the difference?

It was an impressive experience all the same, especially picking up the lingo. One day you're standing there beside a chaotic pile of lumber that they say will be a house. You can't believe it. Only a month later, standing beside another pile of lumber that will form the next house, the confusion clears. You are able to spot the different pieces and can imagine them already nailed into place. The house-building process has begun.

Building a house

Construction work is more specialized now, with different skilled trades handling various parts of the project. The carpenters these days don't show up until the foundation is in. Usually the foundation is made from *poured concrete* or concrete blocks. Generally, a basement is constructed in northern homes but not in southern and western homes.

The carpenters are stars of the construction job because the house takes shape under their hands. They convert the big stack of lumber into a strong, rigid *frame,* the skeleton of the house that supports the rest of its parts. Most of the wood they use has been milled to standard sizes, 2x4, 2x6, 2x10, and so on. Here's where it gets confusing. These sizes represent only labels, not the actual dimensions of the lumber. A 2x4 actually measures 1½ inches by 3½ inches and a 2x6 measures 1½ inches by 5½. But a 2x10 measures only 1½ inches by 9¼ inches. And these dimensions are not always precise. For exact work, even carpenters measure their lumber (*page 188*).

First they lay 2x6 *sill plates* on the concrete foundation. These sill plates have to be rot resistant, because they'll get damp and be subject to decay. Usually a house needs a *beam,* a heavy, strong timber (or steel beam), set in the middle to support the floor (*facing page*).

Next the carpenters lay the *floor joists,* usually 2x10s, in a grid pattern across the sills and beam. These are generally spaced every 16 inches, called 16 inches "on center," that is, the distance from the center of the narrow edge of one joist to the same point on the next joist is 16 inches. They then nail 4x8-foot sheets of plywood or other strong panels to these joists to form the *subfloor.* Often they'll glue down these pan-

THE BASIC PARTS OF A HOUSE'S STRUCTURE

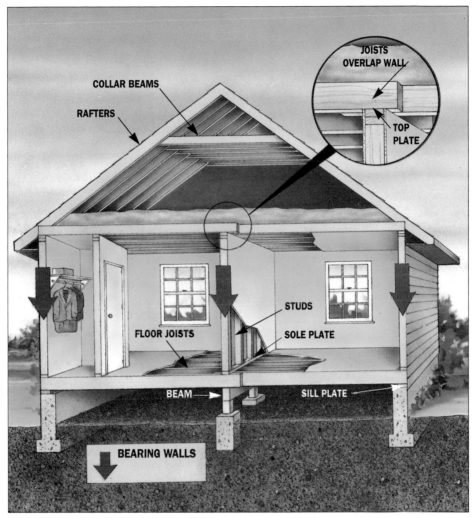

Studs, joists, rafters, and beams all work together to support the frame of a house.

els as well, to avoid the problem of squeaky floors.

With the first platform complete, they're ready to build the dramatic part—the walls. These the carpenters assemble from 2x4s laid on the floor. They nail the vertical 2x4s called *studs* (usually about 8-feet long) to horizontal 2x4s called the *top* and *sole* plates. They also include special beams called *headers* that span openings for doors and windows. Then the builders tilt the whole framework up, plumb it with a level, brace it, and nail it in place. This stage goes quickly, so you soon see the house taking shape. Next they top the walls with another horizontal set of joists to make the ceiling and sometimes the floor above if there's to be a second level.

The crowning touch is the roof. Traditionally roofs were framed by hand with 2x6 or stronger *rafters*, the lumber set at an angle to create the roof slope. *Collar ties* or beams helped keep them rigid. But more often these days you'll see roofs framed with *trusses*, a triangular-shaped frame of 2x4s with 2x4 webbing fastened in between to make them strong and rigid. Truss roofs are faster and easier to assemble than hand-framed roofs, so most pros have switched to them.

Once the frame is complete, the carpenters cover the roof and walls with 4x8 wood panels called *sheathing*. These panels permanently brace the walls and roof and provide a nailing base for siding and shingles. These are the crucial materials that make the house weathertight and attractive.

Generally either the carpenters or roofing specialists nail on the asphalt or wood shingles as quickly as possible, because rain at this stage will delay the work inside. Before putting on the siding (wood, vinyl, brick, stucco, etc.), the carpenters install the exterior doors and windows. Carpenters simply nail them in place, making sure they're all level, plumb, and square (perfectly horizontal and vertical).

The outer shell of the house is complete. Now the carpenters leave and let the next group of specialists take over. The electrical, plumbing,

and heating pros all move in and install the hardware that runs inside the walls. The exterior walls and attic are filled with *insulation* and the ceilings and walls covered by a plastic *vapor retarder*. And finally the drywall crew comes in and screws ½-inch or ⅝-inch thick *drywall* (pure gypsum covered on the front and back with heavy paper) to the walls and ceilings.

This is a messy period, but after the walls are smooth and painted, the finish carpentry can begin. Finish work includes installing the wood trimwork around the windows and doors, laying wood, vinyl, tile, and carpet flooring, hanging cabinets and interior doors, and any other decorative work.

The search for a better wall

Building was not always done this way. To get an idea of how these techniques evolved, consider the history of one part of a house's frame—the wall.

The trail of old walls rendered obsolete extends all the way back to the Colonial period. They're part of a bigger story that combines European traditions, timely innovations and inventions, and the vast forest resources of the United States and Canada.

To European settlers during the first 200 years or so of colonial life, "home sweet home" looked something like the structure you see here (*facing page*). Although houses during the first few decades were primitive earth dugouts and bark houses, Old World timber-framing traditions followed the settlers, who took advantage of North America's vast timber re-

AN EARLY COLONIAL TIMBER-FRAME HOUSE

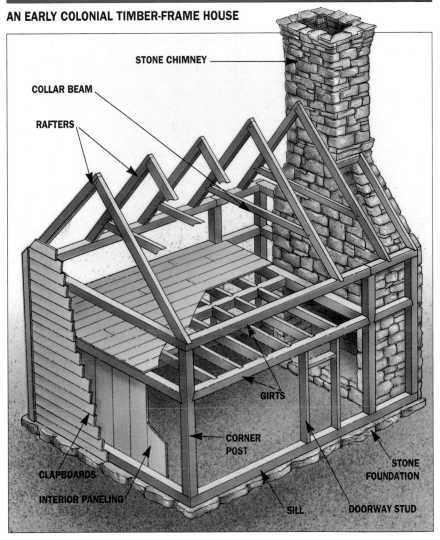

STONE CHIMNEY

COLLAR BEAM

RAFTERS

GIRTS

CORNER POST

STONE FOUNDATION

CLAPBOARDS

INTERIOR PANELING

SILL

DOORWAY STUD

Timber framing relies on strong posts and beams to support the roof, walls, and floors. Colonists often filled the wall with clay and straw to block the wind. Later they added a layer of exterior board sheathing under the clapboards.

sources. Several other styles of building became common later on, including log cabins and brick walls, but houses were most typically framed with heavy timber.

The illustration (*above*) shows an economy model, complete with that era's "central heating," the stone fireplace built in one end of the house. Thick beams rested on sturdy posts, which supported the weight of the entire structure. The forests supplied plenty of good building material, so strength was no problem for the settlers. Many timber-frame buildings standing today are more than 200 years old.

Despite their strength, early timber-frame walls required a lot of maintenance and were too cold and drafty to be comfortable. Following European traditions, those early walls consisted of sticks and branches that were coated with mud or plaster and then woven together between the timber posts. These walls didn't have to support the house's weight; they just had to keep the wind and snow and other bad weather out. This wall left the timber framing exposed, a style we see copied on the exposed "beam"-and-stucco exteriors of some contemporary houses, although this version is purely decorative.

Harsh weather played havoc with these walls, causing the timbers to constantly expand and contract, leaving gaping holes and cracks for the family to regularly fill. Eventually, the colonists covered the walls with a horizontal layer of boards, called *clapboards*, to shut out the worst weather and protect the frame of the house. Then they filled the walls with clay and straw or brick to block the wind and bad weather.

As walls became more refined, they added a layer of interlocking boards under the clapboards to act as sheathing and to help block the wind. They also eliminated the wall fill. On the interior walls, they used wood paneling, plaster, or both, often erecting vertical studs between the top horizontal beams, called *girts*, to act as a nailing base for interior and exterior walls.

As the walls on these houses became more sophisticated, houses became more comfortable, though you still wouldn't want to spend a harsh winter in them. But notice that the main elements of current framing practice were already present—studs, sheathing, and siding.

Timber framing had one major weakness that proved to be its undoing: it was time consuming to build a house this way. Early timbers had to be shaped with axes and other hand tools, though river-powered sawmills later prepared timbers more quickly. And the builder couldn't quickly slap timber joints together with nails. These had to be specially cut, fitted, and fastened with wooden pegs, using hand tools like hammers, saws, chisels, planes, and augers, a type of drill.

The rise of balloon framing

Timber-frame houses, as they are now custom built to simulate the ones early colonists lived in, carry a distinct traditional flavor that's extraordinarily attractive to many modern home buyers who appreciate the massive, hand-crafted superstructure that's left exposed on the interior. However, in the past, as well as now, timber framing was expensive. Wood was relatively cheap, but the skilled labor needed to build the house wasn't.

Three inventions lowered the cost of building a house and brought the age of timber framing to an end: the machine-cut nail, the steam-powered sawmill, and balloon framing (*page 24*).

It's surprising that so small an item as a nail could have so much impact on building methods. But before machines began stamping out nails in 1790, nails were hand-forged one at a time, a labor-intensive and expensive process. By the early 1800s, machines were mass-producing nails, making them cheaper. During that same period, inventors harnessed steam power to the circular saw. Steam power freed lumber mills from their dependency upon rivers for water power, so sawyers could mill their lumber just about anywhere. More standard-size lumber became readily available, if not locally, then by freight car from the expanding railway system.

Finally, in 1833, a whole new type of frame, especially suited to small buildings, appeared in Chicago—the *balloon frame*. It's hard to overstate just how radically the balloon frame changed building practices in the United States. It swept away the timber frame within 50 years, so it's unlikely you've ever lived in a timber-frame house and perhaps have never seen one except as a historical restoration.

Why such a dramatic switch? Just look at the advantages. The balloon frame used light, easily handled lengths of lumber—no board was more than 2 inches thick. That eliminated heavy timbers and difficult joints of timber framing, since the builders could quickly nail the slimmer lumber. Using standardized lumber and nails, one or two people of mod-

erate skill could assemble the frame of an entire house with only a hammer and saw. More people could afford better houses, and they could build them themselves, maintaining a tradition of self-sufficiency that continues today in North Americans' enthusiasm for do-it-yourself projects.

Balloon-framing techniques were quite simple. Timber-frame walls were built much stronger than they needed to be and therefore were a waste of wood. But with balloon framing, two studs nailed together were adequate for a corner and were much easier to handle than a large timber. And each stud in the wall could carry part of the roof and floor load. The sheathing was still needed to block wind, but now it did double duty. It also became a brace for the stud frame and tied the entire wall together in a strong but relatively lightweight unit.

Balloon framing caught on fast. By 1890 you could buy everything you needed for a house from Sears Roebuck or some other catalog company. Balloon framing made wall building more economical, although the walls as yet were not much warmer than timber-frame walls. These houses were still drafty by today's standards. Builders improved the walls by nailing paper between the sheathing and siding to block the wind. Central heating, more common after 1900, made a big step toward improving comfort, too.

Platform framing takes over
Balloon framing dominated building practices until the late 1940s,

BALLOON-FRAME CONSTRUCTION

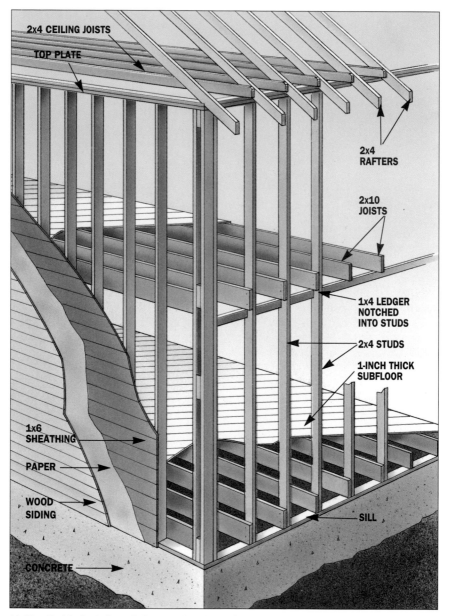

2x4 CEILING JOISTS

TOP PLATE

2x4 RAFTERS

2x10 JOISTS

1x4 LEDGER NOTCHED INTO STUDS

2x4 STUDS

1-INCH THICK SUBFLOOR

1x6 SHEATHING

PAPER

WOOD SIDING

SILL

CONCRETE

Lighter 2x4-inch studs and plates replaced heavier posts and beams in balloon-frame buildings. Wood sheathing stiffens the wall. The second-floor joists hang on a 1x4-inch support board, called a *ledger*, that's notched into the studs.

when *platform framing* became the residential standard that is still used today (*right*). It eliminated balloon framing (*left*) in the short space of about 15 years.

Again, the reason was economy. Less expensive 8-foot studs replaced most of the more expensive 12- to 18-foot studs required for balloon framing. And building one wall at a time on top of its own floor (the "platform" from which this building technique gets its name) was faster and less expensive.

Of course, newer is not always better in all ways. Balloon-frame houses—and, for that matter, timber-frame houses—are inherently stronger than platform framing. But strength was never the issue—cost was. Engineers now scientifically calculate building standards, a process that once was a combination of informed practice and experience. Building officials pared down or beefed up their rules, called *codes*, to comply with the new standards of platform framing.

Recently, our greater focus on energy conservation has led us to place an entirely new burden on our platform frame walls: energy efficiency. Now, in addition to strength, we expect them to provide warm comfort during the winter and cool comfort during the summer at an economical price.

At first, the challenge seemed easy to meet. Those stud spaces are perfect cavities for insulation. Much as the colonials filled their walls with mud, straw, and bricks, we now fill the walls of platform- and balloon-frame houses with various natural and synthetic insulating materials. But filling the hollow wall spaces

PLATFORM-FRAME CONSTRUCTION

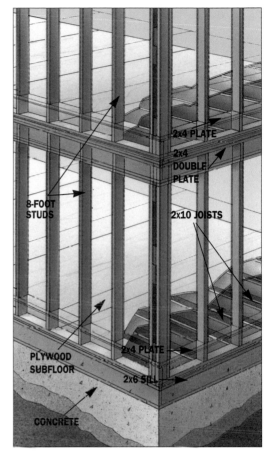

The studs extend only one floor and support the platform above.

isn't always enough to meet the energy conservation standards demanded of today's newest houses. Builders increase energy savings (and the cost of the house) by using wider 2x6-inch studs and thicker insulation, or by wrapping standard walls made of 2x4 studs with a layer of rigid insulated sheathing in place of the old wooden version.

A new problem: moisture

But boosting the energy efficiency of the walls has created a new, unexpected set of problems that continues to vex both builders and home owners—moisture buildup in the house and the walls and the increased cost of stopping it.

Excess moisture is a nuisance when it condenses on windows, but it becomes a major problem when it collects in walls and causes rot. Those older, uninsulated walls were leaky enough to allow air to circulate and dry out moisture long before rot could set in. That's one reason the walls lasted so long. Before about 1950, when builders generally left stud walls uninsulated and hollow, rot wasn't much of a problem. Construction methods inevitably left enough cracks between building materials to allow air to circulate through walls and keep them dry. This was good—as long as wood can dry out reasonably soon after getting wet, it will remain strong and last almost indefinitely.

But look what happens when you stuff those stud cavities with insulation. Insulation traps the air so heat can't escape easily. So far, so good. But if moisture gets into these walls, the insulation will trap it, too. And there's the problem. When the studs and sheathing in the walls are damp for too long, they'll rot, leaving a difficult, costly repair.

Besides insulation, two other factors contribute to moisture problems. First, builders use fairly airtight materials such as plywood and rigid insulation for exterior sheathing jobs. Both make it tougher for moisture to escape. The old sheathing made from boards (usually 1x6 inches) dried out quickly because it leaked air like a sieve.

Second, insulation itself dramatically alters the climate inside a wall. Imagine a wall without insulation. On a cold day, the house's heat would move right out through the walls. As the heat escapes, it warms the outer wood sheathing. But with insulation, the sheathing doesn't warm up. It remains cold, almost the same temperature as outdoors. Like window glass on a very cold day, the cold sheathing will cause moisture in the trapped air to condense or even freeze on it, eventually soaking it. If the wood doesn't get the chance to dry out during warmer weather, fungal growth and rot will surely begin.

Enter the vapor retarder

Before you start anxiously eyeing your insulated walls, wondering if a happy fungal colony is busily living it up inside, remember that good builders have come up with at least partial solutions. The most common one is the *vapor retarder* (sometimes called vapor barrier). This is most often a sheet of plastic stapled over the insulation before the drywall is installed (*facing page*). A vapor retarder doesn't have to be plastic. It can be aluminum foil or even certain kinds of paint—anything that radically slows down the movement of moisture.

Vapor retarders do a good job of stopping humidity, which moves right through highly permeable (water vapor passes easily through) wall materials such as drywall. But humid air can do an end run around the retarder by blowing through cracks along the floor or ceiling, around

ENERGY-EFFICIENT WOOD-FRAME WALL CONSTRUCTION

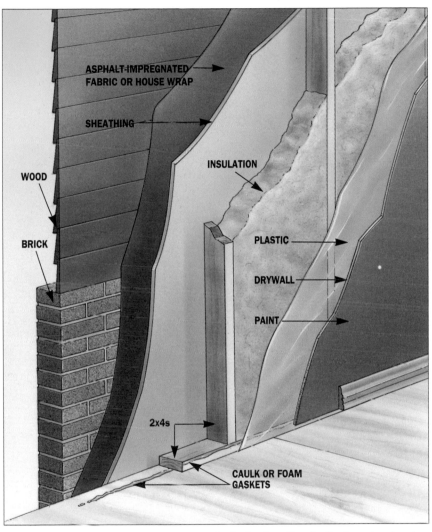

ASPHALT-IMPREGNATED FABRIC OR HOUSE WRAP

SHEATHING

INSULATION

WOOD

BRICK

PLASTIC

DRYWALL

PAINT

2x4s

CAULK OR FOAM GASKETS

An energy-efficient stud wall needs a vapor retarder (such as the plastic shown here) and caulking or gaskets to keep moisture out.

window and door frames, or through gaps around electrical outlets.

Unfortunately, studies have shown that unless builders take painstaking care, plastic doesn't work well to stop air leaks. More often now, well-informed builders rely on airtight construction techniques such as laying rubber gaskets under the bottom of wall framing and behind drywall edges, sealing holes and gaps with insulating foam, and caulking cracks. In fact, even if the builder failed to make the effort, you can still stop many of those leaks yourself after the house is built by using expandable foam and caulk.

No simple solutions

If walls could talk, they would tell us that living in an energy-efficient world is complex. Vapor retarders are doing one thing and air barriers are doing another. Then there is another building material, called a *house wrap*, that manufacturers have designed as air barriers. Rather than caulking your house to make it airtight, you can wrap it tight. Often, builders surround a newly sheathed house with what looks like huge sheets of paper before they add siding. Like plastic, this material stops airflow. But unlike plastic, it allows humidity to pass through.

This water vapor movement is crucial for most walls. At some time, moisture will probably work its way into the wall. To play it safe, the walls must have a way to dry out. The vapor retarder on the inside of the wall has a very low permeability, so it will not let much moisture through. Ideally, materials on the other side of the wall cavity should have higher permeability so moisture can escape to the outside.

But in practice there is one other complication to this line of reasoning. Seasonal temperature changes fool vapor retarders all the time. The general rule for vapor retarders is to place them on the warm side of the wall. They're supposed to block moisture from infiltrating from the warm, humid side. Well, builders in colder northern regions naturally assume that the warm side of the wall means the inside. After all, they want to keep high indoor humidity out of the wall during the winter. But builders in the deep south might find that strategy a bit backwards. They cool the inside of their houses more than they heat them, so for those folks, the predominantly warm, humid side in many cases is the exterior.

In either case, when the seasons change, some northerners turn on their air conditioners while some southerners turn on their furnaces or heat pumps. During that period, the warm side of the wall changes, meaning the vapor retarder ends up on the wrong side of the insulation. Often the walls start absorbing moisture, which dries out when the seasons change.

You probably won't have to worry about rotting walls because most houses are not as airtight as they could be. But as builders push toward higher performance, refining wood stud walls to meet the challenge gets more expensive.

The house of the future?

A few builders are beginning to look for less costly building methods to replace traditional stud framing. One method involves a curious sandwich-like package called a *stress-skin panel*. These panels (*facing page*) get their name from the waferboard panels that form their "skin" and because the sandwich construction allows them to withstand considerable stress.

Manufacturers have come up with several designs of these panels,

STRESS-SKIN PANEL WALLS

Stress-skin panels block moisture movement, insulate well, and, when caulked in place, make airtight walls.

ticular region, and they leave channels and gaps through the foam core of the panels so the builder can run wiring and plumbing.

These walls handle moisture well. A vapor retarder isn't needed because the insulation is waterproof. Moisture cannot get in from either the inside or the outside. And the wood panels make good fastening surfaces for the drywall on the inside and for the siding on the outside.

Once complete, you cannot distinguish houses made with stress-skin panels from houses with traditional stud frames. Although they cost about 5 to 10 percent more, stress-skin panel houses are easier to make airtight and energy efficient, so some home owners are willing to foot the extra cost. The hope is that energy savings and higher resale value will make it worthwhile.

Ironically, the new stress-skin panels are helping to revive an old style of building—timber-frame houses. Timber framing practically disappeared because it was a time-consuming method and therefore too costly. These houses are still expensive, because of the timber framing, but now builders wrap their timber frames with stress-skin panels to speed up the building process and lower the overall cost.

but they all rely on an insulation core, usually expanded polystyrene, with a ½-inch sheet of waferboard permanently bonded to each side. This assembly, sometimes reinforced with a stud every 4 feet, is strong enough to support the roof and the floors of a house. In fact, some builders build the roof itself with stress-skin panels. Manufacturers tailor the thickness of the panels to make them fit the building needs of a par-

29

Stairs and the 8-foot Ceiling

Rules we live by

Not long ago, while visiting my brother, I caught my foot on the top step of his second floor stairway, stumbled, and almost fell. I admit I was in a hurry and wasn't paying much attention to the stairs, but I was also aware that the last step seemed a little off; it wasn't quite where it was supposed to be.

Sure enough, a tape measure proved that the last step was a half an inch shorter than the others. My feet hadn't betrayed me. They were accustomed to the rhythm of the stairs up to the final step. The builder had broken one of the basic rules of stair construction: the rise in a stairway—the vertical face at the front of each step, called a *riser*, (*facing page*)—can vary no more than ⅜ inch between two steps. (Some building codes allow only a ³⁄₁₆-inch variation.) Your feet know that small changes make a big difference!

This example is one of dozens of building rules and standards that have become commonplace in today's houses. Many rules are for safety and strength. You will find most of these rules written into building codes. Others remain informal, having evolved through practice and standardized building materials. Stair dimensions and the standard 8-foot ceiling are two good examples of each type of rule.

Safe stairway dimensions

Stairway construction has become totally regulated by building codes. And for good reason. Accidents on stairways account for nearly a million injuries per year in the United States. Yet most home owners seldom think about their stairs as they dash up and down between floors. A well-designed stairway will hardly be noticed except perhaps as decoration. But to an architect, a stairway hardly noticed means a stairway that's working like a finely tuned machine. It's neither too steep nor too gradual, the handrail is at the right height and feels comfortable, and the *treads*, the horizontal parts where you put your feet, are firm and secure underfoot.

Of course, a good design never occurs by chance. It is the result of experience and experimentation to find the most comfortable and least hazardous arrangement. We now live with the results. Check your own stairs. If you measure the riser of a step, you'll find that it falls between 6½ and 7½ inches. Any step higher than this forces you to lift your foot too far for ease and comfort. You'll

PARTS OF A TYPICAL STAIRWAY

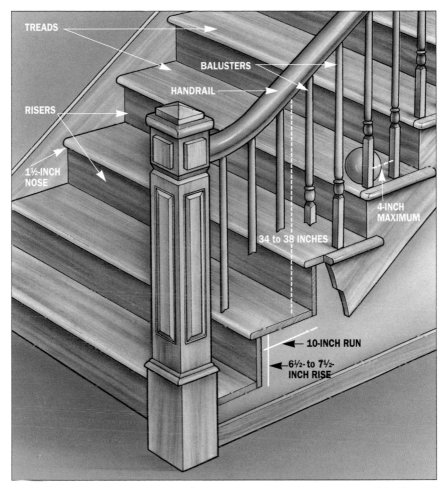

TREADS

BALUSTERS

HANDRAIL

RISERS

1½-INCH NOSE

4-INCH MAXIMUM

34 to 38 INCHES

10-INCH RUN

6½- to 7½- INCH RISE

Stairs are designed for the comfort and safety of an average person. The sum of the rise and run should be 17 to 18 inches, the nose from 1 to 1½ inches, and the height of the handrail from 34 to 38 inches.

feel as if you're climbing a ladder. In fact, you may feel safer backing down such a stairway as if it were a ladder! (You may encounter such stairs with 8-inch risers leading to an attic because they have one big advantage—they require less space. They get you up to the next level using fewer steps, so they need less floor space.) On the other hand, if the rise is less than 6½ inches (and the width of the tread remains the same), you'll find yourself taking tiny steps, which is also awkward.

Now measure the tread. When you subtract the *nose*, the small portion of the step that overhangs the riser, the result, called the *run*, will be between 10 and 11 inches. This measurement reflects a normal, comfortable stride. With a narrower tread, your foot won't fit on the step, making you tiptoe up, and you'll probably kick the risers as you go. If the treads are wider (and the rise is the same), you will have to take longer strides. Either extreme may cause you to trip.

The stair design rule

The rise and the run have to work together to make a comfortable step. One design rule of thumb is this: the rise plus the run should equal between 17 and 18 inches. This also means the rise could be as low as 4 inches (the minimum allowable in most building codes) and the run 14 inches. You'll find a rise and run like this mostly outdoors at entrances to public buildings and monuments. However, you will not find it inside a house. At 4 inches of rise per step, it would take a lot of steps and a lot of stairway space to get up one floor.

Perhaps the easiest way to trip someone is to vary the rise within a single flight of stairs. A variation in tread width can do it, too. Although unconscious of it, your feet are extremely sensitive to any variations in the pattern of a staircase. Once your feet hit a rhythm, they expect to stay in that cadence, with little margin of error. Many architects find the ⅜-inch variance that some building codes allow too liberal, and so they design within the smaller tolerance of 3/16 inch allowed by other codes.

The final design element is the stair nose. While it doesn't add to the run measurement, it gives your foot a little bonus space on each tread, which makes stair climbing easier for the average person. But what if you are not an average person? Then that nose can catch a toe and cause a fall. For this reason the noses on public stairways now tend to be angled (*below*) so they're less likely to catch a foot and cause an accident.

But that doesn't completely solve the problem. Stairways simply can't be designed to fit everyone perfectly. The standards are based on an average person, who turns out to be about 5 feet, 8 inches tall. Of course, that's tall for a woman and short for a man, tall for some ethnic

PUBLIC STAIRWAY REQUIREMENTS

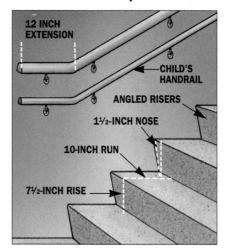

Public stairways increase safety by angling risers to avoid catching toes, adding a lower handrail for easier gripping by children, and extending handrails 12 inches at the top and bottom to help with the final step.

groups, short for others, and gigantic for children.

The role of the handrail

Since no stair design works perfectly for everyone, stairways have come to rely on the handrail to provide a margin of safety. It gives your legs and feet a hand. It's an essential element to help you maintain balance, especially when walking down stairs. The building code regulates handrails closely to make sure they're always within easy grabbing range. They must be securely fastened between 34 and 38 inches above the tread nose (codes vary), be shaped to easily fit a hand's grasp, and be clear from obstruction so a hand can slide up and down them freely. Most building codes also require that the railing be able to be grasped from below to help a person break a fall by grabbing on.

On stairways with an open side, the handrail also must serve as a guardrail, which means that it has to have intermediate rails, called *balusters*, or some other device so that a sphere 4 inches in diameter cannot pass through, according to the Uniform Building Code. A child is not supposed to be able to stick his or her head between the balusters or through any other opening.

Until recently, building codes allowed a 6-inch space between balusters, so most of the time you'll see guardrails on stairways with this wider spacing. The Standard Building Code, followed by most southern states, still retains the 6-inch rule. However, many architects and builders have long considered 6 inches too generous and moved to a closer spacing even before building codes changed to the 4-inch maximum in most of the country.

Public stairways are even more closely regulated than private stairs, so they may have some safety features you don't have in your house, such as nonskid treads and nosing, handrail extensions at both the top and bottom, and better lighting in the stairway. In general, architects and contractors incorporate the rules we live by that govern stair safety and comfort into every project they build. But some of the rules vary in different regions, so if building or remodeling a stairway is part of a renovation project at your house, be sure to check local building codes.

The 8-foot ceiling

In contrast to tightly regulated stairways, the standards that say your ceiling will hang about 96 inches above the floor evolved much more informally. When talking about 8-foot ceilings, you're talking economy of effort and saving money.

There's no particular aesthetic magic to the 8-foot measurement. Many people prefer 9- or even 10-foot ceilings in some rooms. Certainly high ceilings look grander and lend themselves to more spectacular windows, moldings, and other decorations. But 8-foot ceilings work just fine in average rooms. They're high enough to be out of reach (the average reach for design purposes is about 7 feet, 6 inches) and not feel confining. And they're low enough to lend a feeling of coziness to a room, conserve space, and make cooling and heating more efficient because there's less air in the room to cool and heat.

TYPICAL 8-FOOT CEILING

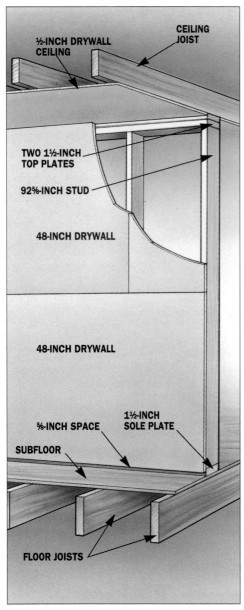

½-INCH DRYWALL CEILING

CEILING JOIST

TWO 1½-INCH TOP PLATES

92⅝-INCH STUD

48-INCH DRYWALL

48-INCH DRYWALL

⅝-INCH SPACE

1½-INCH SOLE PLATE

SUBFLOOR

FLOOR JOISTS

An 8-foot ceiling economizes on material and space and fits the standard 4x8-foot sheet of drywall.

Of course, if you plan a large room for your house, say anything larger than 30 feet on a side, the 8-foot ceiling could seem as low and oppressive as the ceiling in a basement bowling alley. This should serve as a caution if you ever want to knock out a wall to combine two rooms into one. The 8-foot ceilings that worked so well in the smaller rooms can feel cavelike and monotonous in the single larger room if it is not interrupted by an archway or some other visual break between the two rooms.

The standard 8-foot ceiling

Setting aesthetic concerns aside for just a moment, the primary charm of the 8-foot ceiling lies in how kindly it treats the pocketbook. Since the rise of platform framing (*page 25*), the 8-foot ceiling has proven less expensive to build in terms of labor and materials.

You would also suppose that it would be cheapest to build with 8-foot studs, a convenient standard lumber length. Well, that's not the case. Look at the standard 8-foot ceiling construction detail (*left*). Remember, the typical wall contains three 2x4 plates in addition to the stud: two top plates and one sole plate. These add 4½ inches to the height of the wall, which, when added to an 8-foot stud, makes the odd total height of 8 feet, 4½ inches, or 100½ inches. The combined depth of these three 2x4s equals 4½ inches, not 6 inches, because a 2x4 is not actually 2 inches by 4 inches but 1½ inches by 3½ inches. See "Wood and Board" (*page 188*) for a more detailed explanation of why this is so.

Some 40 to 50 years ago, when plaster was used for the wall finish, plasterers didn't care whether the wall height was 8 feet, 9 feet, or any odd size. Their technique of using wood *lath*, small boards nailed close together horizontally across the studs, adapted well to any dimension, including curves. But that wasn't the case with drywall as it became the norm in houses during the 1940s. Drywall is produced in standard-size 4x8-foot sheets, exactly as plywood is. Multiple 4-foot sizes fit well into the standard spacing of wall studs—16 inches on center and 24 inches on center. (Three 16-inch stud spaces and two 24-inch stud spaces equal 4 feet, the width of the narrow side of one drywall panel.)

Drywall installers usually fasten the drywall sheets horizontally to the studs. Even if fastened vertically, drywall hung on a wall built with 8-foot studs would leave a gap because of the added 4½-inch depth of the top and sole plates. Filling that gap would require a lot of extra time to cut and add a narrow piece of drywall and to cover and smooth out the extra joint. And all that would mean greater expense.

So the building industry solved the problem by simply creating a new standard stud length of 92⅝ inches. This, combined with the 4½-inch depth of the top and sole plates, leaves a 1⅛-inch gap after two 4-foot drywall panels are installed. About half of that space is taken by the half-inch thickness of the drywall ceiling (*facing page*), leaving just a ⅝-inch gap at the bottom (drywallers hang the top sheet first), just enough room to insert a wedge to pry the bottom sheet up tightly to the top one. The ⅝ inch is then covered by the flooring or hidden behind baseboards. That's why you'll find most lumberyards and home centers selling 92⅝-inch 2x4s right next to the 8-footers.

Things change, though

Recently, higher ceilings have regained popularity, perhaps in appreciation of older design traditions and a renewed aesthetic sense of room proportions.

Beyond doubt, higher ceilings are an attractive design option. They are becoming more common in expensive houses, but sometimes can also be found in more modest houses, too. A builder told me he charges about $400 per room for an extra foot, so higher ceilings have again become another design feature for home buyers to consider, much like fireplaces, foyers, and fancy woodwork.

Perhaps the 8-foot ceiling isn't quite the standard it was a few years ago. Unlike some standards such as those for stairs, which cannot be changed without changing building codes, this one can be changed. The 8-foot ceiling is an economy standard, arrived at with the pocketbook in mind, but you can certainly have a higher ceiling if you are willing to pay a higher price.

Why Houses Don't Fall Down

How the parts work together

With all the experience and engineering that has gone into the design of a house's structure, you don't expect it to fall down. Sure, old roofs may sag, floors bulge and creak, and walls begin to lean, but we'll eventually either fix them or tear them down and start over. We expect our houses to be forever resilient—withstanding storms, heat and cold, the periodic pounding of our children, and even our own occasionally misguided remodeling efforts.

But for a young fellow named Smith the unexpected happened. A local newspaper reported that while he ". . . was dismantling the second story of his house for purposes of remodeling it, he gave such a solid whack at the chimney that the house collapsed in a cloud of dust and rubble. Smith, who had been standing in the second-story bathroom, ended up in the first-floor kitchen, still standing, still holding the sledgehammer...."

Unfortunately, we don't know why Smith got such a bad break. Houses rarely collapse. Building codes require that their design and construction meet basic engineering and strength standards. If you find signs of weakness or failure in your house—for example, cracked foundations and walls, parted drywall, door jambs out of square so doors won't close, dipping floors, or sagging roofs—it's a good idea to find out what the problem is and whether it needs to be corrected.

How beams carry weight

The roof isn't ordinarily thought of as a beam, since it is sloped rather than perfectly horizontal, but the vast majority of roofs work like one. (Occasionally, a roof has two or more beams.) This beam spans from one exterior wall to the other, with perhaps a support somewhere near the middle. A roof, in addition to keeping rain, snow, cold, heat, insects, and other species of wildlife out, also has to be strong. It has to support its own weight—the lumber, sheathing, and up to three layers of shingles (called the *dead load*)—plus the weight of someone climbing up there to clean the gutters and any extra weight from accumulated snow and ice or the force of the wind (the *live load*).

The illustration (*facing page*) shows the effect of the forces involved. The weight on an angled roof is usually transferred out to the walls. To accomplish this, the triangular roof framing withstands a great deal of tension and stress.

HOW A HOUSE SUPPORTS ITS WEIGHT

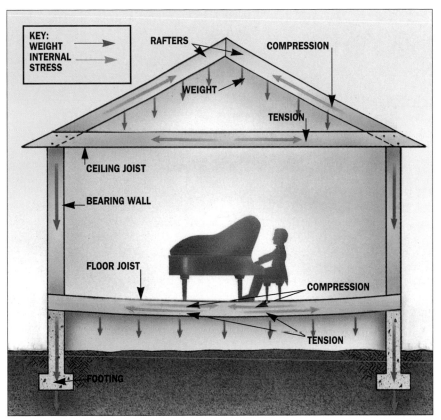

Weight from the roof compresses the rafters and tenses the ceiling joists. These forces, along with well-nailed joints, make the triangle very rigid and transfer the weight to the bearing walls. Weight on the floor joists compresses the wood fiber near the top section and tenses the lower section, which also allows it to transfer weight to bearing walls. The foundation transfers the weight to the ground.

Here's how it works. The weight from above tends to compress the rafters, which in turn tend to stretch or tense the joists below. The stress passes through the rafter-joist joint, which must be securely nailed to keep the entire roof assembly from coming apart.

Wood is quite strong; it neither compresses nor stretches easily. As these forces try to bend it, the wood resists. Wood's internally bonded, fibrous structure is inherently stable and resists both compression and tension forces almost equally well. When roof members are combined in triangulation or in a truss form, they act like beams and transfer the roof load out to their ends and down into the supporting walls.

Floor joists

Weight transfer is very similar in a floor joist, although the shape of the joist is rectangular rather than triangular. The weight of the piano and its player compresses the top layers of wood fibers in the joist and stretches the bottom layers. The wood's resistance to compression and stretching transfers the weight out to the walls. Normally, you'll hardly even feel floor joists bend under your weight as you walk across a floor. They do bend slightly as stress builds, but they're usually deep and thick enough so that it isn't really noticeable.

The normal joist chosen for a good, stiff residential floor is usually a 2x10. If 2x4s were used as floor joists spanning the same distance instead of 2x10s, the floor would bounce like a trampoline and will likely break. As architects and builders design houses, they take into account not only the strength of the beams but also how they feel underfoot. A floor with some bounce may be strong enough, but it won't feel secure.

Floor strength becomes an issue when remodeling an unused attic into living space. The attic joists were originally sized to support only the ceiling below and withstand the tension from the roof. They are usually made with 2x6s, which are not thick enough to support live loads— people and furniture. A comfortable living space requires a stronger floor. The local building inspector probably won't approve an attic remodeling plan unless you upgrade the floor to meet the building code, usually by adding 2x8s or 2x10s as additional floor joists.

Figuring beam sizes

The occasions when you'll be most likely to have to figure a beam size are when building a deck or installing a *header* for a larger window or door in a *bearing* (weight-supporting) wall. When removing studs from a bearing wall to make a window or door opening, the weight the studs support has to be routed around the opening. You have to install a header, which is a small beam, over the top of the opening to transfer the weight to the sides of the opening (*facing page*).

The bearing walls support the roof and floor loads. Because bearing walls must transfer their loads all the way down to the foundation, check the basement or crawl space for posts, walls, and beams directly under interior walls above. That's a sure sign of a bearing wall above. If the house is built on a concrete slab, interior bearing walls may not be as easy to find. Then it's wise to treat all walls perpendicular to joists as if they were bearing.

There are a few exceptions to these guidelines in locating bearing walls. Sometimes a joist pattern changes direction at a wall, or unusual ceiling angles dictate a more complex design.

The building code contains special span tables that simplify the process of determining beam sizes. Even so, there are some variables to consider when choosing the right size. You need to know the load the beam must carry; the distance it spans (between supports for a deck or the rough opening for a window or door header); and the type of wood, since wood strength varies among species.

BEARING AND NONBEARING WALLS

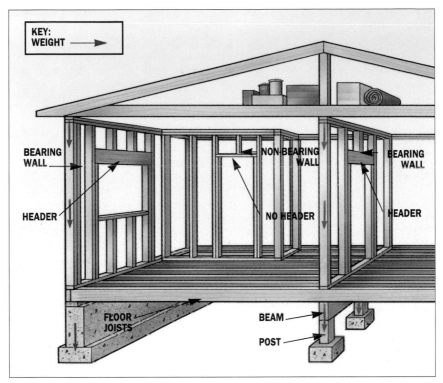

KEY:
WEIGHT ⟶

BEARING WALL

NON-BEARING WALL

BEARING WALL

HEADER

NO HEADER

HEADER

FLOOR JOISTS

BEAM

POST

Bearing walls are continuously supported down to the foundation and are perpendicular to beams or roof rafters. Nonbearing walls are parallel to joists or rafters or have no supporting beam under them.

Obviously, making beam size calculations can get complex. Most builders know the correct dimensions from the sheer repetition of their work. But it's safer to have a building inspector or structural engineer calculate the beam sizes for your deck or header than figuring them out for yourself.

Generally, it's not much more expensive to exceed strength requirements slightly by making the beam larger than the minimum, say, by using two 2x8s rather than two 2x6s for a header, just to make sure it's strong enough.

New beam designs

Knowing the compression/tension principle of beam strength makes it easier to understand the shape of manufactured wood beams. Notice that the bulk of the wood in these manufactured beams (*page 40*) is concentrated around edges where the primary compression and tension occurs. These parts of the beam, called *chords*, carry most of

STRESS PATTERNS IN NATURAL AND MAN-MADE BEAMS

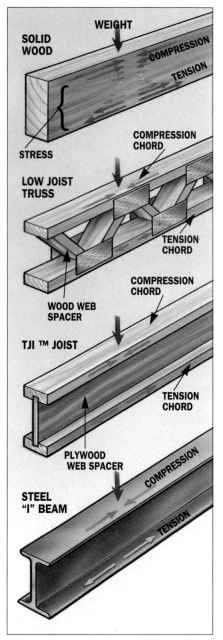

the stress. However, to be effective the chords must be rigidly separated by a stiff *spacer*, a 2x4 system for the low-joist truss and a plywood web for the TJI™ joist (*left*). There is less stress on the spacer, so it requires less material. Both joist types economize on wood, concentrating it where the stress is greatest. In some situations these beams may be lighter, stronger, and less expensive than solid wood.

The design of manufactured beams also illustrates how easily you can seriously damage a beam. Saw cuts, notches, or drilled holes in either the compression or tension chord destroys the wood fiber in exactly the zones where the stress is greatest, compromising the strength of the truss. That's why remodeling a house built with trusses can be tricky. You can't just chop into those critical top and bottom chords without first figuring how to adjust for the loss in strength.

Stress in solid wood beams works almost exactly the same as in trusses. Most of the compression is borne by the top third of the beam, and most of the tension is concentrated in the lower third. You can't cut into either of those sections of the beam without seriously weakening the entire beam. Unfortunately, you'll often find floor joists in houses improperly cut. Remodeling to accommodate toilet waste lines, sink drains, electrical wires, and heating ducts are the primary reasons for

Most stress occurs in the top and lower sections of a solid wood beam. Manufactured beams have material concentrated in these areas.

this offense. Cuts on the tension side of the lower third almost always reduce the joist's strength to the remaining wood thickness above the cut. Notching ends along the lower edge also reduces a joist's strength. Cuts near the ends of the compression edge don't weaken the joist as much. When drilling a joist, always make the holes in the middle third of its width, toward either end of its length, because this area receives the least stress.

Wind bracing

Wood is very strong when compressed along its vertical grain, so wall studs rarely fail unless they become wet and rot. But when the studs are covered with sheathing and siding, another large force comes into play: the wind. It's pleasant to stand in a 10 mph breeze, but try to carry a 4x8-foot sheet of plywood in that same wind and you'll appreciate how strong even such a mild wind can be. If the wind force on that plywood sheet is multiplied by the number of sheets in an entire wall or if the wind velocity increases, there's a sizable force trying to knock the house over (*below*). This force can be long term and steady, as well as short term and violent, as in a severe thunderstorm, a tornado, or a hurricane.

As might be expected, building codes require that walls be built to

BRACING AGAINST THE WIND

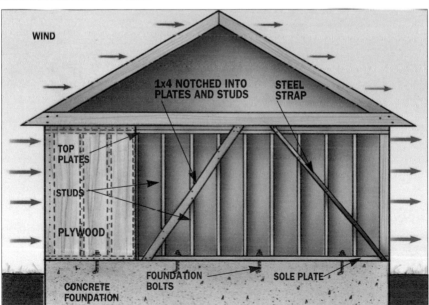

Securely nailed plywood, wood braces, or steel straps must be used in walls to resist the effect of wind. The roof must be securely fastened to the walls, and the walls to the foundation, to resist wind uplift.

withstand wind stress. Each exterior wall of a house must contain at least one steel strap, wood brace, or wood sheathing for this purpose. The steel straps are nailed to the top and sole plates and to each stud, forming either a tension or compression side of a triangle. A 1x4 board may be nailed the same way, although it needs to be notched into the studs and plates; otherwise, it would protrude beyond the wall frame, interfering with the application of the siding. Frequently, builders nail a 4x8-foot plywood sheet in one corner of each wall to handle the stress. Of course, if the entire house is covered with plywood sheathing, that takes care of the wind brace problem, and it provides a convenient backing to support the siding finish.

The wind also causes a roof to lift up. A roof must be nailed down to the rafters, the rafters nailed to the walls, and the walls fastened securely to the foundation to keep the whole house from literally taking off in a really strong wind.

All bracing must be well fastened, since stress is transferred from the wall to the brace through the nails. It may seem technical, but building codes stipulate an exact nailing pattern and number of nails per foot for different types of bracing and roof construction to ensure adequate strength. You need only look at the aftermath of Hurricane Andrew in Florida in 1992 to see the results of sloppy or improper nailing. Photos of damaged houses with roofs blown off and walls blown down clearly show nails that entirely missed the studs or rafters. Some houses were damaged because the

builder cut corners and didn't follow the code for minimum nailing distances. In fact, on some damaged houses, the roofers may have changed crews halfway through the job, because parts of the roof with correct nailing remained intact while other parts of the same roof were damaged.

From the ground up

The house's foundation rests on the ground, making a *footprint,* so to speak. But look at it from the standpoint of the ground; it must hold up the house. It carries the weight of the concrete, lumber, paint, and everything else put in the house. Concrete *footings* spread that weight out a good bit, but there's still a lot of pressure per square foot of soil. Unless the footings reach down to solid rock, that weight causes the soil to compress somewhat as it shoulders the load (*facing page*).

Some types of soil, such as clay and silt, compress more than gravel and sand, so the house must have wider footings or the builder may have to replace silty soil with gravel to avoid excessive settling. A little settling typically occurs in new houses—a lot of it happens before the house is even finished. Continued or uneven settling causes uneven stress on the foundation, potentially cracking it along with the finished walls directly above.

One typical cause of continued settling is poor drainage. Rainwater runoff sinking into the ground along the foundation of the house can carry off fine soil particles of soil as it seeps away, slowly undermining the footing. The remaining soil can no longer carry the load, and eventually the footing sinks lower at that spot.

Another common problem occurs when a foundation is put over disturbed soil. Once soil has been dug up, it contains numerous tiny pockets of air, which aren't easy to force out. Depending upon the depth to which it was disturbed, it may require a year or two to naturally recompress. So unless the soil is mechanically compressed, a foundation placed on it can settle severely. Many foundation contractors simply remove all of the disturbed soil and replace it with gravel, which compacts easily.

Foundations commonly crack and fail when they are not poured deep enough to resist a force called *frost heave*. When water freezes, it expands. Water freezing in saturated soil under a footing can expand and lift an entire foundation and wall, causing it to crack. As the soil thaws and the footing settles again, the problem is compounded. Local building codes, particularly in parts of the country with severe winters, specify how deep footings must be placed to avoid this problem.

Solid design

A properly designed and built structure won't collapse under normal circumstances. The building codes in some regions often require additional bracing for local condition—for example, in areas with periodic earthquakes. When planning a remodeling project, pay attention to how it will affect your house's structure and plan additional support where needed. It's always better—and not that much more expensive—to plan for extra support than to try to get by with the minimum amount allowed by the building code.

Builders and architects design houses so that the parts work together from bottom to top, from the foundation anchored in the ground to the roof that deflects the weather. The structure won't fall down if those designs are properly followed. Smith, the remodeler whose house collapsed around him, was the exception to the rule.

WEIGHT TRANSFER THROUGH THE FOUNDATION

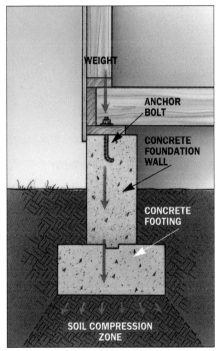

WEIGHT

ANCHOR BOLT

CONCRETE FOUNDATION WALL

CONCRETE FOOTING

SOIL COMPRESSION ZONE

A wider foundation footing spreads the weight of the house over a larger soil area so it settles less.

A Brief Guide to Roofs

How they work, how they're built

On a fall evening, as I sit listening to a cold rain pounding on the roof overhead, I always feel very grateful that my roof doesn't leak. Though the wind-driven rain falls in torrents, my roof faithfully blocks the storm and channels the water to valleys and gutters, which carry it away.

Of course, a roof has to do a lot more. It has to endure hot summer temperatures that can reach as high as 180 degrees Fahrenheit. At the opposite extreme, it must resist bitter cold and ice in winter and stands ready to shoulder tons of snow for weeks on end.

Roofs work in quieter, more subtle ways, too. Frequently they open up enough attic space for an extra room. Where roofs overhang exterior walls, they become built-in awnings that protect siding and windows from the corrosive effects of sun and rain. The angles on many roofs create a natural draft to help ventilate attics, cooling them during summer and flushing out unwanted moisture in winter. And, certainly, a roof makes a house look good. It's an architectural crown whose very geometry shapes a house's character.

When you add up all those expectations, you'd think there would be one ideal type of roof. But not so. The next time you take an evening walk, take a look at all the roofs in your neighborhood and notice the many different sizes and shapes. No matter how plain or ornate the different roofs might look, each style you see represents a unique architectural tradition.

Gable roofs

As you stroll through your neighborhood you will probably see gable roofs everywhere, since they're the most common roof shape throughout the United States and Canada. A gable roof looks like a piece of cardboard folded neatly down the middle and placed over the house's walls (*facing page, inset*). The actual gable is the triangular shape of the wall at either end. When you see that shape, you know you're looking at a gable roof.

They're the easiest and least expensive to construct. Carpenters use three straight pieces of lumber to form the sides of the triangle— two for rafters and one for a ceiling joist. With the corners securely fastened, this triangular geometry creates a strong, stiff structure that can withstand loads of snow, people walking on it, and high winds without collapsing.

Though simple, a gable roof that's designed by an imaginative architect or builder won't look dull or boring. You might find a dozen of them on your street, and not one identical to another. The variety comes from skillfully arranged combinations of gables, roof slopes, and trim styles. Though many gable roofs look complicated, an experienced builder can lay out and frame one relatively easily because the basic shape and framing techniques don't change.

Aside from aesthetics, gables have several practical implications. First, the steepness of a gable's slope determines how much attic space is provided. Steeper slopes mean more attic headroom. Often you can easily convert these attics into an extra bedroom. Add windows in the gable walls and dormers to the roof if more light and

GABLE ROOF WITH GABLE DORMERS

The gable roof on this colonial-style house supports three symmetrical dormers, each with a gable roof. Gable framing uses simple but strong triangular geometry.

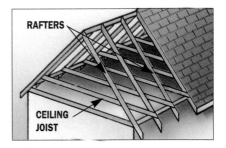

headroom are needed. A shallower slope means less headroom and often only enough space for storage, or perhaps no usable space at all. Second, gables imply a certain kind of wall framing below. The two walls that the roof overlaps support the weight of the roof and are therefore bearing walls.

Gable roofs have another feature that makes them particularly valuable in colder regions: they are excellent ventilators. In particular, gable roofs with lower slopes resemble and work much like the top of an airplane wing. Wind passing over the roof creates a low-pressure zone that exerts a lift on the roof. That lift sucks air out of vents near the top of the roof, ventilating the attic better, keeping it cooler, and removing excess moisture. In winter this venting helps keep the roof colder, so snow on it will not melt, run down to the edge of the roof, refreeze, and cause troublesome ice dams near the edges that will eventually cause leaks.

But in coastal regions, there can be such a thing as too much lift, as some recent destructive hurricanes have so clearly demonstrated. These hurricanes ripped off more low-sloped gable roofs than other types of roof (though other low-sloped styles didn't fare that well either). And if the roof didn't get torn off the house, the gable section of wall often blew off due to the pressure created by the roof. While few of our houses will face wind this extreme, the event illustrates dramatically that roof shapes perform differently. The roof design that best withstands hurricanes is the hip roof, because, as we shall see, this shape eliminates those gable ends.

Hip roofs

Hip roofs look like gable roofs with the ends clipped off at an angle (*facing page*). This angle lowers the profile and makes the roof less visually prominent, especially with steeply sloped roofs. A hip roof also reduces the height of the attic, so you're likely to bump your head on the low, angled ceilings. If you want to convert this area to living space, you will probably have to add dormers to increase the available headroom.

The hip roof framing is slightly more complicated than a gable roof and a bit more expensive to build. It still relies on the triangular structure for strength, but the balance of the forces that work through the *hip rafters* and *jack rafters,* which support the additional slope to the hip roof, is less obvious. Notice that the hip rafter intersects the corner at a 45-degree angle to each wall, and the jack rafters meet the hip rafter at 45 degrees, too, so all the rafters are easy to cut. Rafters lap over every outside wall, spreading the roof weight more evenly but making each wall a bearing wall. You will have to take this into consideration if you plan to add doors or windows, which will need headers (*page 38*).

The style is practical as well as aesthetically pleasing. Because the roof overhangs all sides of the house, it protects the walls and windows from sunlight and rain better than a gable roof does. Hip roofs have a better chance of surviving the strong winds of a hurricane or tornado, too, although

HIP ROOF WITH A HIP DORMER

The hip roof on the American foursquare house reduces the bulk and prominence of the roof. The architect or builder was consistent, putting hip roofs on the dormer, bay, and porch.

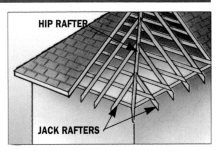

HIP RAFTER

JACK RAFTERS

SHED ROOF

Shed roofs are common in contemporary design and in solar houses, where large, south-facing walls catch maximum sunlight.

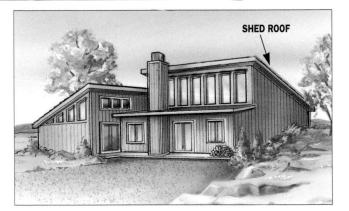

SHED ROOF

sometimes storms are just too powerful even for a well-designed and well-built roof.

Shed roofs

A shed roof (*page 47*) is really half of a gable roof with the upper and lower sides supported by bearing walls. It's one of the simplest structures for protection from the elements, so it's often an economical, quick solution for a room addition or porch roof. There is only one bearing wall, since the house wall is used to support the other side. Many of them are used for dormers, too. Shed roofs, along with flat roofs, are a defining feature of the so-called "contemporary" design. Most of these houses were built in the past 40 years. Often you see shed roofs in solar designs, where the wall supporting the high end of the roof faces south so the windows can catch more sunlight. Still, shed roofs have not become very popular. Gable roofs and hip roofs almost completely dominate residential construction these days.

Two other types of roofs, once common in pre-1950 houses, have virtually disappeared, though they continue to dot older neighborhoods in most cities—the mansard and gambrel.

Mansard roofs

In the 17th century, a French architect named Francois Mansart invented the style of roof that bears his name.

Mansard roofs have two pitches, a shallow top and steep sides, and the roof overlaps and bears on all the side walls (*facing page, top*). It is a big-volume roof containing maximum attic space, which is usually used as a second floor. Notice that the roof framing also frames the walls and ceiling for finishing off the interior. Home builders typically punctured the lower roof plane with dormers and windows to better light and ventilate what essentially becomes a second floor, rather than an attic. While practical, mansard roofs almost disappeared after the 1940s.

Gambrel roofs

A gambrel roof is easy to recognize; it will immediately remind you of a barn (*facing page, middle*). Though the style emerged in the United States during the Colonial period, no one knows who invented it or why. Perhaps its popularity as a barn structure gives us a clue; it offers more interior volume. The wider roof enlarges the attic and makes it a natural living space.

It has an additional advantage from a framing standpoint. You do not need such long and perhaps hard-to-find rafters. Two lighter and shorter rafters can be substituted instead (*facing page, bottom*).

Gambrel roofs allow for efficient, compact houses. They incorporate the maximum amount of usable living space in the smallest and least prominent house exterior shell by cramming more living space under the roof.

Gambrel roofs are a bit more complicated to assemble and their attics are more difficult to ventilate than gable roofs. While these reasons can make them slightly more expensive, nevertheless I suspect that the design has fallen victim to the greater homogenization of our current building styles. Spacious

MANSARD AND GAMBREL ROOFS

Houses with mansard roofs are increasingly rare, although the style often appears on commercial buildings.

The double-gambrel roof on this house creates maximum attic space, virtually an entire second floor.

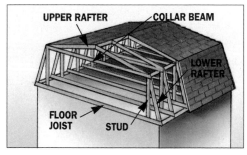

Both roof types create easily used living space. The roof framing also frames the walls and ceiling of the attic room.

suburban lots and bigger houses make their compactness, which is the main advantage of a gambrel, unnecessary. While recently browsing through several current books of house plans, I couldn't find a single gambrel roof. So unless interest in gambrels revives, I suspect that this style will die out.

A move to plain roofs

Although each roof style is distinct, don't be surprised if you see several types on the same house. Architects and builders commonly combine them, so you'll find gable and shed dormers on hip roofs, hip-roofed porches on gabled houses, and shed roofs attached just about anywhere.

But roofs have become plainer in the last 15 years. That's because many builders now use trusses for the roof structure. Trusses rely on a system of smaller width rafters and ceiling joists reinforced by a web of crosspieces. They're built in a factory, often many miles away, and are erected as a unit at the house site. Unfortunately, the cross-pieces render the attic space unusable, except perhaps for lightweight storage, because you cannot cut and remove them to open up attic space without weakening the entire roof structure.

The result is plainer-looking, less interesting roofs on newer houses because without attic living space, dormers and windows in the roof serve no purpose. You get an easier to build economical roof, but regrettably the aesthetics of the neighborhood suffer.

Concrete to Last the Ages

The recipe for a strong mix

When it comes to durability, no part of your house will last longer than concrete. The wood frame will rot, the nails rust, and glass break, but those concrete foundations, floors, and sidewalks can last for centuries.

Of course, not all concrete will last that long. When you see new and growing cracks in your basement walls or floors or when your driveway begins to flake, you might wonder whether your house will stand long enough for the kids to grow up, much less for centuries! At its best, concrete is quite strong and durable, but at its worst, it'll crack, crumble, and flake, sometimes at alarming rates.

What is concrete?

Many people confuse the words *concrete* and *cement*. Concrete is the hard, strong material we walk on and use to construct buildings, the stuff that comes to the job in those big, barrel-shaped trucks. Cement is one of concrete's ingredients, the glue that holds it together.

Cement is made from a combination of lime, silica, alumina, and iron. It's made by heating rocks—limestone, clay, and shale—to their melting points, cooling the molten mass, and grinding it into a fine powder. The process isn't new. The ancient Romans used cement to construct their aqueducts, roads, and buildings, some of which still stand today after nearly 2,000 years.

Unfortunately, the Roman formula for cement was lost for more than a thousand years, until the late 1700s, when it was rediscovered in England. The stronger, improved cement that we use today, called *Portland cement*, was invented in 1824 and went into production in the United States about 1875.

From the outside, concrete looks like a flat, hard, gray stone, but if you slice it open, you'll see that it's a conglomeration of stuff (*facing page*). The larger chunks are stones, called *aggregate*. At first glance, the aggregate looks like a random mix of stones of many sizes. Actually, concrete manufacturers and dealers carefully grade the stones and mix them in exact proportions so they pack together well in the concrete mix. Grains of sand, which are also graded, lie tightly packed around the stones. And if you look closely, you can see a gray material filling the spaces between the sand grains and aggregate, coating their surfaces. This gray stuff is the cement, which gives concrete its characteristic gray color.

Most binding agents, for example glue, harden as they dry. But cement works exactly the opposite way. The chemicals in the powder react and harden as you wet them. That, of course, is why you can't buy

WHAT IS CONCRETE?

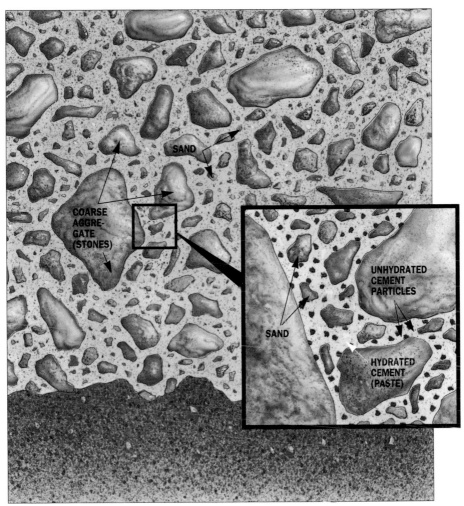

Concrete contains solid stones ranging from ¼ inch to 1½ inches and larger, sand particles less than ¼ inch, and cement, all in correct proportions. The cement is the glue that binds the mass together.

cement off the shelf, premixed and ready to apply. Cement begins to harden as soon as you wet it.

When the cement is mixed with water and the proper proportions of other materials, it creates a whole family of useful products. When you mix it with sand and lime, you make the mortar used for bricks. If you change the proportions of sand and lime, you can make stucco, the hard plaster coating applied to the sides of houses. And if you add cement to aggregate and sand, it becomes the familiar concrete.

Concrete at home

Hard as it is, concrete is versatile stuff. Your home most likely rests upon a concrete foundation, either in the cast form or as premolded blocks that masons mortared and stacked. It also forms the rock-hard durable surface of garage and basement floors and walls, sidewalks, steps, and porches.

Concrete is ideal, not only because it is hard, but because it is easily cast into a great many shapes. The casting technique, called *pouring*, is relatively easy. You mix the dry concrete ingredients with water and then pour the resulting mixture into a *form*. A form is the technical term for the concrete mold, which

you can make out of any rigid material like wood.

But remember, concrete is a very heavy material, especially when wet. You usually have to brace the form securely to keep it from shifting or bowing outward. It's virtually impossible to add effective bracing once you pour the concrete (I've tried!), so a good motto to follow is "brace twice and pour once." (All the professionals tell stories of the concrete they've had to break out with sledge hammers because their forms failed.)

Once the concrete *cures*, that is, hardens, you simply knock off the forms, being careful not to chip the edges of the concrete (*page 54*).

Good mixing means strength

To make good, strong concrete, proper mixing of the various ingredients is critical. A crucial part of that mix is water, which moistens the

---

HOW WATER AFFECTS THE CONCRETE MIX

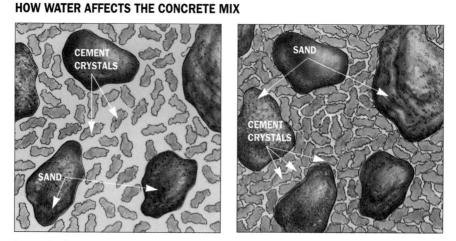

In a wet mix cement (*left*), crystals grow farther apart, producing weaker, porous concrete. In a drier mix (*right*), the crystals grow closer together, making concrete that is stronger and watertight.

powdered cement and transforms it into a thick paste. The paste then coats all surfaces of the aggregate and sand so they'll stick together. Proper mixing will evenly blend the large and small particles so the concrete compacts well.

The water causes the microscopic crystals of cement to react and grow, absorbing water in the process (*facing page*). These crystals intertwine, bind the sand and aggregate tightly, and make the concrete strong. With the correct amount of water, the crystals will grow closer together, hold the sand and aggregate more tightly, and make for stronger concrete. Too much water causes the paste to become thin, however, and the crystals grow farther apart. As a result, the crystals intertwine less and the concrete is therefore weaker.

Ideally, the less water the better—up to a point. Concrete needs enough water to flow like a thick, lumpy syrup so it completely fills the form without leaving any air pockets. Water also lubricates the particles of sand and aggregate, allowing them to slide together and compact tightly. The amount of water added to make a good concrete mix is a compromise between strength and workability.

Too much water can be fatal

Excess water is the kiss of death to concrete in another way. Not only does it weaken the crystal structure, it allows the aggregate to separate (*right*). Excess water causes the concrete to lose its thick, syrupy consistency—its *plasticity*—and become soupy. In a good, plastic mix, the sand and aggregate stick together but still flow slowly. In a soupy mix the ingredients separate, with the heavier aggregate sinking to the bottom and the cement rising to the top. This weakens both the concrete as a whole and the exposed surface in particular.

A mix that's too wet will cause the surface to crack, chip off, and powder. Even worse, the concrete won't compact well because pockets of water remain in it. These pockets dry out, but they easily refill with water and freeze in cold weather, breaking out the surface concrete above (called *pop-outs*). Pop-outs commonly occur in garages in winter where salty water from road de-

PROBLEMS CAUSED BY TOO MUCH WATER

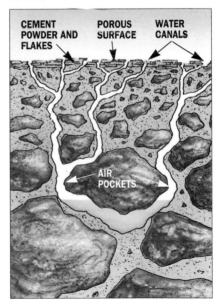

A concrete mix that is too wet or troweled while water is on its surface causes the heavy aggregate to sink and the sand and cement to rise, weakening the surface.

icers soaks into a concrete floor and freezes.

Similar problems with the surface will occur if you try to finish the surface of the concrete too soon after having poured it. When you are pouring concrete, immediately compact the edges and level the surface. But before smoothing the surface, you have to let the concrete set—that is, stiffen to the point where your foot will sink only about ¼ inch into its surface should you stand on it.

During this waiting period, excess water from the concrete rises to the surface. This *bleed water* is normal, and the concrete soon reabsorbs it. Disturbing the surface before the bleed water disappears will cause sand, aggregate, and cement to separate, thus weakening the surface. The more water there is in the mix, the longer you have to wait for the bleed water to be reabsorbed.

There should never be more water in the mix than the manufacturer recommends. If you're mixing the separate materials yourself, follow the exact formula given on the bag. If you order concrete already mixed, the water content should be exact. In fact, if you want to add more water on site, the truck driver might ask you to sign a form releasing the company from liability should the concrete crack and chip.

Advantage of a good cure

Once concrete stiffens and its surface has been troweled smooth, the

MOISTURE CURING STRENGTHENS CONCRETE

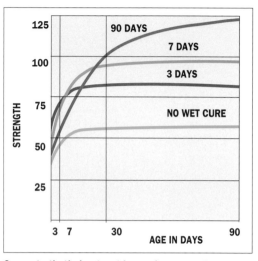

Concrete that's kept wet longer becomes stronger and cracks less.

curing process begins. During curing, more cement crystals react and grow and form stronger bonds with other crystals. The process can extend from three days to a month or longer. The longer the cure, the stronger the concrete (*above*).

Whereas excess water can ruin a good, plastic mix, once the concrete sets, water becomes the key ingredient for curing. The longer the concrete is wet, the stronger it gets. If it dries out, the hardening process stops. Keep concrete wet by covering it with plastic and pulling the plastic off every few days to sprinkle more water on the concrete with a garden hose. Unfortunately, the plastic causes uneven surface coloration, so for better appearance, simply water it frequently. Pros sometimes spray a white moisture-retardant paint over concrete to keep moisture in. They sometimes even dam up the edges of the freshly poured project and flood the surface of the concrete with a pool of water.

When opting for a long cure, not only will you get stronger concrete, you'll get fewer cracks. But cracks always appear in concrete. There's no escaping them. When concrete dries, it shrinks. Not much, about 1/16 inch in a 10-foot span, but unfortunately, concrete won't give that much. Shrinkage will fracture any large span, whether it's a sidewalk, driveway, or basement floor.

Concrete masons have long since learned that if you can't stop concrete from cracking, the next best thing is to control the locations of the cracks. So before the concrete dries, usually while troweling the surface, they deeply groove the surface to make weak spots, called *control joints*, so the concrete cracks at those lines, and not randomly. The concrete masons make those control joints at regularly spaced intervals determined by the length and thickness of the project.

Wire mesh or steel reinforcement bars, called *rebar*, can help reduce cracking, too. Rebar won't stop cracks, but it will keep them from widening. Rebar also ensures that one section of concrete doesn't pull away and drop below the level of an adjacent section, creating a safety hazard. Rebar is set in the form before concrete is poured so the concrete surrounds and encases it.

Is concrete waterproof?

When concrete is properly mixed, *air entrained*, and cured, it is waterproof. Air entrainment is a process developed in the 1940s in which the concrete dealer injects millions of microscopic air bubbles into the wet concrete mix. This injection has two purposes: first, the bubbles lubricate the aggregate and sand, making the mix flow and consolidate easier so you can reduce the water content. As mentioned earlier, less water means stronger concrete.

Second, the air bubbles relieve pressure from ice forming inside the concrete during the freeze and thaw cycle. This makes concrete more durable in regions that use salt and other de-icers in winter. When ordering ready-mixed concrete, check with the dealer to make sure it's air entrained.

For those of us who struggle with wet basements, it's hard to believe that concrete is waterproof. Moisture still comes through in the form of vapor and dampness, but water can't flow through a good concrete mix.

Handle concrete safely

The chemical compounds in concrete are corrosive, meaning they can cause mild burns if left on your skin for long periods of time. Wet cement can even etch glass. So wear protective clothing—long sleeves, long pants and rubber boots—and waterproof gloves when working with concrete.

Building Doors and Windows to Last

Why do doors and windows perform so well?

For all its size and complexity, it might come as a surprise to realize that your house has only two moving parts—the doors and windows. That's good news. Moving parts wear out, so the fewer the better. The bad news is that some of those doors and windows take a lot of abuse.

Consider the minor explosion that rocks the walls and floor of my kitchen every time my teenage son goes out the back door. I'm continually amazed that the old door survives all those wood-jarring thumps.

And consider the effort that it takes to pry open some of my old double-hung windows, because several generations of well-intentioned painters gradually clogged up the tracks. Frankly, you can no longer classify all my windows as moving parts. They're painted shut.

Given the tough life ahead for doors and windows, it's no surprise that new ones arrive at the building site already assembled and ready to install. Carpenters at the construction site don't do any of the meticulous hinge fitting or window frame assembly, because the woodworking specialists at the factory can hang the doors and frame the windows far more precisely and quickly. That precision counts when you expect your doors and windows to open and shut thousands of times without wearing out.

Although doorknobs loosen, latches stick, the paint fades and peels, and the glass breaks, doors and windows are durable. With a little upkeep and repair, they usually last a lifetime.

The traditional panel door
When browsing through the door section of any home center or lumberyard, you'll find two types of doors: *panel* and *flush*. Both are easy to identify. Panel doors have decorative rectangular indentations, while flush doors have perfectly flat, smooth faces. Of course, there are doors made in many other designs, but these two dominate the residential landscape.

Panel doors were popular in houses built before World War II. They fell out of favor for a while, but now they're popular again. Panel doors are assembled from a fairly complicated-looking framework of vertical *stiles* and horizontal *rails*. Rectangular panels fill the frames (*facing page*).

While this door assembly looks attractive, the value of this design is primarily practical. It takes into account wood's tendency to expand

THE MAKEUP OF A WOOD PANEL DOOR

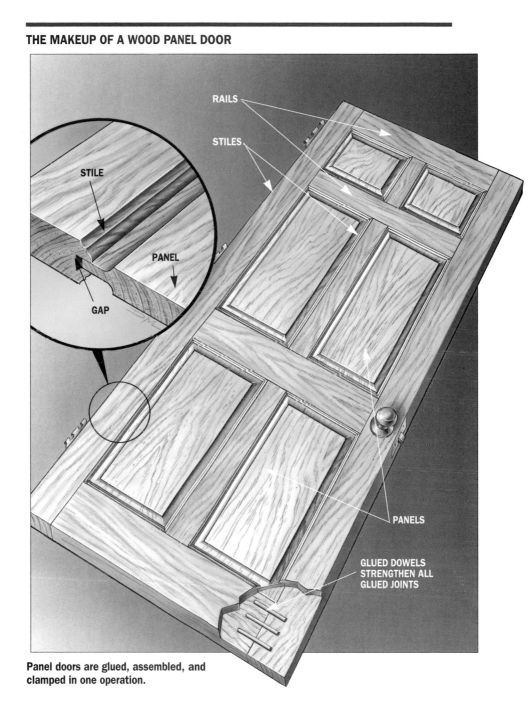

Panel doors are glued, assembled, and
clamped in one operation.

and contract with changing humidity. Doors made from solid boards or planks absorb moisture and expand in humid weather, causing the door to bind and stick in its frame. Our wooden storm door did this every summer, and I'll bet yours did, too. Then, during dry periods, the wood shrinks, opening cracks between the boards and widening gaps around the door edges.

The panel door solved most of these problems. Its wood still expands and contracts, but most of the movement occurs in the wide panels, which are ingeniously designed to "float" in the framework. Makers of panel doors leave small spaces between the panels and the framework and hide the gaps with molded edges on the stiles and rails. The molded edges, rather than nails or glue, hold the panels in place. In fact, look closely at the edges of the panels in dry weather and you can often see that a panel has shrunk, exposing a narrow unpainted or unstained band of wood along its edge. The upshot of this is that the panel's expansion and contraction never affects the door's overall dimensions. Rather, the only parts that could affect its fit in the door frame are the solid wood stiles and rails at the sides, top, and bottom. And these are quite narrow and therefore not prone to as much expansion and contraction.

Higher quality panel doors, the kind usually used as main entry doors, go even further to ensure stability by having laminated stiles and rails. In the laminating process, door makers glue together narrow strips of a softwood such as pine, which expands less in humid weather than a hardwood such as oak. They then cover these cores with a durable and decorative hardwood veneer to make the stiles and rails. Laminating strengthens and lightens the door while reducing the likelihood of warping. This is a real danger if the door gets wet.

Laminating and covering doors with veneer is not a new idea. It goes back to the 1800s. What was new in the early 1900s was higher quality plywood. This became the chief component in a new kind of door that became popular after World War I, the flush door.

The flush door

Flush doors delivered strength and stability, but in a new way. They consist of two plywood "skins" about ⅛ inch thick that are glued to a wood frame (*facing page*). The plywood, usually two or three layers thick, is stable and strong. It expands and contracts little with changes in the humidity. And the plywood layers are usually hardwood, which makes the door surfaces more durable.

Originally, the core of the flush door was partially laminated, much like high-quality panel doors. However, as adhesives improved, door cores (called *stave cores*) were made from rows of short blocks of wood glued together inside a light frame and sandwiched between the plywood. Today, these cores are usually made from particleboard.

In terms of style, flush doors represent a major step away from the elaborate, hand-crafted decoration of the Victorian era and a step toward "industrial modern" design. You can just imagine the skilled woodworkers assembling

58

LOOKING INSIDE SOLID-CORE FLUSH DOORS

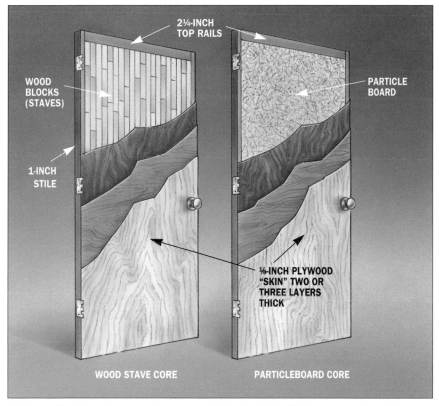

Solid-core flush doors have wood cores sandwiched and glued between two plywood, or sometimes hardboard, skins. Particleboard cores are gradually taking the place of wood-block cores.

panel doors by hand. But not so with flush doors, which are made with high-pressure presses used to clamp the whole assembly until the glue sets. The result is a solid but simpler and less expensive door. And they fit a growing consumer interest in the 1920s for less ornamentation and a lower price.

Flush doors have several other advantages over panel doors, too. They're better insulated, block sound better, and are easier to clean in rooms such as bathrooms and kitchens where sanitation is an issue. They also are more fire resistant than panel doors and came to be used in apartments, in commercial buildings, and in houses with attached garages.

The hollow-core door

Solid-core flush doors initially took hold as exterior doors in the 1920s, but they didn't become popular inside the house until about 25 years later, after World War II and the development of the hollow-core flush door (*below*).

The end of World War II unleashed pent-up demand for affordable housing, which in turn changed residential construction for good.

House builders streamlined building by ordering more precut and assembled components from lumberyards and dealers so carpenters wouldn't have to make them by hand at the job site. Hollow-core doors fit this process well because they were easier to produce than panel doors and cost half as much. They soon became the standard for interior doors.

Manufacturers simply eliminated wood staves from the solid-core door and replaced them with an inexpensive but ingenious alternative—a lightweight wood lattice. Later, they replaced the wood lattice with cardboard that was arranged in a honeycomb pattern. Both of these materials made the skins stiffer and the door lighter and easier to handle. The hollow-core door did not have to be exceptionally rugged because it was designed for interior use only. A wood block that was glued along the stiles helped support the knob and latch.

As you can clearly see in the illustrations of both solid-core and hollow-core flush doors (*page 59 and left*), the solid-wood framework around the door edges is fairly narrow. This limits how far you can cut them down to fit smaller openings.

HOLLOW-CORE FLUSH DOOR

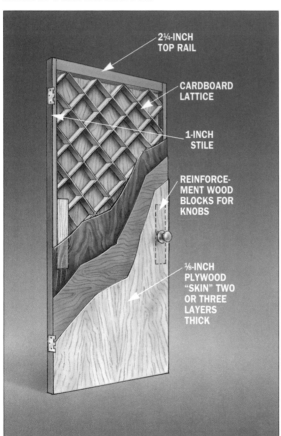

- 2¼-INCH TOP RAIL
- CARDBOARD LATTICE
- 1-INCH STILE
- REINFORCEMENT WOOD BLOCKS FOR KNOBS
- ⅛-INCH PLYWOOD "SKIN" TWO OR THREE LAYERS THICK

A hollow-core door is a solid-core door whose wood core has been replaced by a cardboard lattice. Wood blocks support the knobs and latch. The hollow-core door is light yet strong and perfectly suited for interior use.

A return to panel doors?

Post-World War II modernism was a plain style with no fancy detailing or reminders of the past, so panel doors fell out of favor. In the 1950s and 1960s, simple slab cabinets, flat paneling, and plain doors were in vogue. Now panel doors are again popular, though still expensive. A basic panel door costs about $100, compared to about $25 for a hollow-core door.

However, a new type of hollow-core door may make the paneled look more affordable for inside the house. These doors have hardboard skins molded to look like the rails, stiles, and panels. They must be painted, but some look sharp, and they are worth checking out at a local lumberyard or home center when shopping for interior doors.

Better exterior doors

In the last 20 years, manufacturers have replaced wood skins with steel and fiberglass to eliminate the main weakness of wood—its vulnerability to the weather (*below*). To last a long time, a wooden exterior door needs the protection of wide roof overhangs or porches, or else it should be located on the north side of the house where it's protected from direct sunlight. Otherwise, you'll have to sand and refinish it every five years or so. In addition, home owners should use light-color finishes on wood doors that are exposed to direct sunlight so they do not absorb heat and there's less chance of warping.

Steel doors, as tough as they are, can also temporarily warp from excessive heat if painted a dark color. But they straighten out as the temperature moderates. Steel and fiberglass doors have become popular because they're rugged and virtually maintenance free. You can repair dents in steel doors on your house the same way you repair a car

STEEL OR FIBERGLASS EXTERIOR DOOR

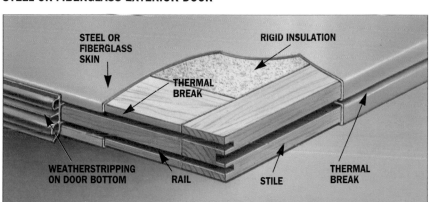

STEEL OR FIBERGLASS SKIN

RIGID INSULATION

THERMAL BREAK

WEATHERSTRIPPING ON DOOR BOTTOM

RAIL

STILE

THERMAL BREAK

Steel or fiberglass skins make exterior doors more durable and maintenance-free than those made from wood. They insulate better, too. The thermal break keeps the inside steel skin from cooling and developing a film of condensation or frost.

door—with auto body filler. And their cores are filled with foam insulation to make them more energy efficient than wood doors.

To make them more attractive, manufacturers mold the steel or fiberglass skins to mimic traditional wood panel doors. Some even go so far as to apply a wood grain pattern that you can stain with wood stains. While they are seldom mistaken for wood panel doors, some higher-priced brands just might fool you.

But when you buy an exterior door, shop for more than appearance alone. A high-quality door will be tightly weatherstripped in its frame so drafts don't blow in around it. (It takes an expert and experienced carpenter to hang a door correctly, so it's almost always better to buy an exterior door already prehung in its frame, since it will be hung correctly and snugly at the factory.) Brand-name doors are tested and have an air infiltration rating. Ask the dealer for this rating. A low rating, about .15 cubic feet per minute or lower, indicates good weatherstripping performance. In addition, make sure the aluminum sill, the angled frame piece on the bottom that you step on, has a thermal break. A thermal break is a gap in a good heat-conducting material such as aluminum or steel; the break keeps heat from flowing out through the metal. It also keeps cold weather from cooling the inner surfaces of the sill or door and causing a buildup of condensation or even frost inside the door. Usually a more heat-resistant material such as wood or rubber fills the gap. Most steel doors and aluminum

sills have thermal breaks, but check to make sure.

Windows improve, too

Windows improved at the same pace if not faster than doors. Gone are the popular old-style *double-hung windows*, so called because both the top and bottom sash were counterweighted with iron weights. These weights hung from a cord that ran over pulleys mounted in the window frame. Unfortunately, this entire arrangement was always drafty. New double-hung windows have springs to counterweight the window, have good weatherstripping, and are far more energy efficient.

The same goes for *single-hung windows*, which are like double hung except only the bottom sash opens.

A new version of the *casement window* has come into vogue in the last 20 years or so and now rivals the double-hung in popularity. Casement windows swing open on side-mounted hinges. The newer style, dating back to the 1960s, substituted a crank mechanism for the old adjustable extension arm that held the window securely open. Now you open and shut the window with the simple twist of the crank.

Casements have three practical advantages over the double-hung. You can open the entire window, rather than just the lower or upper half of a double-hung. An insect screen on the inside of the sash eliminates the hassle of putting up or maintaining a separate outer screen. And modern casements are more weathertight than even the new double-hungs.

Perhaps equally telling for the casement's popularity is its plain,

THE BASIC PARTS OF A DOUBLE-HUNG WINDOW

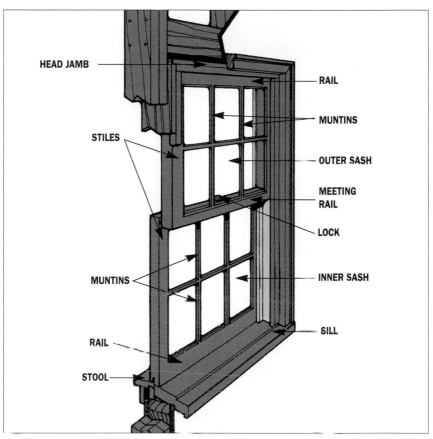

HEAD JAMB

RAIL

MUNTINS

STILES

OUTER SASH

MEETING RAIL

LOCK

MUNTINS

INNER SASH

SILL

RAIL

STOOL

Most windows contain these basic parts, particularly rails, muntins, and stiles. On many modern windows, the muntins are purely for decoration, as the sash contains only one pane of glass.

modern-looking style that blends well with contemporary architecture. It's interesting to note that you're beginning to see modern casements with grids of *muntins* (the dividers between small panes of glass), a distinctly classical touch!

Windows have become more maintenance-free too. The exterior wood on windows has always suf-fered from exposure to the sun and rain. You had to scrape and re-paint the sash, sills, and trim every 5 years or so to keep them from rotting, especially on the south side of the house where the sun was most harsh. Windows with vinyl or alu-minum cladding on the exterior completely eliminate those chores, as do solid vinyl and aluminum windows. All are welcome to maintenance-weary home owners. But you still have to wash them!

These window improvements come at a price, of course, so it's probably not worth rushing out to buy replacement windows until your old ones deteriorate. But when replacement time comes, they may be just the ticket.

Skylights and roof windows have become popular during the past 25 years. These once had a reputation for causing roof leaks. Home owners wisely stayed away from them. But once manufacturers were able to offer a better glass seal, a *curb system* that mounted the glass in a frame a few inches above the roof, and good flashing techniques, they could guarantee a leakproof system.

The popularity of skylights took off. These windows proved to be an excellent way to brighten a room with dramatic natural light. In fact, manufacturers soon developed special shades because they often let in too much light and heat. On the other hand, the style that you can open makes for great ventilation (*page 134*).

Skylights work best when installed over poorly lit hallways and stairways, because both usually have little available natural light. They're also pleasant additions to kitchens and bathrooms, although you can enjoy them anywhere. (But if you open your skylights, make sure you close them when it rains!)

SINGLE-HUNG WINDOW

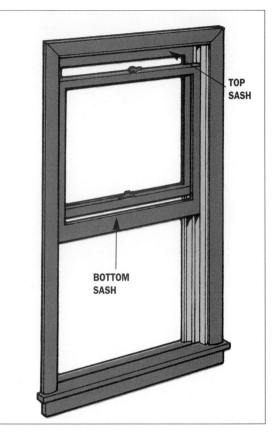

TOP SASH

BOTTOM SASH

Only the bottom sash moves on this single-hung window. On a double-hung window, both sashes move.

The earliest glass windows

Improvements in the glass itself are even more impressive. Glass isn't new. Its recipe has been around for about 3,000 years. It is made with a combination of sand (silica), soda (sodium), and lime that, when heat-

CASEMENT WINDOW

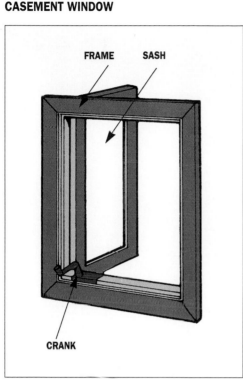

A modern casement window swings on side-mounted hinges and opens with a crank arm.

ed to its melting point and then allowed to cool, creates a transparent, brittle, but extremely hard and durable material.

Large sheets of clear window glass were developed only during the last two centuries. Two hundred years ago, the most notable characteristic of glass was that it was made in very small pieces. There had not been many improvements in glass making since the Middle Ages, when large cathedral windows were painstakingly constructed from thousands of small and varied-shaped pieces of colored glass.

Cathedral architects of this period would have been awed and even inspired with the prospect of a decent, clear, 4x4-foot sheet of glass. But they didn't have any; it hadn't been invented yet. Glass windows were purely decorative. In fact, if you bought a secondhand castle, you wouldn't get the window glass; the former owners removed it along with the other furnishings.

Since such large panes of glass weren't available, early windows were assembled from many small panes set in a larger supporting grid. Nowadays, of course, the fancy gridwork of muntins that manufacturers lay over large glass sheets to make them look like small divided panes is primarily decorative, not functional. The early glass used in muntins, called *crown glass*, was not very clear either. Often it contained swirls, air bubbles, and other distorting imperfections. The first step in producing modern window glass was to make it larger and more transparent.

Clarity and brightness

It was not until 1851 that a workable manufacturing process for flat glass was invented. It made a bright, daytime room interior a common design feature of houses well before the invention of the electric light bulb, especially when the glass was set in a bay window.

However, achieving the nearly flawless clarity that we now take for granted took another 100 years of technical advances.

OLD SHEET GLASS WINDOW

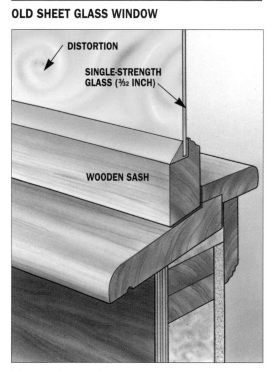

DISTORTION

SINGLE-STRENGTH GLASS (3⁄32 INCH)

WOODEN SASH

Wavy surfaces and distortion characterize many older sheet glass windows.

The flat glass of this 100-year period is called *sheet glass* (*above*). It was, and still is, made by drawing a wide ribbon of molten glass into a thin sheet, somewhat like pulling taffy. The glass was then cooled slowly. Because the molten glass surfaces were never touched, they cooled to a brilliant luster.

You can often recognize sheet glass by its distortions. If you are looking through a window and notice that objects on the other side of the glass seem to change shape slightly when you move your head, you're seeing the distortion that sheet glass produces. It's caused by the front and back surfaces of the glass not being parallel because of small variations in thickness.

You may recall seeing distortion in the windows of older houses, since they usually contain older sheet glass. Those wavy surfaces were created by uneven pressure in the process of drawing the glass, or they might be small imperfections caused by impurities in the material while it was still molten.

Sheet glass is no longer made in the United States or Canada, so if you prefer those distinctive distorting effects as you look through a window, try rummaging through the old windows in a salvage yard or check with local suppliers of art glass. But even though it's no longer manufactured, the old sheet glass has given us two standard measures of glass thickness that are still in use today—*single-strength glass* and *double-strength glass*.

Thickness and strength

Single-strength sheet glass satisfies virtually all of today's household window needs. When your old window breaks, you'll normally replace it with single-strength glass, or actually its modern equivalent—3⁄32-inch-thick glass. You'll almost always want to replace broken single-strength glass with glass equally thick. Rather than measuring its thickness, simply take a piece of it with you to the glass store for comparison. This glass is cheap and easy to replace if broken. It is usually set with its edges encased in putty. Occasionally, when a larger window breaks, you'll need double-strength replacement glass, which is thicker (⅛ inch).

The thicker the sheet of glass, the greater the effect of distortion, so another production process was developed to create distortion-free thick glass for use where greater strength was needed, as in picture windows, store fronts, and doors. This thicker glass, called *plate glass*, was literally rolled flat while molten, then cooled. Later, after hardening, its surfaces were ground smooth and polished. This way, precisely controlled sheets could be made to any thickness without distortion.

You're not likely to find plate glass in your house unless you have a large picture window more than 10 years old. Like sheet glass, it's no longer made in North America except as specialty glass, since more precise production methods have made surface grinding obsolete.

Both sheet and plate glass have been replaced in the United States by *float glass*, made by pouring molten glass over a bed of molten metal. The molten glass, being lighter, floats on top of the metal's very flat surface and cools. This process produces two very smooth parallel faces, virtually free of distortion. Actually, the top side is more brilliant than the bottom, but it takes a practiced eye to be able to see the difference.

Glass that's safe

If you've ever accidentally struck the *tempered glass* in a patio door or some other exterior door, you know

it doesn't break easily. It takes a good whack with a lawn chair, and then it doesn't shatter into razor-edged shards; rather, it crumbles into a multitude of blunt, relatively harmless pieces.

What you've encountered is the toughness of tempered glass. It's about four times as strong as regular glass. Its superior strength is created by putting regular glass under stress. Regular float glass is heated to a high temperature, then cooled rapidly. The outer surfaces cool most quickly and compress against the slower cooling inner zone. This stress pattern remains in the cooled, hardened glass, making the product much tougher. That is, until a fracture occurs. While it's tougher

TEMPERED GLASS

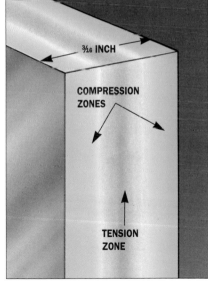

The combined stress of compression and tension makes this glass four times as strong as regular glass.

to break through the compression zone, once penetrated, the tension releases and the stress pattern breaks down. The entire sheet of glass self-destructs and disintegrates into small fragments.

You probably have some of this glass in your house. According to building codes, it should be used in exterior and interior doors, shower doors, and windows that extend to within 18 inches of the floor. It's one type of *safety glass.*

The term "safety glass," however, can be confusing. Safety glass is not a special kind of glass; it's simply a technical rating for glass that meets certain impact and breakage requirements. The development of safety glass has had a major impact on house design. Safe glass shower stalls became possible, as well as sliding glass patio doors, full-view exterior doors, and clear skylights. Tempered glass, if it's thick enough, meets the safety-glass requirements. It's used in locations where it may receive severe or repeated blows.

You can buy tempered glass (at about twice the cost of regular glass) and install it yourself, but there's a catch: you must buy an exact-sized piece. Tempered glass can't be cut without upsetting the internal balance of stresses, causing it to disintegrate. So measure carefully when you order it!

The other common type of safety-rated glass is called *laminated glass* (*above, right*). To make laminated glass, any type of glass, including the decorative glass for entrance doors, is sandwiched around a thin sheet of plastic and securely bonded under heat and pressure. It's no stronger than a sin-

LAMINATED GLASS

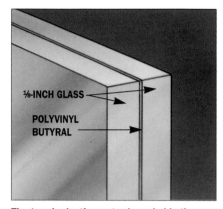

1⁄8-INCH GLASS

POLYVINYL BUTYRAL

The tough plastic center layer holds the sharp glass shards together when the pane breaks.

gle piece of glass of equal thickness, but when it breaks, the tough plastic layer usually remains intact. The sharp shards of glass remain bonded to the plastic in one whole piece. Auto windshields are made of laminated glass so flying pieces of glass do not injure the occupants of the car if the windshield breaks during an accident.

Laminated glass is not often used in houses because it's generally thicker (and therefore heavier) than tempered glass. Glass manufacturers can also laminate tempered glass to achieve even greater strength but still keep the pieces from flying apart if it breaks. Both tempered and laminated glass are available only at a glass specialty shop. Laminated glass costs about twice as much as regular glass.

Energy-efficient glass
Perhaps the most important advance in glass technology was the

development of the energy-efficient window. Glass is a poor insulator, so windows always tend to be cold spots in winter and hot spots in summer. As concern for better energy conservation increased after the oil crisis in 1974, researchers focused their attention on those energy-wasting windows. This was doubly important because the trend among home owners is to want more windows in the home than ever before. The double-pane window, better known as *insulated glass*, is the best solution to date.

Insulated glass consists of two layers of glass permanently bonded together at their edges but separated by a ½- to ¾-inch air space. An old-timer would describe it as a window with a permanent storm panel stuck to it (*page 142*).

Insulated glass now dominates the residential window market, not only because it works, but because it eliminates the need for that extra storm window in all but the most severe climates. It doesn't cost more either—if you include the cost of the extra storm window that you previously had to buy.

One major drawback to these energy-efficient windows is the replacement cost if they break. With a single-pane window, you simply scrape out the old putty, buy a $7 (or less) sheet of glass, and putty it back into place. Not so with insulated glass. Since the two panes are permanently bonded, they have to be replaced as a unit. An average size unit will cost about $50. Unfortunately, they are difficult, if not impossible, to reinstall into their wood, vinyl, or aluminum frames. Normally the easiest approach is to take the entire sash with the broken glass to a glass-repair specialist. In fact, by the time you add up the costs, the least expensive approach might be to simply buy an entire replacement sash.

Caring for glass

Although production methods have evolved, the nature of the window glass itself hasn't changed much. You can't scratch it with a knife point, but you can with a hardened metal file. Scratches weaken glass. In fact, that's how glass can be cut. It's scratched with a hardened steel or diamond wheel and snapped along the scratch mark. Of course, if the glass already has scratches or flaws, it might snap randomly. That's one reason you may have trouble cutting used glass; its surface is already full of scratches.

Glass rarely fractures because of scratches. It usually breaks from an overwhelming impact. Scratches destroy the glass clarity and leave distracting marks and a dull finish. When it comes to scratches, the main culprit is grit caught in a cleaning cloth rubbed across the window. Otherwise, the only other things around the house that usually damage glass are misguided baseballs and soccer balls. And you can't blame the window for that.

HARNESSING ELECTRICITY

E lectricity is powerful stuff. Remember when you shuffled across the carpet and planted a stinging shock of static electricity to the ear lobe of a brother or sister? What power at your fingertips!

An equally accessible but far more powerful form of electricity waits behind the walls of our homes in outlets and switches, ready to spring into use. Electricity is perhaps the most magical of all the services in our homes. It's almost like having an army of supercharged gnomes, tiny kilowatts of power, packed into the wiring of your home, all eager to charge out and spin a drill or food processor, light up a bulb or TV screen, or brown our toast. Electric power works silently and swiftly, and by now it's hard to imagine living without it close at hand.

But despite the benefits, electricity has a dark side. Unlike an irritating but harmless static shock, a shock from your electrical system can kill you. This ever-present danger has dogged scientists, engineers, and building code officials ever since electricity came into the home about 80 years ago.

How do you contain all that electrical energy more safely? The National Electrical Code, the rules that determine the design of residential systems, has addressed that issue squarely over the last 50 years and introduced several solutions. These solutions appear in new homes and can be added to older homes. Electrical engineers have figured out ways to protect sensitive electronic equipment from glitches inside the electrical system as well. But protection isn't without a cost.

And perhaps more successfully, engineers have improved the old faithful light bulb, and now, as you will see, have challenged its favored status with new energy-efficient compact fluorescents.

Making Electricity Safer

Harnessing the force of modern life

A thunderous crash of lightning hardly compares to the clear, precise musical notes coming from a stereo, but they're more alike than you might imagine. They're both electrical discharges, one immense and wild, the other tempered and controlled by your house's electrical wiring system. And they are both potentially dangerous. There are a number of ways residential electrical systems keep the power of electricity in safe bounds. Before examining those, take a look at how your wiring system harnesses that power in the first place.

How an electrical system works

You're already familiar with the business end of an electrical system: the wall outlets, technically called *receptacles,* and switches that make things happen. But let's trace the system backwards to the source of electricity. Behind the switches, cords, and outlets—inside the hollow walls and ceilings of your house—wind a maze of wires that carry electrical current. They stretch out like octopus arms from a single center, the *main service panel,* the heart of the operation usually located where the power line enters your house (*facing page*). If you have a basement, you'll probably find the main panel on a wall down there. Otherwise, it'll be in the wall of a utility room.

The main electrical power line to your house, called the *service,* probably comes in overhead from a nearby utility pole, although in new houses it usually comes in underground. You can spot it by looking for three cables twisted together (sometimes running separated in old houses). Don't confuse it with telephone or cable TV wires; these are usually single cables. The electrical wires on the utility pole link up with the electrical grid that connects the entire neighborhood to powerful electrical generators.

The recipe for power

If there's anything close to the awesome power of lightning in the electrical system, it's in the electrical wires at the very top of the utility pole. They carry in the neighborhood of 10,000 volts. Think of *voltage* as the electrical equivalent of "push." The higher the voltage, the harder the push. When you were a kid, you discovered that the longer and harder you scuffed your feet on the wool carpet, the bigger the static shock you could generate. You could actually generate about 400 volts, enough to make a visible spark jump between your finger and a metal object (or kid brother). That is a pretty good push. Ten thousand volts has considerably more push than that; a residential wiring system

NATURAL AND MAN-MADE ELECTRICITY

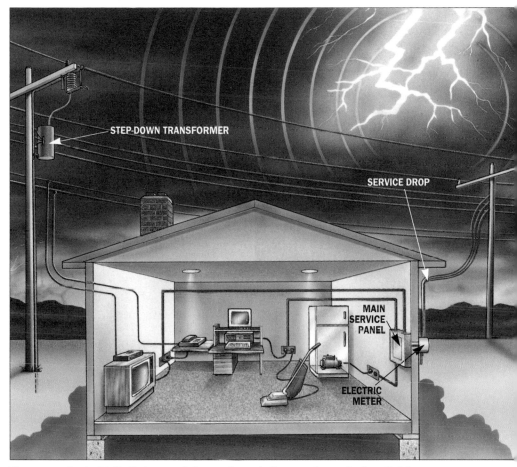

STEP-DOWN TRANSFORMER

SERVICE DROP

MAIN SERVICE PANEL

ELECTRIC METER

The man-made electricity that comes into your house is the same force of nature that is contained in a flashing bolt of lightning. We have tamed that force to power the devices used in everyday life.

couldn't contain it. So *transformers* on the utility poles, those big cylindrical objects you see hanging up there, reduce the voltage to around 120 volts, our household standard.

Still, 120 volts can be fatal, a fact that might surprise you since you can generate 400 volts from the car-

pet. The explanation for this lies in the second component of electrical power—*amperes*. Amps (short for amperes) are the actual amount of current that flows. It's the combination of volts and amps that's deadly. A static shock has an extremely tiny current flow, thus its effect, despite the high voltage, is startling rather than harmful. However, the current flow available from the utility grid is almost unlimited, making our 120-volt household systems powerful and dangerous. The electrical current could easily melt all the wiring in your home.

Thanks to special devices that limit current that are located in the main panel, such household disasters rarely occur. If you open up the door of your panel, you will find either *fuses* or *circuit breakers,* each rated to withstand a certain amount of current, usually 15 amps. If the current exceeds the listed amount, the fuse will burn out ("blow") or the breaker will trip, shutting off the current and protecting the wiring system from an overload. It's a clear signal that you're trying to draw too much power through the wires.

How you get a shock

The big picture of how your electrical system works might seem a bit abstract, but it gets personal when the system reaches out and zaps you. Electrical shocks always take you by surprise. Most of the time you'll experience a harmless tingling sensation. Even such a mild shock is a sober reminder that the same energy that lights our homes, browns our toast, and spins our power saws can also do us in.

To receive a shock two things must occur simultaneously. One, you must touch a hot wire (or metal object in contact with a hot wire) and two, you must be grounded. Each of these is worth a closer examination because each one uncovers some of the mysteries of the electrical system.

Why electrical power flows

An electrical *circuit* usually has three wires. The *hot* ("live") wire, which is covered by black insulation (or any other color except white, green, or gray) runs side by side with two other wires—a *neutral* wire, which has white or gray insulation, and a *ground* wire, which is either bare copper or has green insulation (*page 76*). (Homes built before 1960 often won't have a ground wire. I'll come back to this wire later.)

The hot wire carries the electrical power generated by your local utility. It's always poised and waiting to deliver its charge from inside an outlet or behind a switch. But current won't flow and release its power until it has a way to get back to its source, a way to close a loop, so to speak. That, as you might expect, is the job of the neutral wire. Whenever you throw a switch to turn on an electric drill or a light bulb, you are essentially connecting the hot and neutral wires and creating a path for electricity to follow. This path is called a circuit.

The hot wire immediately senses this path and reacts and releases its energy. And if nothing impeded the current flow, most of that energy would be lost. But here is the genius of electrical design. Standing in the path between the hot and the neutral wire is a job to be done—a motor to be spun, a lamp filament to be lit, or a TV screen to be animated. These devices use up virtually all the energy available in the hot wire, leaving little for the neutral wire to carry. This is why you get a shock from touching a hot wire but not the neutral one, even when current is flowing.

You receive a shock when you touch a hot wire because your body acts like a neutral wire and completes the circuit. How? It so happens that the damp ground, the earth itself, is also an excellent path that leads back to the power source and closes the loop. In fact, it's so good that the electrical system uses it as an alternate path for safety purposes. The neutral wire is connected to the ground at the main service panel through a wire to a copper-coated steel rod driven deeply into the earth beside your house or, on older houses, to a metal water pipe that enters your home from underground. The power source (essentially the transformer on the utility pole) also has a wire that runs into the ground. All residential wiring is grounded. If you're not in contact with the damp ground, either by touching it directly or indirectly through other wires, metal pipes, or damp concrete in contact with the soil, you won't get a shock.

Why shocks are dangerous

Fortunately, your body isn't as good a neutral path as a wire. Wires are good conductors. Your body is not. Although it contains about 90 percent water, it resists most electrical charges. Water, when it contains impurities like the salts in your body or soaps in a bathtub, tends to be a good conductor, but your skin thickness, muscle, and other traits make you a poor path for electric current. Don't get overconfident though. You're surprisingly vulnerable.

Shocks kill by stopping your heart. A steady, beating heart relies on tiny electrochemical nerve pulses that carry a current in the range of .001 amp. Even a charge as small as .006 amp can shatter the heart's microcircuitry and disrupt its beating rhythm. Often the nerves can't stabilize quickly enough to restore the circuitry and save your life.

Those .006 amp look almost insignificant compared to the 15 or even 20 amps available in a typical residential system. And consider for comparison: an electric drill draws about 3 amps and an electric mixer draws about 1 amp. There would be far more fatalities if people received anything like these current flows every time a shock occurred.

Fortunately, it takes a fairly high voltage to push a significant amount of current through us. Generally, you won't get a shock from circuits under 24 volts. Electric toys fall into this range, as do doorbells, thermostats, telephones, security systems, and cable TV lines. (Folks with pacemakers need to be careful even in these low ranges.)

The best defense against a shock when you're handling electrical devices or appliances is to make sure your body is not grounded. Remember, current will go through you only when you are a path to ground. Don't work with electricity while standing on damp ground or damp concrete, nor work on a metal ladder that's resting on damp materials. Using electric tools and other electrical devices around the plumbing system can be dangerous, too. All these connect you with ground. Some electricians are so careful that they do critical work in which they might touch a hot wire with one hand in a pocket, just to make sure they don't absent-mindedly reach out and grab a grounded object.

COMMON LEAKS IN AN ELECTRICAL SYSTEM

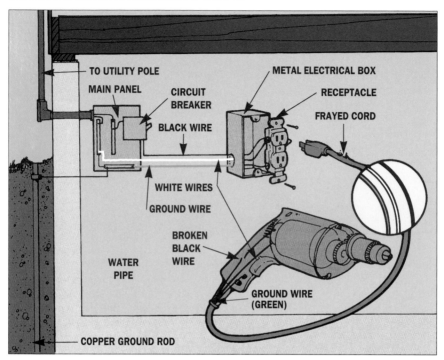

A safe system routes electricity through insulated wires, closed boxes, and appliances. Leaks, as in a faulty outlet or drill, are absorbed within the system by the ground wire. The potential leak at the frayed cord is not grounded and many be dangerous. The cord should be replaced.

Taming electricity: innovations that make it safer

The National Electrical Code, called the NEC, sets standards for electrical systems. It has introduced three features that made these systems safer: the *equipment ground, ground fault circuit interrupter,* and *polarized plugs.*

Adding the equipment ground

The equipment ground is that third wire, either bare copper or having green insulation, that runs alongside the hot and neutral wires. If you haven't seen it, you'll know it's there by the type of outlets and plugs you use. The equipment ground is that third prong on a three-prong plug, the one that slips into the half-round hole in an outlet.

While the ground wire appeared well before the 1950s, it wasn't required in residential wiring systems by the NEC until about 1960. If your home was built before 1960 and hasn't been remodeled, your wiring system probably doesn't have an equipment ground.

The purpose of the equipment ground is to solve the problem of electrical "leaks." Usually a hot wire is covered by insulation, buried in an electrical box inside a wall, or covered by motor housings and light sockets where you can't touch it. But equipment wears out, as anyone with an old, frayed extension cord knows well. Then electricity can escape. Look for trouble where vibration and other types of movement wear out a wire's insulation or break the wire itself. Old refrigerators and washing machines, which vibrate a lot, are typical culprits. So are lamps and portable trouble lights, whose insulated cords harden as they age but still receive a lot of heavy use. When such leaks occur, a hot wire can be exposed or an entire metal appliance can be electrically charged (hot). You risk a shock every time you touch them.

The ground wire runs alongside the hot and neutral wires and is attached to the metal parts of electrical boxes, outlets, and electrical tools and appliances, all those parts that could carry an electrical charge should a leak occur. The ground wire siphons off those leaks by providing a good path back to the main service panel, exactly like the neutral wire. In effect, any leak that's picked up by the ground wire will probably blow a fuse or trip a breaker and shut the circuit down. That's your signal that you have a serious problem somewhere in the system.

An electrical bargain: the GFCI

While the ground wire brought a new level of safety to our homes, researchers found that shocks were still especially common in the damp or wet areas of our homes—the kitchens, bathrooms, basements, and yards. Part of the problem was the proliferation of plug-in devices such as hair dryers, power tools, and coffee makers that you now commonly use around sinks, in the basement, or out in the garage.

The old saying "water and electricity don't mix" holds true here. Dampness in the soil or in concrete that rests in the soil makes both surfaces good electrical conductors and good grounds. It is here that your body could easily become the perfect ground path for an electrical leak from a frayed cord or faulty tool. Even worse, metal faucets and drains are also excellent grounds, because the water supply lines and sewers that they connect with are usually underground. Shutting off a faucet with one hand while holding a faulty hair dryer with the other could be fatal (*page 78*).

It's tempting to think that the fuses or circuit breakers in the main service panel will protect you from a lethal shock in such circumstances. They won't. Fuses and circuit breakers protect the wires in your house from overheating, melting the insulation, and causing a fire. They do not protect you! Fortunately, a special type of circuit breaker called a ground fault circuit interrupter (or GFCI for short) was invented about 20 years ago.

A GFCI's role

A GFCI is that odd-looking outlet you might have seen in the wall near the bathroom sink, the one with the tiny buttons that say "test" and "reset." The role of the GFCI is to protect you.

The illustration (*below*) highlights the scenario for a potentially dangerous shock. With one hand you pick up the hair dryer to move it away from the sink while at the same time you shut off the water faucet. In lifting up the hair dryer, even though it is turned off, you accidentally touch an exposed hot wire in the frayed cord. An electric current immediately flows from the cord, through your body, through the plumbing system, and eventually to ground. This is called a ground fault, sometimes known as a short circuit. In the meantime, the circuit breaker in the main panel might never shut off the electricity, nor will the fuse burn out.

In contrast, a GFCI instantaneously senses misdirected electrical current and reacts within one-fortieth of a second to shut off the circuit before a lethal dose of electricity escapes. This ingenious process explains how the ground fault circuit interrupter gets its name. When it senses the ground fault, the device "interrupts" the circuit and switches it off.

Let's take a look inside a GFCI outlet to see how the device senses an electrical leak. Normally, the currents passing through the hot and neutral wires are equal, although they travel in opposite directions. The doughnut-shaped transformer senses both currents, but because they're equal and opposite, their effects cancel each other out. However, when current leaks through a worn cord or a faulty appliance, the current through the hot wire will be greater than the current through the neutral wire. The transformer immediately senses this imbalance. When the difference exceeds .005 amp, a switch inside the GFCI reacts instantly and breaks the circuit, shutting it down.

If you happened to cause the imbalance by touching a frayed wire

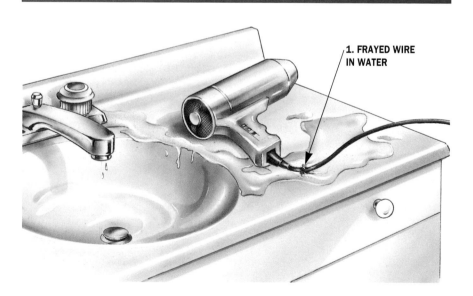

1. FRAYED WIRE IN WATER

or by holding a damaged electric tool, for example, you might feel a light shock, that initial .005 amp of current before the GFCI reacted. Engineers didn't pull that amperage figure out of thin air, by the way. Remember, .006 amp can stop the heart, so .005 is the limit at which GFCIs are set.

To make sure that GFCIs are working, manufacturers added the "test" and "reset" buttons that you see on them. Pushing the test button creates a small electrical fault, which the GFCI should sense and immediately react to by shutting off the circuit. The reset button restores the circuit. You should test your GFCIs every week and replace them immediately if they are not working properly.

GFCIs have a relatively short history in the NEC. The 1971 code initially required them on circuitry controlling lights and other electrical equipment for swimming pools.

HOW A GFCI WORKS

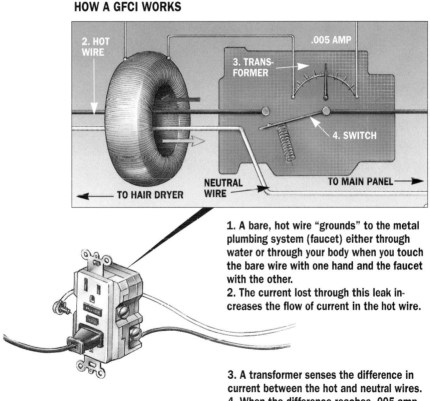

2. HOT WIRE

.005 AMP

3. TRANS-FORMER

4. SWITCH

NEUTRAL WIRE

TO MAIN PANEL →

← TO HAIR DRYER

1. A bare, hot wire "grounds" to the metal plumbing system (faucet) either through water or through your body when you touch the bare wire with one hand and the faucet with the other.

2. The current lost through this leak increases the flow of current in the hot wire.

3. A transformer senses the difference in current between the hot and neutral wires.

4. When the difference reaches .005 amp, a switch opens the circuit and stops the flow of current.

It also gave a deadline for including GFCIs in outdoor locations (1973) and construction sites (1974). The 1975 code required GFCI outlets in all new and remodeled bathrooms.

Initial GFCI locations were undoubtedly limited to the most dangerous areas by the relatively high price of the device, about $25. As the price dropped to below $10, however, the cost became insignificant compared to the safety gained. More recent versions of the NEC expanded GFCI requirements to include garages and basements. The 1993 code requires GFCI protection for readily accessible outlets located outdoors, in crawl spaces and unfinished basements, in garages, in bathrooms, and within six feet of a kitchen or wet bar sink. Code officials wrote these rules to protect users of portable power tools and hand-held kitchen appliances from receiving shocks in these damp, high-risk areas. Incidentally, the code treats spas, hot tubs, and Jacuzzis as if they are swimming pools. Outlets, lights, and electrical equipment within a certain distance of pools all require GFCI protection.

Polarity and plugs that don't fit

Have you ever tried to shove a two-prong plug into an outlet and found that it doesn't go in until you turn it around? If so, you've encountered the third level of shock protection now mandated by the NEC. Plugs that fit into an outlet only one way, including three-prong plugs, are called polarized plugs.

Polarity means that the neutral wire in an electrical cord connects with the white neutral wire in the electrical system and the hot wire in the cord connects to the black hot wire in the system. Remember, the black wire in the electrical system carries the power. The white neutral wire carries little power. Yet both are necessary to allow current to flow. When you flip a switch, you release the power in the black wire waiting to go to work spinning a motor or lighting a bulb.

Polarized plugs keep you from switching the hot and neutral wires around when you plug a cord into a receptacle. The wide blade that connects to the neutral wire will not fit into the narrower slot reserved for the hot wire, and the round prong on a three-prong plug fits only into the round opening in the outlet, which automatically positions the hot and neutral blades. Polarized plugs fit only one way. These polarized plugs reduce the chance of a dangerous shock because you cannot reverse the connections and make the neutral wire in a cord hot, as shown in the illustration (*facing page, bottom*).

Normally, reversing the connection wouldn't cause a problem. The lamp lights up either way. But unfortunately, in many cases the neutral side of the circuit in a lamp fixture is less well insulated than the hot side. Notice in the illustration (*page 82*) that the lamp's internal wire that is connected to the hot wire of the cord runs through the switch and becomes exposed deep in the socket, where it makes contact with the bottom of the light bulb. It's virtually inaccessible and difficult to touch accidentally.

The neutral wire, on the other hand, connects to the screw base,

COMMON HOUSEHOLD PLUGS AND OUTLETS

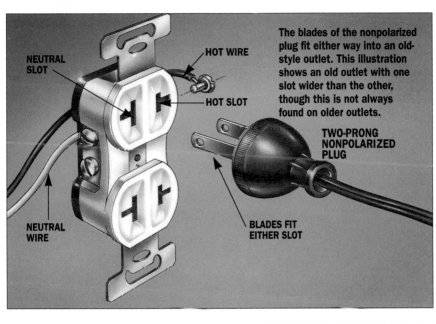

NEUTRAL SLOT

HOT WIRE

HOT SLOT

NEUTRAL WIRE

BLADES FIT EITHER SLOT

The blades of the nonpolarized plug fit either way into an old-style outlet. This illustration shows an old outlet with one slot wider than the other, though this is not always found on older outlets.

TWO-PRONG NONPOLARIZED PLUG

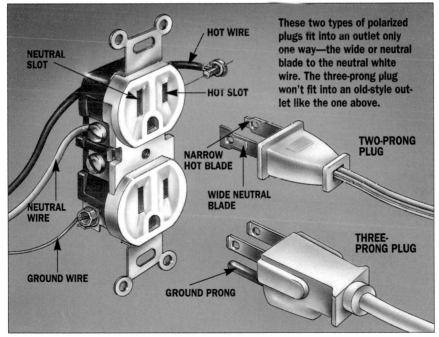

NEUTRAL SLOT

HOT WIRE

HOT SLOT

NARROW HOT BLADE

WIDE NEUTRAL BLADE

NEUTRAL WIRE

GROUND WIRE

GROUND PRONG

These two types of polarized plugs fit into an outlet only one way—the wide or neutral blade to the neutral white wire. The three-prong plug won't fit into an old-style outlet like the one above.

TWO-PRONG PLUG

THREE-PRONG PLUG

which you are much more likely to touch. Historically, the insulation around the screw base has proven to be the weak link in the system. It consists of little more than a cardboard tube that becomes brittle and cracks or even falls out as the fixture ages. With the cardboard worn or gone, the screw base can easily make contact with the outer metal socket. As might be expected, that contact often occurs precisely when you unscrew a bulb, holding onto the socket or another metal part of the lamp with your other hand.

If the neutral wire is hot when you hold the lamp and that crucial contact occurs, causing a ground fault, you could suffer a dangerous shock. In fact, because the socket touches the rest of the metal lamp, the entire fixture could be electrically charged, even though the light isn't turned on! It's an accident just waiting to happen.

And let's face it, people don't pay much attention to how they plug in their lamps. With nonpolarized two-prong plugs the chances are 50/50 that the neutral side is

SCENARIO FOR A DANGEROUS SHOCK: A LAMP PLUGGED IN BACKWARDS

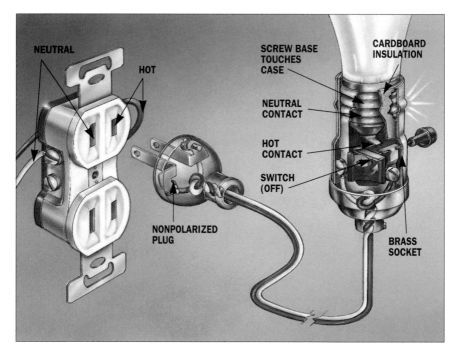

Inserting a nonpolarized plug backward will electrically charge the white wire and all metal touching it. Worn insulation around the screw base allows contact with the brass light socket and the entire metal lamp, electrically charging the entire fixture. The scene is set for a dangerous shock when you touch the light fixture.

actually hot. That's why so many shocks occurred with old light fixtures. Polarized plugs eliminate this hazard by keeping the hot wire properly connected. Even if the neutral wire accidentally touches the fixture while the light is on, you won't get a shock.

Exceptions to the rules

Despite the NEC's insistence on polarity and grounding, you've probably noticed plenty of electrical plugs with two identical blades. These plugs were on equipment produced before the code change in the 1960s. But you also will find nonpolarized two-prong plugs on some brands of new power tools. The NEC allows an exception to the polarized plug rule if the device is *double insulated*. In these devices, manufacturers encase the electrically conductive metal parts such as the motor and wire connections in an extra layer of a nonconductive material. You can't receive a shock as easily because of the extra layer of insulation.

You'll discover another unofficial exception when trying to replace a worn-out two-prong plug. It's difficult to find a polarized two-prong replacement plug. You can easily find a three-prong replacement plug for a cord with a ground prong, however. Why? Because even if you're aware of polarity, there's no foolproof way to ensure you'll wire a polarized two-prong replacement plug correctly—that is, with the neutral wire to the wide blade and the hot to the narrow blade. Improper wiring here will guarantee an improper connection every time you plug the cord in while cre-

ating the illusion that it's proper. Code officials, of course, can't look over your shoulder to check your work, so they haven't pushed retailers to make polarized two-prong replacement plugs more available, nor do they require home owners to use them.

Bypassing the system: a bad idea

So you want to insert the three-prong plug of your new power drill into the electrical system of an old house and you can't find a three-prong outlet? It's tempting to try to bypass the whole system and make polarized and grounded electrical devices work anyway. Some people break off the third, round grounding prong or file down the wide neutral blade. These actions sabotage the equipment's safety features and increase the potential for dangerous shocks.

Another popular but unsafe bypass is to replace the old two-slot outlets with the newer, three-slot, grounded types. Three-slot outlets will accept all types of household plugs and will conveniently allow a three-prong cord to be plugged in anywhere. Of course, old two-wire systems do not have an equipment ground, so the grounding prong on the plug does not really go to ground. Installing a proper ground wire for these outlets is time consuming and costly, but if it's not done, you have created the illusion of a grounded outlet when in reality it isn't.

Electrical inspectors might not like ungrounded outlets, but they consider false impressions even more dangerous. That's one reason you can still buy old-fashioned, ungrounded outlets to replace the old ones when they wear out.

Another commonly used approach is the three-prong/two-prong adapter, more popularly known as a *cheater plug* (*below*). The NEC accepts this device provided you insert the screw that attaches the cover plate through the equipment ground tab. This screw connects to the metal yoke, which in turn connects to the metal electrical box. But, unfortunately, that's where the "grounding" usually ends. Many metal electrical boxes were never grounded to earth in old two-wire systems, so using an adapter again creates a false impression of a safe, grounded system. And this false sense of security puts you one step closer to receiving a dangerous or even fatal shock.

Good solutions

The best solution for old systems is to run grounded circuits from the service panel or other grounded electrical boxes to easy-to-reach parts of rooms. You can run cables up from the basement into walls or

---

A BAD SOLUTION TO NONPOLARIZED OUTLETS: THE *CHEATER PLUG*

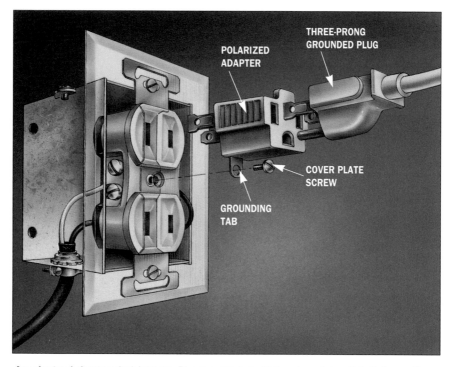

An adapter (*cheater plug*) lets you fit a grounded plug into a two-slot outlet. But even if you connect the grounding tab to the outlet with the cover plate screw, many times neither the outlet nor the metal box is grounded, so the plug isn't grounded either.

drop them down walls from the attic. That's a start.

The 1993 NEC allows one exception to help resolve the grounding problem: you can substitute a GFCI outlet for an ungrounded outlet because a GFCI *behaves* as though it is grounded, even if it isn't. A GFCI contains a hole for the grounding prong on three-prong plugs. It's particularly useful when you want to upgrade an old two-wire electrical system that doesn't have an equipment ground. You get safety at a bargain price. Paying less than $10 for a GFCI outlet is a lot cheaper than tearing open walls to run new wiring.

As usual, be sure to obtain an electrical permit when doing your own electrical work. It gives you the opportunity to review local codes with your local building inspector and have your work inspected to make sure you did it right.

A different kind of problem: electrical surges

Not only can electricity rear up and shock you, it can also flare up and destroy many of our electrical appliances and devices.

The scoundrels in the system are sudden power increases, called *surges*, that momentarily disrupt a house's steady power flow and can rocket it from its normal 120 volts all the way up to 400 or 500 volts.

Despite such impressive voltage rises, surges are invisible and give no warning. You won't see a bright flash in the steady glow of a light bulb or hear the refrigerator motor change its rhythm. Surges zip right through the main electrical panel so fast that the circuit breakers and

fuses don't notice them either. Fortunately, most such surges are small and don't pack much of a punch. Except for the massive surge caused by a direct lightning strike, which is extremely rare, surges used to be a minor eccentricity, a curiosity more than a problem.

The invention of sensitive electronic devices changed all that. We now live in the age of the microprocessor. The microprocessor is a tiny package that shrinks a virtual truckload of old wiring circuits, tubes, and other rugged electrical gadgets onto a delicate silicon chip. They've flooded our houses, not only in home computers, calculators, and stereos, but also in the controls of TVs, VCRs, garage door openers, and telephones.

Microprocessors don't operate at the voltage of our electrical systems. They would burn up with that much power. Instead, each has a built-in power supply that converts 120-volt electricity to about 5 volts. And there's the rub. To keep their data properly channeled, microprocessors like a nice, steady current. Small changes in power, even the split-second hit from a surge, can scramble the electrical signals. A surge that slips by the power supply or blasts through it can easily punch through delicate chips, burn out circuits, and leave you with a pile of worthless electronic junk.

Where do surges come from?

You don't have to be an electronics junkie to understand surge basics. By far the most dramatic and catastrophic surge comes from a lightning strike. If your electrical system takes a direct hit, you can kiss good-

ELECTRONIC DEVICES WITH SENSITIVE MICROELECTRONICS
- Computers, printers, fax machines
- VCRs, TVs, stereos
- Kitchen appliances with microprocessor controllers such as ranges, dishwashers, ovens, and microwaves
- Intercoms, security systems
- Clothes washers with microprocessor controllers
- Garage door openers
- Plug-in radios
- Answering machines
- Smoke alarms
- Programmable thermostats
- Telephones
- Dimmers, motion detectors, microprocessor timers
- Microprocessor-controlled power tools

bye all the electronics that are plugged in and often stuff that isn't. But the chances are low that this will ever happen. It's more likely that lightning will induce a surge in your house's electrical system (*page 73*). A lightning strike generates a brief but very powerful magnetic field in the surrounding atmosphere. Any electrical wiring from the utility pole and throughout the house acts like a radio antenna and picks up an electrical charge from the magnetic field as it briefly forms and collapses. But lightning does not even have to hit nearby power lines to cause damage. It could generate a charge from some distance away, and any power lines between your house and the lightning strike will conduct the surge.

Surprisingly, some of the most troublesome electrical surges come from right inside your own house. Large electric motors like the ones in your refrigerator, freezer, or air conditioner generate a surge every time they switch on. Lightweight electric motors like the one in your vacuum cleaner also cause surges.

Surges aren't one-way affairs, either. The surge can run through any wire in the system in any direction and out to any device on the branch circuits. Not all of these surges are harmful, but they occur regularly as motorized appliances cycle on and off.

Shopping for surge protection

Good surge protection is expensive, easily costing about $75 or more. That presents the home owner with a dilemma. Is it practical to invest that much money to protect moderately expensive devices such as TVs and VCRs that cost $300 or $400, much less relatively inexpensive items such as telephones and garage door openers? Is it wiser to settle for less expensive but less complete protection and gamble that a big surge won't come?

Unfortunately, there's no simple answer. There are a wide range of plug-in protective devices called *surge suppressors* or *protectors*. As you might expect, higher quality surge suppressors cost more, and it's easy to get lost in electronic jargon when you're trying to choose the best one for your money and your needs. In general, look for these three things in a suppressor: a quicker response time, lower clamping voltage (as explained below), and higher energy-handling capability.

• *Response time:* Suppression devices have to react fast to sudden rises in voltage. Otherwise, the most damaging part of the surge, the initial burst, will pass through to the sensitive electronic components before the suppression kicks in. Look for devices with response times of less than 10 nanoseconds (that's 10 billionths of a second). That information should be stamped on the device itself or on its package.

• *Clamping voltage:* Suppressors react to the voltage level. When the voltage rises, the suppressor kicks in and diverts all voltage above that level. Essentially, the surge voltage that gets through shouldn't be able to exceed that clamped level. Look for surge protection that clamps at 300 volts or less.

• *Energy handling:* The longer the surge lasts, the more energy it carries and the more energy the suppressor must divert or absorb. A suppressor will burn out immediately if the surge exceeds its energy-absorbing capability.

Utility companies in many parts of the country sell a suppressor designed to absorb most lightning-induced surges; it costs about $160 installed. It's mounted at the electric meter or main panel and reacts relatively slowly, but it can absorb the intense energy induced by most nearby lightning strikes. You can choose this type and still install faster responding protectors to handle the residual charge that gets in as well as lighter surges produced from inside the house.

Look for two other features. First, the suppressor should have so-called three-line protection. That simply means that the device protects all three wires—the hot, neutral, and ground—since surges can travel through any one of them. Second, make sure the suppressor has some sort of indicator so you know it is no longer working. Most suppressors can take only so many hits before they start to wear out. You need to know this so you can replace it. Just as with polarized plugs and reverse polarity, a false sense of security can be worse than having no protection at all.

How much protection should you buy? Unfortunately, there are no easy answers when it comes to deciding how much to spend. Buy good suppressors for all your expensive equipment and those items that would cause you grief if they failed. Expect to pay at least $100 or more for these. If you live in a region with frequent thunderstorms, such as Florida, it might be worthwhile to protect your less expensive equipment, too. And remember, there's always one inexpensive solution. Simply pull the plug on your electronic devices when you're not using them.

Electric Lights: Yesterday and Today

The new glow in home lighting

Much of the way electricity works in the house is invisible. All the wiring is hidden behind the walls and in the ceiling with the electrical outlets and switches as the only visible reminders that the electricity is close at hand. Perhaps there's no better symbol of that convenience than the first electrical device to enter the home—the electric light bulb.

In the last few years, new kinds of light bulbs have proliferated like fireflies on a warm summer night. When you shop for them you'll encounter a bewildering array of sizes and shapes, and your confusion may be compounded by many newly invented bulbs that look identical to the old standard ones.

There are at least four types of improvements to electric light bulbs: (1) more efficient bulbs that use less electricity while casting the same amount of light, (2) bulbs that last longer and virtually won't burn out, (3) brighter bulbs that highlight colors brilliantly, and (4) compact fluorescent bulbs that are efficient and color balanced.

You can clear up some of the confusion caused by this vast array of light bulbs by looking at the tinkering that scientists and engineers have done to improve the incandescent bulb, changes that improve home lighting so as to make it more maintenance-free, less expensive, and more brilliant.

Making incandescence work

Incandescence is the light produced by a hot, glowing wire. Light bulbs that produce light from such a glowing wire have come to be called incandescent bulbs.

It took the genius of inventor Thomas Edison in 1879 to recognize not only that driving an electric current through a wire caused it to heat up and glow, but also that if it got hot enough, it might produce enough light so you could read the newspaper in the evening.

Spurred forward by this idea and blessed with stubborn persistence, Edison tested thousands of types of thin wires, called *filaments,* before coming up with a strand of carbon, which made his new light bulb a commercial success. While modern filaments are made from a metal called tungsten, it's surprising that today's familiar light bulb (*facing page*) still closely resembles an early Edison bulb. In fact, the screw base on today's bulb is the same and is called an Edison base.

The problems Edison faced still plague scientists today. How do you get the filament to glow brightly enough to emit light without burn-

THE STANDARD INCANDESCENT BULB

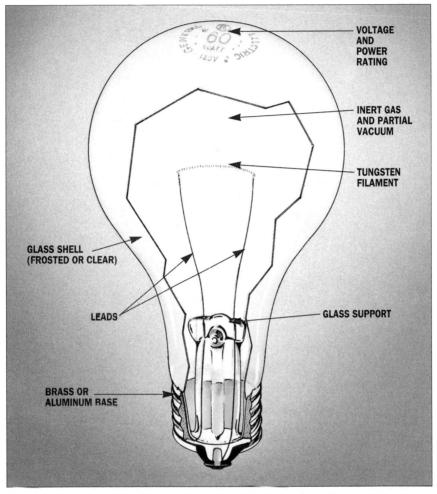

VOLTAGE AND POWER RATING

INERT GAS AND PARTIAL VACUUM

TUNGSTEN FILAMENT

GLASS SHELL (FROSTED OR CLEAR)

LEADS

GLASS SUPPORT

BRASS OR ALUMINUM BASE

Electricity flows through the fine wire filament, making it glow (incandescence). The glass globe contains a partial vacuum and inert gases to help cool the filament.

ing out? The dull red glow of a hot wire won't do—it doesn't produce nearly enough light. To be worthwhile, the filament must get white hot, roughly to the temperature of 3,800 degrees Fahrenheit. Very few materials can withstand that temperature without vaporizing. Eventually, tungsten proved to be the best, and it became the filament standard that is still in use today.

However, even tungsten needs help. The tungsten inside the glass walls of the bulb is surrounded by a partial vacuum and inert gases that won't react with the hot metal filament and cause it to decompose. Those gases perform another vital function: they cool the filament by transmitting heat away to the glass walls of the bulb, which then release it to the surrounding air. If that heat were held in, either the filament would overheat and break or the glass walls of the bulb would melt.

That's why you can buy standard light bulbs in different sizes. You'll see that a 150-watt bulb is larger than a 60- or 100-watt bulb. On any bulb, if the glass walls are too close to the filament, they'll melt.

Unfortunately, all this heat is wasted energy. (Typically, more than 99 percent of the energy a bulb consumes is wasted as heat.) All we want is the light; the heat is just an inconvenient by-product. This didn't matter much when electrical energy was cheap. But as the energy costs and the demand for electricity began to rise, engineers took another look at incandescent bulbs to try to reduce the amount of energy they wasted and make them more efficient.

Standard incandescent bulbs are bright, but not really white hot. Light from the sun, produced at several million degrees Fahrenheit and reaching our eyes at midday at an apparent temperature of 18,032 to 117,032 degrees, better represents white light. Of course, sunlight isn't that hot. The apparent quality of its light makes it *seem* as if it were that hot. Standard light bulbs produce a yellower light because the filament burns at 3,812 degrees Fahrenheit, much cooler than the temperature needed to produce the very white light similar to sunlight.

But here's the rub. A hotter and whiter burning filament is more efficient because it converts more electricity to light and less to heat. Does this sound like a contradiction? A hotter filament creates less heat? Imagine a 60-watt bulb that's been made brighter without increasing the electrical flow. Then to reduce the light back to the old level, you decrease the electricity to perhaps 55 watts and save 5 watts of power.

This is exactly what engineers did. Much as Edison did more than a hundred years ago, they tinkered with the filament, trying to get it to burn brighter without consuming more electricity. They succeeded by improving the metallic composition of the tungsten and by thinning or lengthening the filament. They also added at least one support, perhaps only a single thin wire, to stabilize the more fragile filament.

Unfortunately, these new energy-efficient bulbs haven't really caught on. A 10-percent savings in energy consumption doesn't seem like much when the bulb costs perhaps 20 percent more in the first place. The energy savings eventually pay back that extra cost, but only a dollar or two is saved over the life of the bulb.

Bulb failure and the long-life bulb

Most standard bulbs are rated at a life span of about 1,000-hours. But why not 2,000 hours, or 3,000? A partial answer lies in bulb design. The filament is the weak spot. An electrical charge jolts it suddenly and violently every time you turn on the light switch.

We all know how readily metal expands and contracts with changes in temperature. Imagine the violent seizure the thin tungsten wire experiences when it heats up from room temperature to 3,800-plus degrees in a split second. It goes crazy, heaving about violently and erratically. Finally, once heated, it settles into a rhythmic vibration. It's that initial shock, however, that in time fractures the filament and causes the burnout. That's why incandescent bulbs burn out most often when you turn on the light.

Engineers devised two ways to avoid this problem. First, they added filament supports (*below*) to reduce those initial contortions. Second, they made the filament thicker and stronger. That heavy-duty filament is indicated by the voltage rating that is stamped on the package and on

THE LONG-LIFE BULB

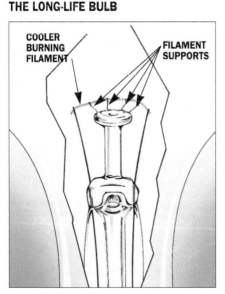

COOLER BURNING FILAMENT

FILAMENT SUPPORTS

A long-life bulb has more filament supports to reduce filament vibration when the bulb is switched on.

the glass tops of most light bulbs. A standard bulb reads 120 volts; the long-life bulb reads 130 volts.

Without getting too technical, the difference is this: the 120-volt bulb burns hotter and brighter than the 130-volt long-life bulb of the same wattage. Because the 130-volt bulb burns cooler, it lasts longer. But, unfortunately, it also burns less efficiently and gives off less light.

Does the energy waste negate the long-life advantage? Initially, you would have to say yes, except in a few instances where it isn't worth the effort to replace a burned-out bulb as often as a standard bulb—for example, in a night light, ceiling fixture, or yard light.

But on the other hand, more often than not long-life bulbs will be worth their extra cost. First, most manufacturers now make long-life bulbs that also use energy-efficient filaments. Second, in most cases the electrical service that reaches your house from the public utility is no longer set at 120 volts. To increase the electrical supply through existing power lines, electrical utilities have often cranked up the voltage to 125 volts or higher. This makes the 130-volt long-life bulb burn more efficiently, but it actually decreases the life of a standard 120-volt bulb. This factor alone makes the long-life bulb a good deal despite its higher initial cost.

There is yet another way to save money, both on electricity and for replacing burned-out bulbs. Engineers have recently developed bulbs that turn themselves off after a certain length of time—say, 10 minutes. A computer chip in the base of the bulb senses how long it has been on and cuts off the power after a preset time. These bulbs are ideal for basements, closets, or attics where you might accidentally leave a light on for weeks at a time. You can also buy special adapters with this computer-chip technology that let you use ordinary light bulbs but get the same benefits.

Creating a brilliant light

A quick glance at the earlier bulbs sets the stage for the most spectacular incandescent bulb of all, the *tungsten halogen,* sometimes called the quartz halogen (*right*). This bulb produces an extraordinarily white light, much closer to the light of the noontime sun, that renders colors brilliantly. Its very high temperature makes it more efficient, so it uses less electricity to produce the same amount of light. But engineers had to solve a problem of excessive heat buildup around the filament. Of course, the heat in a 60-watt tungsten halogen bulb is no more (and actually slightly less) than the heat produced by a standard 60-watt bulb because the energy consumed is the same. But that heat is produced by a much smaller filament in a smaller area, so it has to be cooled faster.

Quartz halogen technology has solved that problem. The peanut-sized quartz envelope withstands the high temperature while encasing the halogen gas whose job it is to transfer heat away from the filament quickly. The quartz envelopes get extremely hot, more than 1,800 degrees Fahrenheit. Since we're talking serious burns here, manufacturers usually encapsulate the quartz envelope inside a sealed glass shell as well.

THE TUNGSTEN HALOGEN BULB

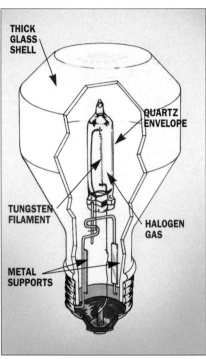

THICK GLASS SHELL

QUARTZ ENVELOPE

TUNGSTEN FILAMENT

HALOGEN GAS

METAL SUPPORTS

The quartz glass envelope in the center of the bulb allows the filament to burn hotter, creating a whiter light.

In fact, the high heat of these bulbs limits how you can use them. They'll melt ordinary plastic sockets. You should screw them only into ceramic sockets because the filament is so hot and close to its base that it drives the intense heat back through the electrical connections into the base material.

Cost is another limiting factor. Currently, halogen bulbs are three to five times the cost of an ordinary bulb. They're more efficient and last at least twice as long, but it's doubtful that these savings will pay back their initial high cost.

THE REFLECTOR BULB

QUARTZ
ENVELOPE

GLASS
SHELL

TUNGSTEN
FILAMENT

HALOGEN
GAS

REFLECTOR   QUARTER

The tungsten halogen reflector bulb is a small, powerful spotlight that dramatically highlights colors.

But designers love these bulbs because they bring a new dimension to home lighting. They're small, so they can be put in smaller, less conspicuous fixtures without reducing the overall amount of light in the room. And they perform particularly well in reflector bulbs (*above*), as spotlights, or as floodlights, where their whiter light illuminates objects brilliantly, highlighting colors in a strikingly vivid way.

Fluorescent lights come home

When it comes to energy efficiency and longevity, you already have an excellent choice. Fluorescent lights, long the standard style of lighting for supermarkets, department stores, business offices, schools, and factories, have slowly but surely invaded our houses.

Of course, they aren't completely new to houses. They first gained a foothold in our workshops and laundry rooms, those utilitarian work spaces where people didn't give a hoot about aesthetics. Forget how the bulb looked; they just wanted the lighting to be bright, even, and glare-free so they could make sure the clothes came clean or that the small scale on the measuring tape was easy to read.

Fluorescent light bulbs next crept up to the kitchen, another busy work area that needed good, even lighting. Again, the bulbs were practical but not very attractive, so designers hid the fluorescent tubes behind translucent plastic panels in suspended ceilings or they tucked them out of sight beneath the cabinets or in the spaces over the tops of the cabinets. Now, thanks to a new compact design, fluorescent light bulbs wait at the thresholds of other rooms in the house. To understand the significance of this, step back a moment and look at how a fluorescent light bulb creates light.

How do fluorescents work?

A fluorescent tube generates light in a much different way than an incandescent bulb does. The tungsten filament is still there in the form of an

HOW A FLUORESCENT BULB WORKS

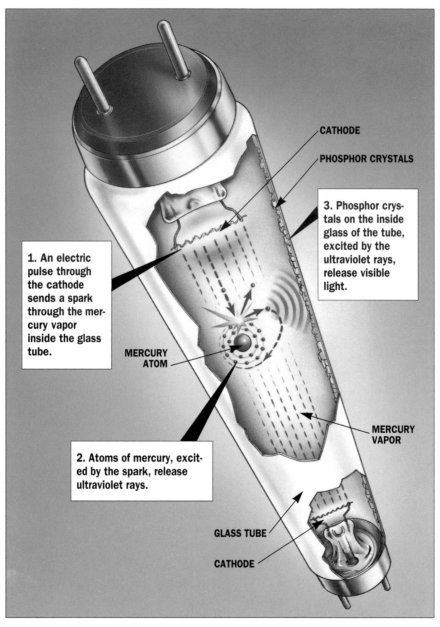

CATHODE

PHOSPHOR CRYSTALS

3. Phosphor crystals on the inside glass of the tube, excited by the ultraviolet rays, release visible light.

1. An electric pulse through the cathode sends a spark through the mercury vapor inside the glass tube.

MERCURY ATOM

MERCURY VAPOR

2. Atoms of mercury, excited by the spark, release ultraviolet rays.

GLASS TUBE

CATHODE

Fluorescent bulbs emit light in rapid pulses, 120 times per second, that our eyes perceive as a continuous glow.

electron-emitting *cathode* to generate energy inside the bulb, but it doesn't actually generate the light. Rather, it creates an electrical spark that jumps from a cathode at one end of the tube to a cathode at the opposite end (*facing page*).

Normally it would take a lot of electric power to make that long of a jump, but mercury vapor, sealed inside the tube, makes that leap easier. You can't see the spark itself. Its purpose is to start a chain reaction. It energizes the mercury atoms in the vapor, causing them to release ultraviolet rays. The ultraviolet rays in turn strike the many tiny crystals (called *phosphors*) that coat the inner surface of the bulb and energize them. These phosphors emit visible light. While this process is complicated to explain, it occurs instantaneously. In fact, the cathodes emit 120 sparks each second.

Two other pieces of hardware are needed to make the fluorescent bulb work. One is an electric transformer, called a *ballast*, which controls the power supply. The other is a *starter*, which gives the bulb a good, swift electrical kick to get it going.

The fluorescent bulb was first introduced in 1939, but by that time the incandescent was well established, so the future of fluorescents might well have been dim except in the garish form of their well-known cousins, neon lights. But fluorescent bulbs have two distinct, important advantages over incandescents. Fluorescent bulbs are about four times as energy efficient, requiring only one-quarter the electricity to produce the same amount of light. And they won't burn out for a long time, usually lasting 10 to 20 times longer than an incandescent bulb.

It is not surprising that these efficiencies made fluorescent bulbs popular where costs mattered most, in commercial and industrial uses. They became the lighting of choice for the workplace, stores, and most large commercial buildings, where they had other advantages as well. By emitting light over the length of the tube rather than from single-point sources as incandescents do, fluorescents eliminate most shadows and glare, making detailed work easier and faster.

Bring them home?

Perhaps it's that very image of efficiency that sharply limits our interest, as home owners, in fluorescent lights. After all, home is supposed to give us a break from the daily pressure of an efficient routine. We want to come home to a comfortable and relaxed setting that leaves the workplace behind.

There were other drawbacks to fluorescent lights. Designers had difficulty making those long, tubular bulbs attractive. They looked, well, *industrial*. Bending the tubes into a U-shape or circle helped somewhat, but otherwise, designers had to hide these bulbs to cloak their commercial, workplace aura.

Then there's the problem of color. Fluorescents cast a nice white light that brings good color rendition and definition to objects, but unfortunately it "feels" cold. Of course, we don't really feel the light, but somehow our minds register a cool sensation from fluorescents. And that's not the feeling we want when we're at home trying to relax.

95

COMPACT FLUORESCENT BULBS

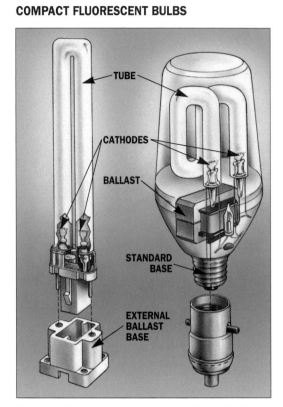

Compact fluorescents conform more closely to the shape and size of traditional incandescent bulbs. They often can fit into regular light fixtures.

On the other hand, incandescent lights, which give off light that is much more yellow than sunlight, seem warm to us, making them the overwhelming choice for a pleasant home atmosphere.

Fluorescent bulbs shrink...

Recent developments in fluorescent lighting have solved most of these problems. The so-called compact fluorescent bulbs, which have been available since about 1990, give designers a smaller bulb to work with.

Some of these bulbs come with the bulb, the ballast, and the starter all crammed inside a single unit, while others are available with an adapter that screws into the standard socket used by incandescent bulbs (*left*).

That puts these bulbs in head-to-head competition with incandescents, even though some compact fluorescents are too long to fit in a standard fixture and some are too wide. In principle, however, engineers have tried to make compact fluorescents interchangeable with standard incandescent bulbs.

...and take new colors

They've also succeeded in warming up fluorescents by altering their color mix. As you recall, phosphors deposited on the inside surface of the tube emit the visible light. Since different phosphors release different colors, lighting engineers have been able to develop an array of fluorescent colors simply by changing the mix of the phosphors in the bulbs.

Different combinations of phosphors vary to give white light slightly different effects. Some shadings strike us as cool and efficient while others appear warm and cozy.

So-called *cool white* bulbs would probably feel too cool for all but the most utilitarian task lighting such as that found in a workshop or over a laundry countertop. The cool white "deluxe" bulbs distribute their energy more to the red side of the color spectrum, which makes them feel warmer, though still not as warm as incandescent bulbs feel.

Lighting engineers have recently been able to develop a range of color-balanced bulbs by adding rare earth elements such as barium magnesium aluminate, yttrium oxide, and cerium aluminate to their mix of phosphors. They've concentrated these phosphors in the part of the spectrum where the eye is most sensitive yet still sees the color mix as white. These trichromatic (three-color) lights render colors better and provide light more efficiently.

The benefits

Fluorescents should become more popular because of their improved color and smaller size. But as energy costs rise, their strongest selling point will be their superior efficiency. A fluorescent bulb consumes only about one-fourth the electricity of an equally bright incandescent bulb, and they last about 10 to 20 times longer. They're by far the best deal for heavily used lighting and for lights that stay on all night.

The limitations

Then why haven't cost-conscious home owners embraced fluorescent bulbs more quickly? There are five reasons for the lack of enthusiasm.

First, the savings aren't as large as you might first imagine. You may save five times as much electricity, but the average cost of lighting for an average house is less than $100 per year to begin with. You're not likely to save more than half of that, since you'll still prefer incandescents in many places.

Second, fluorescents are expensive. You're used to buying incandescents that cost less than a dollar each and last long enough that you don't think twice about replacing one. But compact fluorescents cost $5 to $15 each. They'll save in the long run, but the initial purchase price hurts.

Third, until recently manufacturers produced compact fluorescents primarily in lower wattages, corresponding to 60-watt and less incandescent bulbs. A 60-watt bulb is not very bright. Even two such bulbs placed around a bathroom mirror will seem dim. And you need at least 100-watt incandescents for reading and larger still for general room lighting. Manufacturers had trouble figuring out how to pack enough phosphors into a compact bulb to give off more light. They've been partially successful, and now brighter bulbs are available.

Fourth, compact fluorescents tend to be larger sized and more oddly shaped than incandescents. This is part of the price of making brighter bulbs. They don't always look good in standard fixtures and the brighter ones are often too large to fit. Manufacturers have partially corrected this problem by developing a wider array of bulb styles and designing fixtures specifically for use with compact fluorescent bulbs. These fixtures are well worth a look when buying fixtures.

Fifth, you can't put a fluorescent bulb on a dimmer. Well, you actually can. But the special ballast and dimmer cost about $100, as compared to about $5 for a simple dimmer for incandescents.

Perhaps the greatest advance in home conveniences occurred the day plumbing moved inside the house for good. No more wet, cold trips to the outhouse; no more chamber pots at night; no more hauling water from the pump and dumping waste water into the garden; and no more bad smells from the sewers. Fresh water was piped in and waste water ran out.

PLUMBING COMES HOME

Of course, a few held out even after they had indoor plumbing. Year after year my grandfather took a daily afternoon stroll down to the mountain ash grove to sit and "meditate" in the old 2-seat outhouse. Convinced that indoor plumbing was a mixed blessing, he continued this ritual until he died.

It was about that time, the late 1960s, that the popularity of those rooms that contained plumbing, the bathroom and kitchen, took off. Kitchens, once small, grew larger and became the center of family life. And since then, busy families have discovered that one or two bathrooms aren't enough. No one wants to wait in the morning.

None of this would have been possible without good sanitation and the equipment that make cleanliness possible. Pipes lead the way. Always strong and durable, they've recently become more user-friendly for home owners who want to jump in and repair their own plumbing.

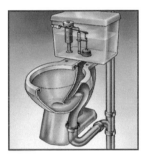

Sinks and bathrooms finally moved inside once plumbers developed smoothly functioning drain systems that rarely clog up and, most important, keep the stench of the sewer out. The invention of the one-piece ceramic toilet solved the problem of the sanitary disposal of waste. And that continues to evolve under pressure from the need for water conservation.

The Evolution of Pipes

Convenience and sanitation go hand in hand

A historian might tell you the keys to civilization's pulling itself from the primordial muck and heading for the modern city were high ideals, capital accumulation, and big brains. Go ask any plumber, though, and he is more likely to point to good pipes. And for good reason. In the past, citizens of large cities were at the mercy of periodic epidemics that killed them by the thousands. These plagues were unstoppable. It wasn't until the mid-1800s when physicians discovered that waste, garbage, filth, and disease go hand in hand that any notion of sanitation began to evolve and prevent the devastation of infectious diseases.

The key to good sanitation is a plumbing system that gets rid of waste and garbage without leaving a pool of bacteria and scum to foul our homes and pollute the fresh water supply. The solution was to construct two completely separate systems, a *water supply system* that delivers clean water to your home and a drain system (called drain, waste, and vent or *DWV system* by the pros) that channels all the waste downward through your house to the sewer below.

The supply system enters your house underground, far enough down so that it doesn't freeze in winter. You'll find a valve where it emerges inside called the *main shut-off valve*. Knowing where to find this valve can come in handy should a broken pipe or leaky faucet force you to shut off the entire system. From the main valve the supply lines branch out to faucets throughout the house.

The DWV system begins at the sink, bathtub, toilet, and shower drains. From here it carries waste water downhill, joining pipes from other drains until it connects with the sewer buried beneath your house. From there it leaves your house and empties into the municipal sewer system or a septic tank. The DWV system has another element, as well, the vents, which run upward, join together, and eventually poke through the roof. (There is more about these vents, which release harmful sewer gases, in the next chapter.)

None of this was possible until we had good pipes. You might say that modern plumbing began only about 130 years ago when a new specialist called a plumber began to figure out how to put pipes in homes. Most of these systems lasted a long time; you can still find these early types of pipe, mostly lead and cast iron and later galvanized steel, in older homes. But during the last 40 years less expensive and easier to install copper and plastic pipe have gradually replaced lead, iron, and steel (*facing page*).

100

CHANGE IN WATER SUPPLY LINES: STEEL TO COPPER

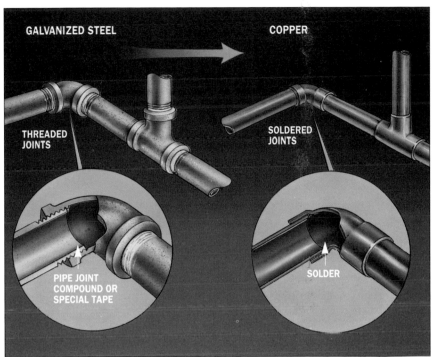

GALVANIZED STEEL

COPPER

THREADED
JOINTS

SOLDERED
JOINTS

PIPE JOINT
COMPOUND OR
SPECIAL TAPE

SOLDER

Threaded galvanized steel systems required professional tools to thread and fit. Copper pipe is much easier to use and has largely replaced steel for water supply lines.

Lead pipe

Many people have probably never even seen lead pipe other than in the board game *Clue*. (Remember "Mr. Green did it with the lead pipe in the billiard room"?) Unfortunately, neither the picture nor the game token shows a lead pipe but rather shows a galvanized pipe with threaded ends.

Lead pipe is too soft to receive threads, so soft you can easily bend a 2-inch pipe with your bare hands. For this reason, plumbers commonly used lead pipe for toilet and sink drains up through the 1950s. They could snake it around and through the framework in floors and walls.

Using lead to make pipe isn't a new idea. Two thousand years ago, Roman plumbers fabricated and installed it to supply running water to public baths and the houses of the upper classes. In fact, the word "plumbing" itself comes from the Latin word for lead, *plumbum*. And lead pipes generally serve trouble-free for decades.

In the past decade, however, health officials have become more aware of the toxic effects of lead and the ways it can enter the human body. The Environmental Protection Agency and local health departments are keeping an eye on lead pipes and copper pipes joined with lead solder. They're concerned that lead will leach out of the pipes and solder and enter the drinking water.

Fortunately, lead on the inside surface of a pipe quickly reacts with sulfates, carbonates, and phosphates in the fresh water supply to form a coating that keeps it from leaching out. Experts believe, however, that the lead content in water is likely to exceed safe guidelines when the water is highly acidic or is allowed to sit in the lead pipes for a long time.

Cast iron

On the other end of plumbing fixtures, the DWV side, cast iron used to be standard. Sewer pipes running underground to the street were also cast iron or sometimes clay tile.

Cast iron contains about 4 percent carbon, which makes it so hard that you virtually can't cut it with a saw. To cut it, plumbers first score it and then crack it with a hammer and chisel or they use a special tool called a chain cutter. If you live in an older house, you can spot that rough, black-painted or rust-colored cast-iron pipe (*right*) beneath the house or in the basement. It doesn't corrode easily, so it lasts a long time. It's too hard to thread for screw joints, however, so until recently plumbers had to join it at its hub joints using molten lead.

These days, plumbers rarely use cast-iron pipes in new residential construction, although it's still commonly used in the plumbing for commercial buildings because of the greater load the pipes in these

CAST-IRON DWV PIPE

Old-style lead joints on cast-iron pipes had to be joined by pouring molten lead.

busy buildings must carry. In those cases, thanks to a recent invention, plumbers don't have to pour those lead joints. A sleeve made of a special flexible plastic called *neoprene* makes so-called hubless cast-iron joints possible (*facing page, right*).

DWV PIPES BECOME EASIER TO WORK ON: PLASTIC AND HUBLESS IRON

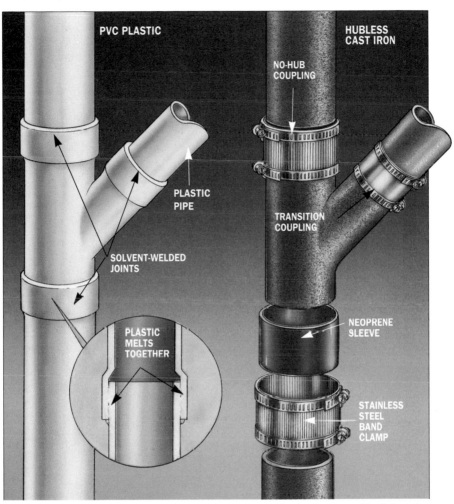

New hubless joints make the job easier. Plumbers now run plastic pipe for residential waste lines because it's even easier and more economical than cast iron.

Galvanized steel pipe

Galvanized pipe is the old standard material so familiar to our parents and grandparents. It supplied water to our faucets for more than half a century until copper took over during the 1960s. It's easy for you to rec- ognize those old gray galvanized pipes, threaded on both ends and joined by knobby-looking elbows and couplings (*page 101*). They were supposed to last only 20 to 30 years, but in many houses they've lasted twice as long.

Steel pipes do have weaknesses, though. They rust and eventually spring leaks. In addition, they allow mineral deposits to build up inside, which then reduces their inside diameter and results in reduced water pressure at the faucets.

Copper pipe

In the 1950s the price of copper, which had been quite expensive up to that point, finally dropped far enough for plumbers to begin to use it regularly in place of galvanized steel. By 1970, copper water supply lines had almost completely replaced galvanized steel in new house construction. Copper pipe lasts twice as long (about 50 years), resists mineral buildups that tend to clog steel pipes, and, most important, is easy to cut and join.

Copper is a softer metal than steel, so a plumber can quickly cut it with an inexpensive tube cutter or hacksaw. To join copper, a plumber solders the joints—*sweats* them, as they say—with a propane or acetylene torch and solder. It so happens that tin and antimony bond easily to copper and melt at low temperatures, so they make an easy-to-use solder. Earlier solders were made from a 50/50 ratio of tin to lead, but building codes recently changed to get the lead out and reduce the chances of lead leaching into drinking water. Solder is now 95 percent tin and 5 percent antimony.

Plastic: ABS and PVC

About the same time that pipes made of copper began to replace steel supply pipes, plastics began to replace steel and cast iron in the household DWV system. Plastic, of course, is lightweight and easy to cut. Plumbers use a hand saw to cut both of the two types of plastics most commonly used in houses—*ABS* (acrylonitrile-butadiene-styrene) and *PVC* (polyvinyl chloride). You can tell them apart because ABS is black (the "B" in ABS can remind you) and PVC is usually white, although it comes in many shades of off-white and gray. Manufacturers usually mark the type of plastic on all fittings and lengths of pipe for easy identification.

Using solvents to weld ABS or PVC joints gives plastic a huge advantage over cast-iron and steel joints. Plastic fittings have hubs that fit snugly over the ends of the pipes. To bond them, you apply a special solvent to the surfaces being joined, then simply push the pieces together. The solvent melts the top layers of plastic on the pipe and fitting, allowing them to fuse and become one when the solvent evaporates. Solvent welding doesn't work on all plastics, only on so-called thermoplastics, which include ABS and PVC. (Thermoplastics are materials molded under heat. They can be melted and remolded any number of times. Because of their sensitivity to heat, ABS and PVC are not used for hot water lines.) In addition, PVC must be cleaned with a special primer to remove the surface glaze from the factory before applying the solvent and bonding.

Plastic: CPVC and PB

Plastic water supply systems are not as popular as copper, probably because copper established itself first and performs well, although copper costs more (*facing page*).

CPVC (chlorinated polyvinyl chloride), which is similar to PVC, is designed to handle hot as well as cold water. It can usually be identified by its cream color, but check the manufacturer's stamp on the plastic to be sure. CPVC, like PVC, is a thermoplastic and therefore can be solvent welded.

PB (polybutylene) pipe, on the other hand, cannot be welded with solvent. Its primary advantage is its flexibility. Plumbers can snake long lengths of it through walls, much like a garden hose, so it needs fewer of the joints that other types of pipes would need to get around minor obstacles. It is also less susceptible to damage from freezing.

Since PB joints can't be solvent welded, plumbers must use compression fittings instead. These fittings cost considerably more than other types of fittings, but fewer of them are required. There is one disadvantage to using PB pipes, however: builders must leave these joints easily accessible in case the fittings need to be repaired, so the pipes can't be closed up inside walls.

PLASTIC SUPPLY LINES

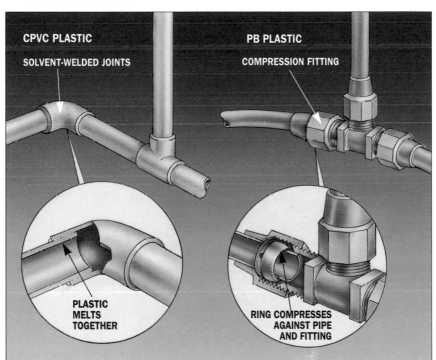

CPVC PLASTIC

SOLVENT-WELDED JOINTS

PB PLASTIC

COMPRESSION FITTING

PLASTIC MELTS TOGETHER

RING COMPRESSES AGAINST PIPE AND FITTING

CPVC is rigid but is easily cut with a hand saw and joined with a special solvent. PB is flexible and must be joined with special compression fittings.

Making Drains Work

Inventing the P-trap and opening clogged drains

Drains may look simple, but there's a lot more going on than first meets the eye. A length of pipe from the sink drops down through a U-shaped "squiggle," then runs horizontally until it disappears into the wall, presumably taking all the drain water and waste with it. When I was 8 years old, I figured the squiggle, actually called a *P–trap*, was a special blessing for little kids with slippery fingers. If I should happen to accidentally drop my fish down the drain while cleaning the fish bowl, I'd find it swimming around inside the trap, if not happily, at least alive.

But my childhood notion about what a P–trap does and how it works was mostly wrong. While it is able to catch some dropped treasures, that is not its primary purpose. As simple as it looks, a P–trap is actually a sophisticated piece of hardware (*page 109*). It took generations of plumbers working through trial and error to perfect it.

The problem of bad odors

Draining the waste water from a sink was never particularly difficult; any downward sloping pipe would do. But doing it while keeping the smells of the sewer out of the house was the big hurdle. The same pipes that carried waste water to the sewer system brought the smelly and potentially lethal sewer gases back up into the house. For all practical purposes, these bad smells kept the outhouse in business (and outdoors) well into this century.

Some earlier solutions to this odor dilemma simply weren't practical. Several thousand years ago, Roman plumbers solved the problem for nobility by directing a steady stream of water through the indoor bathroom. The stream was a flushing mechanism that washed the waste and smells away. Of course, this luxury worked well only if you lived upstream. But you quickly lost your popularity with the neighbors downstream! So the idea never really caught on.

When concern for better sanitation arose in England in the mid-1800s, inventors came up with many solutions for blocking out sewer gas. Few solutions proved to be sanitary, but the *S–trap* (*facing page*) stood above the rest. When you filled the low bend in the S–trap with water, it effectively plugged the pipe and prevented sewer gases from flowing back into the house.

While the theory was good, the S–trap didn't work that well. First of all, you could not assume that the bend in the pipe would fill automatically. Water rushing down through the drainpipe created a suction that pulled most of the remaining water along with it. This suction, known as *siphoning*, pulled the water seal through the S-shaped bend in the pipe. To restore the water seal, you had to remember to pour a little water down the drain after draining a sink or flushing a toilet to make sure the trap filled. You'd quickly smell the problem if you forgot.

Today's toilets work exactly on this S-trap principle, except that the siphoning action is deliberate, which ensures the waste will be sucked from the bowl (*page 118*). Then, as the water tank refills itself, a small amount of water remains in the bowl to seal out sewer gases.

Occasionally, the S-trap caused another problem called a *blow-out*. A blow out occurred when a charge of water (called a *slug*) came down a drainpipe shared with a fixture on the floor above. As the slug rapidly dropped, it compressed the air in the pipes below it. This sudden compression forced the water seal in the traps of connecting drains back up into their sinks. Then, once passed, the slug often created a suction that siphoned water from traps as well.

The key invention

The solution to the siphoning problem came through trial and error. Finally, a plumber experimenting with vents in 1874 came up with a unique idea. The trick to keeping the water plug in place was to equalize the air pressure in the drain system. To do this, plumbers added an extra pipe, called a *vent*, to the traps that led out to open air, a kind of pressure-relief system.

THE S–TRAP

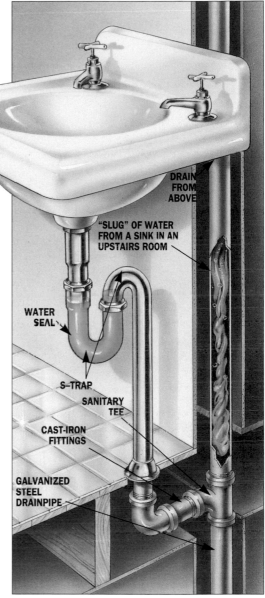

DRAIN FROM ABOVE

"SLUG" OF WATER FROM A SINK IN AN UPSTAIRS ROOM

WATER SEAL

S–TRAP

SANITARY TEE

CAST-IRON FITTINGS

GALVANIZED STEEL DRAINPIPE

The S–trap was a big stride toward blocking sewer gases and allowing plumbing to come indoors.

The pipe ran upward so water would not fill it and clog it up (*right*). Eventually, plumbers ran the vent pipe up through the roof so that sewer gases wouldn't stink up the house. This vent pipe finally put the outhouse out of business for good.

Plumbers continued to improve this vent system, and they eventually developed a basic rule of plumbing: every fixture must have a trap, and every trap must have a vent. As a result of this, the drain system in today's house has nearly as many pipes extending up to fresh air as it has going down. You might never know it because you can't see the vents unless you have a sink in an unfinished room where the pipes are exposed. Otherwise, plumbers enclose vents inside walls. Look at the roof of your house; one or more pipes, 2 to 4 inches in diameter, will be poking out. At least one pipe will be large, 3 to 4 inches in diameter. This one is called the main vent or the *soil stack* because it usually vents a toilet and the main sewer leading away from the house.

From S–traps to P–traps

The S–trap represented state-of-the-art drain technology in the early part of this century. In fact, while I was browsing through a 1910 edition of

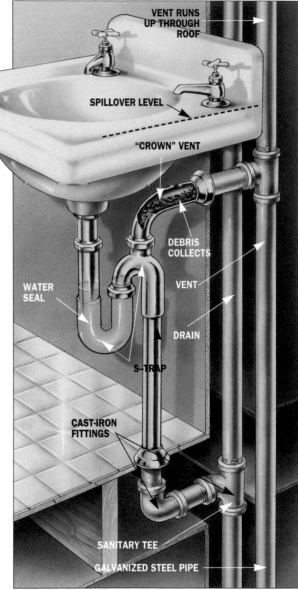

VENTED S–TRAP

VENT RUNS UP THROUGH ROOF

SPILLOVER LEVEL

"CROWN" VENT

DEBRIS COLLECTS

WATER SEAL

VENT

DRAIN

S–TRAP

CAST-IRON FITTINGS

SANITARY TEE

GALVANIZED STEEL PIPE

Adding a vent solved the problem of siphoning and kept the water seal in the S–trap. The vent tended to collect debris and clog up, however, and had to be cleared.

HOW A P–TRAP SEALS A DRAIN

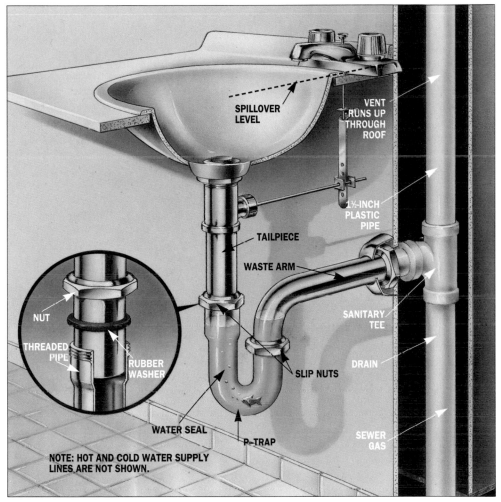

SPILLOVER LEVEL

VENT RUNS UP THROUGH ROOF

1½-INCH PLASTIC PIPE

TAILPIECE

WASTE ARM

NUT

THREADED PIPE

RUBBER WASHER

SANITARY TEE

DRAIN

SLIP NUTS

WATER SEAL

P–TRAP

SEWER GAS

NOTE: HOT AND COLD WATER SUPPLY LINES ARE NOT SHOWN.

A plug of water remains in the low bend in the trap after the sink drains, sealing the pipe and preventing potentially hazardous and foul-smelling sewer gases from entering the room. The vent prevents that water plug from being sucked out.

Sears Roebuck Home Builder's Catalog, I found the S–trap pictured on almost every sink shown. During the next 25 years, however, the S–trap was gradually replaced by the half S–trap or what we now call a P–trap (*above*), so named because it looks like the letter "P" lying on its side.

The change occurred because the vent system for the S–trap proved unreliable. In theory, the vent worked well enough, supplying air to prevent siphoning. But in practice, over a period of years it sometimes failed. Every time water in the drain slowed down, say, because sludge temporarily clogged the waste line, water backed up into the vent. Although it eventually drained out, this waste water left behind oil, grease, and other debris that collected in the horizontal part of the vent pipe. After several years, this sludge could clog up the vent, block the airflow, and allow siphoning to happen in the S–trap itself.

Once again, by trial and error, plumbers learned that the vent had to run vertically to a point above the spillover line on a sink before running horizontally so that the debris wouldn't collect in the vent if the drain clogged. Plumbing officials eventually put this requirement into the plumbing codes.

The P–trap solved these problems because plumbers no longer had to connect the vent directly to the trap. Now, plumbers can install the vent some distance away, conveniently back inside the wall where it's out of sight. From there the vent can run straight up, keeping it clog-free. Once the vent rises above the spillover line of the fixture, it can run horizontally and then join up with other vents, eventually exiting through the roof.

But several problems persisted. To make the system work smoothly, plumbers found that waste water, flowing between the trap and vent in a piece called the *waste arm*, must move at just the right speed. If it flows too slowly, it will leave behind debris, which clogs the pipe. But if waste water moves too fast, it will tumble, fill the pipe, block balanc-

ing air from the vent, and siphon the water from the trap.

As a result, plumbing codes now closely regulate the waste arm section of the drainpipe. It should drop between ⅛ and ¼ inch per foot and extend no more than 42 inches (in most cases, although this figure varies with the diameter of the pipe) before reaching the vent. This arrangement results in the most efficient flow of waste without siphoning any water from the trap.

The *sanitary tee* makes sure the plumber gets the right slope. This joint is designed so that if the vent and drainpipes are exactly plumb (straight up and down), the waste arm that attaches to it will slope ¼ inch per foot.

Another old trap: the drum trap

You're not likely to find an S–trap anymore; most have been replaced. But chances are you will find a *drum trap* (*facing page*) connected to the bathtub drain in an older house. It looks a lot like a 2-pound can of coffee, made from iron, lead, or occasionally brass, with a screw top or bottom. Water from the tub enters near the bottom and exits near the top so the waste water fills the trap and creates a water plug before flowing out. Sometimes the screw-off top, called a *cleanout*, is plated with chrome or brass and left exposed in the floor so you can open the trap to clean it out.

The water seal will not siphon out as easily from a drum trap, so plumbers didn't always vent them. This saved the hassle and expense of running extra pipe, although codes eventually required vents on drum traps, too. Unfortunately, the drum trap causes drainage problems because debris settles and collects in the trap. If not cleaned out regularly, a chore that home owners often ignore, these traps eventually get completely clogged up.

THE UNVENTED DRUM TRAP

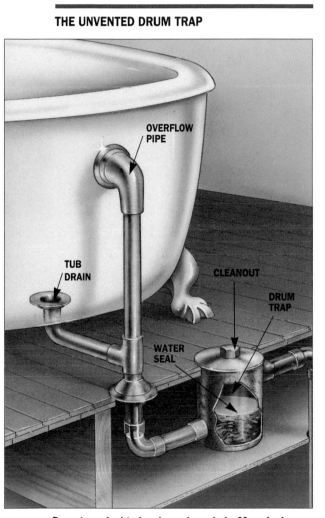

Drum traps had to be cleaned regularly. Many had no vents, even as late as the 1950s in some regions. They were usually made from lead or cast iron. The brass style with copper pipe shown here is a bit unusual.

The problem of the drum trap highlights one important advantage of a P–trap (or even an old S–trap): it is self-cleaning. Each time you pull the plug, the waste water scours the inside and washes debris away.

So P-traps rarely clog up. Toothpaste tube tops, goldfish, and even toy spider rings generally slide right through. But drop a toothbrush or some silverware down the drain and it's another story. Other parts of the drain system, as you well know, can clog up, too.

The drain system

The drain system spreads through the house like the branches of a tree, serving every sink in the house.

Suppose you have just finished taking a bath on the second floor of your house. When you pull the drain plug in the tub, the water charges through a short pipe to the soil stack. The water then passes by the toilet drain and the kitchen and laundry drain before hitting bottom and flowing out through the underground sanitary service to the local sewer system or to the septic tank.

The pipes colored red in the illustration that rise from the drainpipes are the air vents (*page 112*). No water should flow through them. You should also find one or more cleanouts to give access to the sanitary

COMMON BLOCKAGE POINTS IN A DRAIN SYSTEM

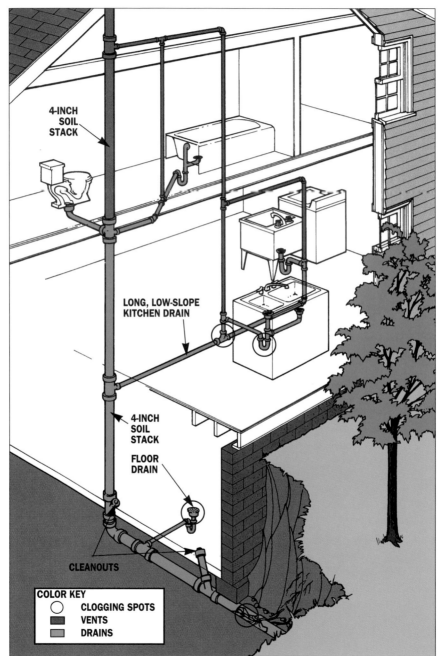

4-INCH SOIL STACK

LONG, LOW-SLOPE KITCHEN DRAIN

4-INCH SOIL STACK

FLOOR DRAIN

CLEANOUTS

COLOR KEY
○ CLOGGING SPOTS
VENTS
DRAINS

service underground. These clean-outs should be on the ground floor, one at the base of the soil stack and the other at the service entrance on the inside or outside of an exterior wall. (If the soil stack is close to the service entrance, there may be only one cleanout.) Their covers can be unscrewed should you need to get at any clogged pipes below ground.

Pipes that clog up

The illustration (*facing page*) also shows locations most likely to have pipe blockages. Blockages in the 4-inch soil stack or the sewer service do not occur very often. But when they do happen, they can be especially troublesome to reach. Tree roots can penetrate the sewer service at pipe joints, particularly if the pipe is clay tile. Roots are very tough to cut through. You'll probably need professional help with this problem, and, once such a problem has happened once, it is likely to recur again. It is possible that the sewer service might also become blocked by a crushed pipe, which is frequently the result of old age and deterioration. An experienced plumber should be able to diagnose whatever the problem is before making a decision to dig up the system.

A basement floor drain should not normally get clogged unless you leave the drain screen off. The trap for this drain is reached easily by simply removing the screen.

The kitchen sink is the drain that is most vulnerable to blockages. A lot of solids go down it, especially from electric disposal systems. But the real gunker is grease. It adheres to inside pipe surfaces, and then other grease and food particles stick to it. Furthermore, kitchen drains frequently run a long distance at a minimal slope before dropping vertically, giving grease a lot of pipe surface to stick to. It's even worse if an adjacent laundry drain dumps into the same line. Laundry water carries a lot of suspended clothing fibers, which readily stick to grease and, in fact, help bind the gunk together. It doesn't take much imagination to see a malignant clot growing in a kitchen drain system!

If you have a disposer, be sure to run cold water through the system both before and after you drop food in so grease will flow through and won't stick. The running water also builds up momentum to allow the ground-up waste to slide through more easily. Eliminate some of the normal grease buildup in the sink drain by running the hot water for a few minutes each week.

The bathtub drain

Clogged bathtub or shower drains usually result from a combination of hair and various soaps, beauty aids, and other gummy stuff. A clog is frequently made worse by the mechanical obstruction of the drain plug. Hair catches on the various levers and then snags all the gummy bathroom crud. To unclog it, pull the mechanical parts out through the drain opening and get at the gunk through the tub overflow, which is a hole located above the drain. To avoid these problems in the first place, consider buying one of the several simple stoppers on the market that eliminate the mechanical lever system and all the trouble that it causes.

HOW A TUB CLOGS

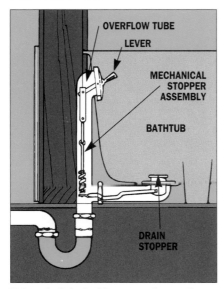

Hair and sticky bathing soaps frequently catch on stopper mechanisms, eventually clogging the drain. Stopper systems may be removed for cleaning.

HOW A TOILET FLUSHES

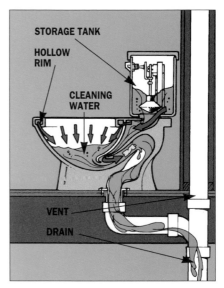

When you press the flushing lever, the tank ball lifts and allows water from the storage tank to force waste material down the drain and to swirl around the toilet bowl to cleanse it.

The overflowing toilet

The toilet drain is the most repulsive drain in the house that can get clogged up (*above, right*). When the flush water from the storage tank can't force the waste from the bowl, the bowl will simply fill up and even spill over. About the only good news is that the blockage is most likely right there in the toilet itself. Usually an object gets stuck in the bend of the S–trap. A couple of thrusts with a plunger should move softer obstructions through, or you can use a *water closet auger*, a flexible cable running through a shaft (*facing page*) that you simply insert into the drain and twist in order to pull out solid objects.

Opening clogged drains

There are several easy home remedies for clogged drains. Try using a plunger first, since it's the quickest and easiest. Cover the drain completely with the bell-shaped part and push on the handle, forcing the trapped water through the system. Bathroom sinks and tubs have overflow outlets that you must plug with a wet cloth before using a plunger.

If the plunger doesn't work, loosen the slip nuts on the P–trap with a pipe wrench or a large adjustable pliers and remove it. (Wrap the jaws of the wrench with electrical tape so they can get a better grip and so they don't scratch chrome fixtures.) Check the trap for hard obstructions and other clogging. If the problem isn't there, it's most likely somewhere between the trap and the soil stack.

Insert a flexible wire *snake* into the drain at the P–trap and work it in as far as it will go. The snake (*below, right*) is a variation on the closet auger used on toilets. It is longer and more flexible than the closet auger because it is designed to reach into narrow drains. When you feel the snake encounter an obstruction, rotate it with its adjustable handle to "drill" the end into whatever's clogging the system. Either the rotation will break down the plug, or you can pull it out when you pull the snake back out. Once clear, reconnect the P–trap, tighten the slip nuts, and run water through the drain to make sure that it's open. Be sure to test the trap for leaks.

Removing the P–trap and running a snake through the drain will be messy work. The drain water isn't very pleasant either, so you may wish to wear rubber gloves for this project, and have a bucket handy to catch any water that runs out of the trap and from both ends of the pipe. Don't run a snake down through a drum trap to unclog it because it'll get stuck inside the drum itself, or worse, the snake will pierce the soft side walls of a drum trap that is made of lead.

You can use chemicals to open clogged drains as well, but they usually have a limited effect. Because they must be heavier than water to work their way down to the obstruction, they'll settle in the low part of the trap and won't go much farther. It's usually more effective simply to remove the trap and clean it out.

All drain cleaning chemicals can be extremely dangerous if they are ingested or splashed onto your eyes or on your skin. Even the drain cleaners that you buy in the supermarket can be very harmful. Use them carefully; be sure to read the directions carefully, and store leftovers out of reach of children. If the chemicals fail to unclog the drain, under no circumstances should you then try to use a plunger. This is a surefire way to splash the chemicals into your eyes.

Don't hesitate to call a plumber if you can't unclog a drain. Describe the procedures you have tried; this may help the plumber make an accurate diagnosis of the problem. Above all, let the plumber know if you've already put chemicals into your drain.

HOME REMEDIES FOR CLOGGED DRAINS

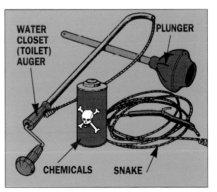

The plunger and a snake will handle most clogged drain problems. The plunger pushes the blockage down, and the snake pulls it up and out. Chemicals can be dangerous; follow manufacturer's directions carefully.

Designing a Better Toilet

The search for a perfect flush

Developing a good, dependable flush toilet was even more of a challenge for inventors than was the trap problem in drains. But once a sanitary solution was found, the toilet quickly came indoors, putting the outhouse out of business.

Now the modern flush toilet occupies a central place in our bathrooms, but not, let's face it, in our hearts. Most people don't even notice their toilets until they have to clean them. That dependable ceramic pedestal sits virtually ignored in the bathroom corner, conveniently flushing waste out of sight and out of mind. And so it would have continued to sit, conforming only to new shapes and colors as demanded by current fashion, were it not for water shortages in some regions.

Just how much water is really needed to flush a toilet? That question has drawn toilets from the shadows and put them squarely in the center of a debate among plumbers, conservationists, and manufacturers of bathroom fixtures.

In some parts of the United States such as California and Massachusetts, legislation mandated a change in toilet design as long ago as the late 1980s. Building codes in those regions required new and replacement toilets to be *ultra-low-flush* (ULF) models that use no more than 1.6 gallons of water per flush. That's a huge reduction from the 5 gallons most older toilets use and is more than twice as efficient as so-called water-saver toilets.

Beginning on January 1, 1994, it became illegal to make or sell anywhere in the United States any toilet that uses more than 1.6 gallons of water per flush. And no, you don't have to go out and buy a new toilet. No one is going to burst into your house and arrest you for having an old 5-gallon toilet in your bathroom, but when it comes time to buy a replacement toilet, you'll have only 1.6-gallon ULF models to make a selection from.

A little arithmetic shows how fast the benefits add up for a municipal water supply. Assuming that each person flushes the toilet three times a day, home owners can save from 5 to 10 gallons of water per day using ULF toilets. Even a small town of 100,000 people can save between half a million and a million gallons of water daily!

With less water flushing down the drain, these new toilets take a load off strained municipal sewer systems and, even more important, relieve fresh water supply problems

COMMON 1910 TOILET

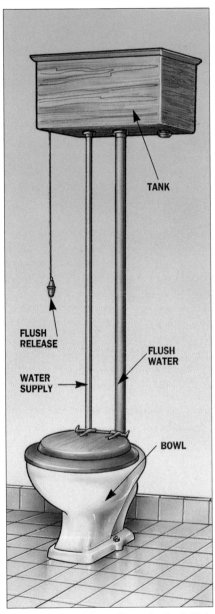

TANK

FLUSH RELEASE

FLUSH WATER

WATER SUPPLY

BOWL

Using gravity and force: the water tank high on the wall increases the velocity and effectiveness of the flush water.

in those regions suffering periodic water shortages.

Making a good flush

Although there have been many minor modifications over the years, most of the components of the modern toilet were introduced about 120 years ago, including the flushing rim around the top of the bowl and the jet siphon that accelerates the removal of waste.

On those older toilets, a 5- to 8-gallon tank containing flush water was placed high on the wall above the bowl (*left*). This was typical of many toilets of that period for one good reason: the key to a good flush was the amount of thrust that could be applied to get the siphon action going at its highest velocity. Water dropping from a height of, say, six feet entered the bowl with more force than it would if the tank was mounted lower on the wall, thus providing a strong, thorough flush. A larger tank could also provide a good flush, since a greater water volume resulted in greater flushing momentum.

When height and water volume were combined, the result was an effective, dramatic flush. Of course, if force should fail and a bad blockage develop, you'd have a dramatic toilet overflow as well.

Noise from the rushing water echoing throughout the house was considered a problem, as well. So the tanks were lowered, the flushing actions were made smoother, the jet action was improved, and our modern toilets emerged in the 1940s with tanks that hold about 5 gallons of water mounted on the backs of the bowls.

How a toilet works

Let's take a look at how older toilets work (*facing page*) so we can better understand the new ULF toilets. All toilets have two jobs—to flush waste away and rinse the bowl clean. When you trip the handle on your toilet, a flapper valve opens in the bottom of the tank that releases the water to do both those jobs. A portion of the water flows out around the top rim, swirling to wash down the sides of the bowl. Most of the water, though, flows rapidly through a hole near the bowl bottom and propels waste out through the drain trap. The volume of water needed to do a thorough job determines the size of the tank, so some tanks are bigger than others, depending on the bowl design. Once the tank empties, the job is done, the flapper valve falls closed, and the tank and bowl refill from the household water supply.

The flush is so simple and dependable that it's easy to underestimate the subtle engineering that goes into a toilet. There's a purpose behind that contorted path. Flush water from the tank rushes into the bowl and begins to force the waste through the drain. To complete the process, water that's pushed through the back section of the drain creates a suction that pulls the rest of the water and waste inside the bowl on through the drain, too. That's why the toilet bowl completely empties after a flush until air gets into the drainpipe through the bowl and breaks the suction.

That effect, called *siphoning*, is the same as what happened with the old S–traps (*page 107*). In 1775, Alexander Cumming, an English inventor, was the first to use this well-known hydraulic principle in an early S–trap arrangement under a toilet. Cumming thus invented the first "water closet," the old term for toilet still used by some.

Early water closets consisted of a simple valve to release the waste and a water supply to rinse the inside of the bowl, much as modern marine and airline toilets use. One of several problems with this design, however, was keeping enough water in the trap because the siphoning action would often suck it all out. Without the water plug in the drain, sewer gas drifted up through the toilet and could stink up a house so badly that it would have to be abandoned. That is a big reason why toilets were slow to come inside; the outhouse might have been cold, but at least it was well ventilated!

Soon inventors eliminated the trap in the drain line and incorporated a loop-shaped path right in the bowl itself. This "trapless" toilet, which was patented in 1852 by J. G. Jennings, also English, became the forerunner of today's modern toilet bowl design.

The final step was to deal with leaks. Toilet bowls could never be leakproof and free of contamination until all the metal and moving parts were eliminated. In 1885, a potter named Thomas Twyford, yet another Englishman, succeeded in building the first one-piece earthenware toilet that stood on its own pedestal base. His toilet design is essentially the same as the one used in the modern bathroom.

Conserving water

Our toilets use the same clean water supply as our sinks, tubs, and out-

THE INNER WORKINGS OF A TOILET

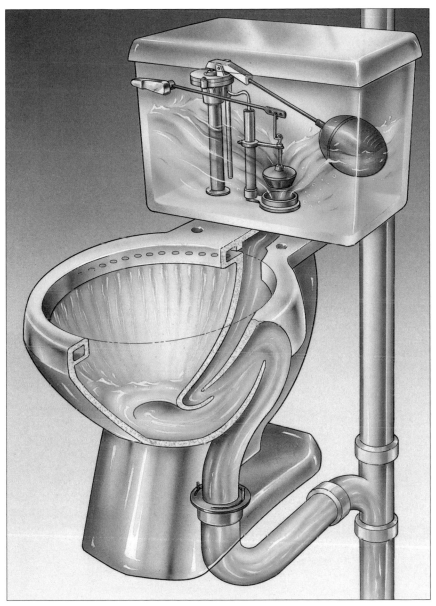

When flushed, water from the storage tank flows into the hollow rim and out along the sides of the bowl to rinse it and into the bottom of the bowl to accelerate the siphon action of the drain. The siphon action pulls the waste from the bowl.

door faucets. As long as fresh water was plentiful, a 5-gallon flush was acceptable. But faced with water shortages, conservationists looked to Europe, where countries long ago learned to deal with water shortages and use 6-liter toilets. Whether home owners can adapt successfully to the new low-flush standard has touched off an intense debate within the plumbing industry. Like it or not, though, the ULF toilet is here to stay.

At issue is whether 1.6 gallons is enough to consistently produce a good, sanitary flush. If it fails and leaves waste on the sides of the bowl or fails to clear all waste from the remaining water, naturally you'll flush a second time and perhaps a third time if necessary. Obviously, repeated flushes cancel any water-saving advantage. It is the designers' goal to come up with a ULF toilet that works right on the first flush.

There are two types of water-saving toilets currently available to home owners: the *gravity ULF* and *pressurized ULF*. The gravity model operates like a standard 5-gallon toilet does, although plumbing engineers have reshaped it in several subtle ways.

The interior of the bowl has been modified and streamlined to make the flush as smooth as possible. You might not be able to notice any difference between it and an

THE GRAVITY ULF TOILET

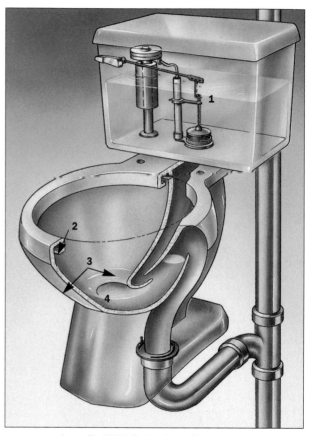

A gravity ULF toilet looks and operates like a standard toilet but usually incorporates one or more design changes, depending on the model:
1. A smaller, slimmer, or taller tank, perhaps with a device that limits water flow.
2. A slit along the rim rather than holes.
3. Steeper bowl sides.
4. A smaller water reservoir.

older toilet. With some models, however, the changes will be much more obvious; the gravity ULFs have steeper-sided bowls to increase the flushing velocity.

Some manufacturers produce smaller tanks, although, curiously, the tanks on other models of gravity ULFs appear as large as on the old ones. Designers made those tanks taller and slimmer, which raises the flush water higher and thereby increases its flushing power. They harness the same principles of gravity and velocity used with the high, wall-mounted tanks on toilets of old.

Ironically, these taller tanks also hold more than 1.6 gallons of water. Of course, that would violate the 1.6-gallon limit, except that the flush valves don't release it all, harnessing only the force of the topmost 1.6 gallons. The tank never empties its entire capacity, and it's a clever way to increase flushing power.

Pressurized ULFs (*right*) look conventional from the outside but use a unique air-assisted flush mechanism inside the tank. As the home water supply fills the plastic tank, the water pressure compresses air in a closed compartment as well. This compressed air is used to accelerate the water in the tank whenever the flush button is pushed. The extra velocity provided by the air pressure leads to a more powerful flush.

Do they work?

It's no secret that because of the legal mandate from Congress, toilet makers have had to hustle to come up with ULF toilets that work well and are attractive to home owners. All the ULF models from major manufacturers must now meet the minimum flush standards estab-

THE PRESSURIZED ULF TOILET

A pressurized ULF toilet contains a special tank that compresses air as it fills, adding velocity to the water when flushed.

lished by the American National Standards Institute, which most local plumbing codes accept. But whether they perform as well as the older toilets and satisfy home owners is a practical problem for both professional plumbers and do-it-yourselfers who choose to install the toilet themselves.

So far, plumbers give the ULFs mixed reviews. And they have a lot invested in ULFs working well, since it is plumbers who have to return to unclog drain lines and face irate customers. That's a good clue on how you can shop for a low-flush toilet. Visit the showroom of your local plumbing contractor, compare the various ULF models, and ask which ones the installers like best.

Year-round comfort. Not too long ago it seemed that every advertisement promising year-round comfort was a real estate promotion to buy bargain-priced land in southern California or Hawaii.

How times have changed! Now you can have comfort all year long by simply pushing a button that controls the heating and cooling systems in your house. No, it isn't going to deliver soft warm breezes on a frigid January morning, but neither will you feel the chills or the oppressive heat of the climate outside.

HEATING & COOLING

The heating and cooling system is the heart of the comfortable house. Central heating and air conditioning lie tucked away in the dark corners of the basement, closet, or utility room. The controls are automatic. Where your ancestors had to throw another log on the fire to warm up or escape to the front porch to keep cool, you now just nudge the thermostat a degree or two to adjust the temperature to your liking.

But the magic goes beyond new heating and cooling hardware. Comfort is the happy marriage of the system to the unique structure and character of the house. But the best heating system can't make a drafty house comfortable.

You can't reduce heating and cooling bills unless you've taken steps to make your home energy efficient.

To make the relationship between your house and its heating and cooling system a good one, be aware of how your system works, how air circulation and humidity affect it, and how the amount of insulation in the walls and ceilings help preserve your comfort. Natural cooling methods can significantly reduce your air conditioning needs, too. And energy-efficient windows promise even more energy savings, although they can cause some headaches, too.

Keeping Warm, Staying Cool

Keeping a house comfortable and energy efficient

Comfort comes in a small envelope, especially in winter. Even the tiniest shiver seems to violate the cozy feeling of a warm home. Cold feet at dinner, a cool draft in the living room, or a chilly bathroom floor are all reminders of how winter comfort depends upon a well-designed heating system.

Our skin is actually quite sensitive to drafts and temperature variations. The body's comfort zone tends to be narrow, ranging from 65 to 75 degrees Fahrenheit during the winter. The comfort zone may be even smaller because your body generates very little heat while resting. And those relaxing times at home are exactly when comfort is most important. Our own internal heating systems are slowing down, and we expect our home heating system to pick up the burden. A dependable furnace is one part of the story, but heating system design, air circulation, drafts, and relative humidity also affect our comfort.

What kind of heating system do you have?

Chances are that your house has a *forced-air furnace*, by far the most common modern heating system. A forced-air system (*facing page*) usually burns gas or oil inside a closed chamber called a *heat exchanger*. A large blower located inside the furnace compartment forces cool air across the hot outer surface of the heat exchanger, heating the air before sending it on through a system of ducts located inside the walls and under the floors. Another system of ducts draws cool air back through return air registers to be reheated and recirculated. The return air ducts generally sit low against an inside wall, somewhat distant from the heating registers, which you'll usually find in the wall or floor beneath windows.

A *hot-water system*, (*page 126*) the residential standard until about 60 years ago, has a boiler that works much like a furnace except that it heats water rather than air. The hot water circulates through pipes to the radiators that you'll find in every room (the sure sign of a boiler system in the house), then returns to the boiler for reheating.

Folks with hot water systems generally love them because they heat without blowing air and creating drafts. Although the system costs more to install, a small percentage of home owners still install them. But a hot-water system has another big drawback—you can't adapt it for air conditioning.

124

A TYPICAL FORCED-AIR HEATING SYSTEM

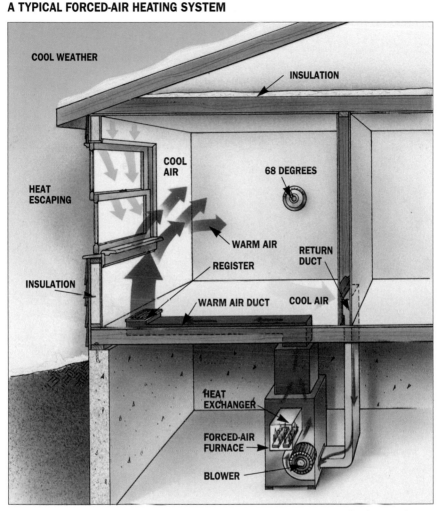

A forced-air furnace burns oil or natural gas in a closed heat exchange, which is vented out-doors. The blower flushes cool air across the hot surface of the exchanger, where the air heats. Warm air then flows through ducts into rooms. The register positioning helps elimi-nate drafts.

Those who want air conditioning usually choose a forced-air system, whose ducts and blower can deliver cool air in summer as well as warm air in winter. It's less expensive to go this route, although the system isn't ideal. The registers blow warm air in low where its natural buoyancy will cause it to rise and mix with cooler air. Cool air blown in low has no natural buoyancy, so it won't rise and mix well. Ideally,

HOT-WATER HEATING SYSTEM

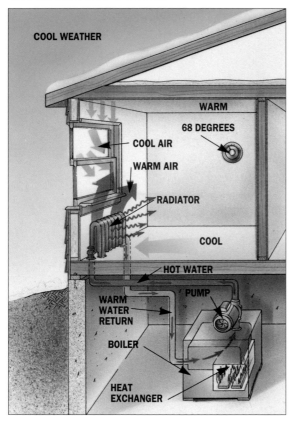

COOL WEATHER

WARM

68 DEGREES

COOL AIR

WARM AIR

RADIATOR

COOL

HOT WATER

PUMP

WARM WATER RETURN

BOILER

HEAT EXCHANGER

Hot water from the furnace heats the metal radiator, which in turn heats the surrounding air. The warm air rises and mixes with cool air off the windows and walls, inducing an even temperature without a fan. The water returns to the furnace through a separate system of pipes. In a steam-heat system, it returns through the same pipes.

wires heat up when you turn it on. Most of the time such a system consists of baseboard units or small, wall-mounted heaters, both of which contain the hot wires. The heaters do not cost much and are perfectly clean, so you don't have to worry about properly venting fumes as you do with oil- and gas-fueled boilers and furnaces. Electricity costs about twice as much on average as gas and oil, however, so few choose this option except for "spot" heating a bathroom, a small addition, or a workshop.

A heat pump is also an electrical system, but the current powers a compressor rather than directly creating heat. Think of a heat pump as an air conditioner that works in reverse. Whereas air conditioners extract heat from indoor air and pump it outside, heat pumps extract heat from outdoor air and expel it indoors to warm the house. The beauty of the system is that the heat is free, although you have to pay the electrical cost of running the compressor. As you might guess, a heat pump has to work harder to extract heat from cold air in winter. And that's the time you need it most. So heat pumps aren't popular outside the temperate middle and southern

cooled air should come into the room high so when it drops it'll mix with the warm air (*facing page*).

Heating with electricity

Electrical heating comes in two forms: *resistance heat* and the *heat pump*. An electrical resistance systems works just like your toaster—

AN IDEAL COOLING SYSTEM

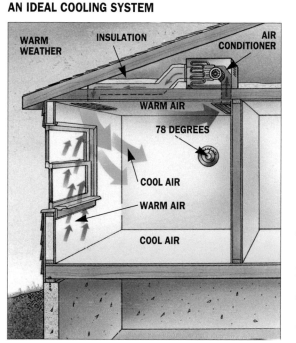

Cooled air from a ceiling register mixes with heat rising from the warm exterior wall. Cool air mixes as it falls toward the floor. Warm air reaching the ceiling is drawn back into the air conditioner for cooling.

regions of the United States, with one notable exception: heat pumps that use the earth itself as a heat source have shown promising results. Such pumps circulate water through pipes in the ground to pick up heat, then extract the heat from the water. This system can work in even the coldest climate.

What about solar heat?

The most powerful heater at our disposal is the sun, but harnessing its free energy to serve both the night-time hours and on cloudy days has proven difficult and costly. You can find successful solar heating systems that use large panels filled with fluid to capture and store the sun's energy. But these *active solar systems* usually cost more than conventional systems. As the price of fuel rises in the future, however, expect them to become more competitive. (Solar heating is already competitive in some sunny regions, for example, as hot water heaters in Florida.)

The good news is you can benefit from *passive solar heating* for almost no cost at all. The principle of passive solar heating is simply to make the most of the sunlight that comes in through your windows. Most of the sunlight comes through south-facing windows, because during the winter the daytime sun dips low toward the southern horizon. Leave the windows uncovered during the day, but make sure to pull drapes or another insulated covers over them at night so you won't lose the free heat you've captured. You will not have to run your conventional heating system as much, which can significantly reduce your fuel bill.

Many homes built since about 1980 feature passive solar design by incorporating more south-facing windows. These home owners are lucky, because it's expensive to adapt older homes to benefit from passive solar heating unless you're already planning to build an addition or plan to remodel with windows or skylights.

Planning for efficiency

While you might be grateful for your heating system on a cold winter morning, your heating system does not monitor how you feel when you crawl out of bed. It responds to what is going on in your house. When the temperature outside drops, the system has to make up for all the heat the house loses through its walls and windows. Its performance is directly related to the energy efficiency of the house.

Heating contractors work out a complicated heat-loss estimate when designing a properly sized system. They measure the total exterior wall and ceiling area of the house, the number of windows and doors, insulation thickness, the expected air infiltration, and other factors. Then they take into account the average low temperatures for the coldest period in your region, when your system must work hardest to maintain an even room temperature. They choose a system with adequate capacity to make up for the house's heat loss in extreme conditions.

Natural air movement

It's interesting to note, however, that the solution for a cold house may not be a larger furnace. Cutting energy losses by plugging air leaks to lessen infiltration, covering windows with curtains, or adding to the existing insulation may actually be less expensive than upgrading a furnace. In fact, after you make energy efficiency improvements, your new furnace may even be smaller than the old one.

That's because there is a lot more to comfort than simply making up for heat loss. Warmth must be uniformly spread throughout a room so you don't get chilled when sitting in a corner or have to wear wool socks to keep your feet warm.

Warm air rises and cool air falls. If poorly mixed, the air in a room will stratify—that is, warm air rises to the ceiling and cool air drops to the floor. The thermostat, usually located somewhere in the middle, may read comfort, but your feet won't believe it.

Radiators or registers are set near outside walls, usually under windows, to prevent indoor air from stratifying. As the outside cold air absorbs heat from the walls, the walls cool and then cool the inside air next to them. That cooled inside air tends to drop. And because the insulation value of a window (R-2) is much less than a wall (R-13), windows cool inside air very quickly, causing it to fall downward more rapidly. (An *R-value* is a measure of resistance to heat transmission. The higher the R-value, the greater the resistance.) Heated air from the register or radiator rises to meet this cooler air, counters its flow, and acts to create a more even mix. This natural process of air movement is called *convection* (*page 125*).

Hot-water systems and electrical heating systems also use convection, but they have a big advantage over forced-air systems: in addition to heating the surrounding air, they radiate heat that warms the floor, furniture, and you, much like the sun does but at a much lower intensity. While this *radiation* is a smaller component of their heating process than convection, it's an especially comfortable heat. Also, since hot-water and electrical heating systems rely on the natural air currents in the room, no new air is blown in or sucked out, making the room quieter and less drafty.

Drafts

But proper mixing of the hot and cold air doesn't always occur. When cool air currents sliding off a window aren't stopped by curtains or a warm airflow, a very noticeable cool air flow can develop. Even a small breeze can be chilling. Cool drafts flow off of the windows and walls, across floors, and even down stairs.

Ironically, the heating system itself can create the drafts. Although the furnace blower may be pushing warm, 80-degree air out a register, the air velocity alone might make it feel like a cool draft. Drafts from a forced-air system can be particularly uncomfortable when the heating system must operate for a long time in cold weather or in a house with a lot of air infiltration (as cool air enters, warm air escapes). Such problems with drafts can increase with newer, high-efficiency furnaces or heat pumps because they have larger blowers to move more air, especially in houses with older duct systems that were designed to handle lower air velocities.

Adding more heat isn't necessarily going to solve a draft problem. Instead, additional heating ducts, curtains, or an extra storm panel, which raises a window's R-value, can ease the intensity of drafts from windows. Plugging infiltration leaks and closing doors near stairways also should help. Sometimes merely rearranging room furniture can alter the airflow pattern, especially if a chair or carpet is blocking a register. Nevertheless, despite their potential for creating drafts and the fact that they are frequently less comfortable than hot-water or electric systems, forced-air systems continue to dominate the heating market in most regions.

Relative humidity

A forced-air system provides an easy way to deliver additional humidity to the house in winter. Consider the discomforting effects of low relative humidity: increased evaporation from your nose and throat, causing more respiratory irritation, dry skin and hair, and large static electricity shocks from dry fabrics. Low relative humidity causes deterioration of the house and furnishings as well. Wooden furniture may crack or develop loose joints, and wood windows may shrink, rattle in the wind, and allow more air infiltration.

Furthermore, very low relative humidity in winter, below 30 percent, begins to narrow the temperature comfort zone. This happens because our bodies are continuously cooled by moisture evaporation from the skin. At lower relative humidity, skin moisture evaporates more rapidly, cooling our bodies faster. This also explains why winter drafts can be particularly irritating; a dry draft cools skin more quickly than a humid draft. In fact, at an indoor relative humidity of less than 20 percent, it's difficult to be comfortable at all, no matter how warm the inside of the house is.

The optimum level of relative humidity for good health is about

OPTIMUM HUMIDITY LEVELS FOR HEALTHY LIVING

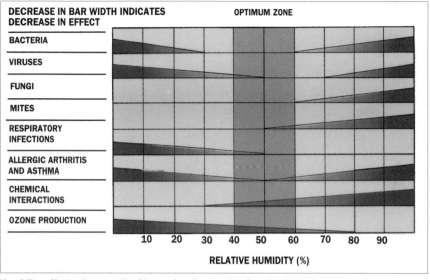

DECREASE IN BAR WIDTH INDICATES
DECREASE IN EFFECT

OPTIMUM ZONE

BACTERIA

VIRUSES

FUNGI

MITES

RESPIRATORY
INFECTIONS

ALLERGIC ARTHRITIS
AND ASTHMA

CHEMICAL
INTERACTIONS

OZONE PRODUCTION

RELATIVE HUMIDITY (%)

Humidity affects the growth of bacteria, viruses, fungi, and mites. They cause, in part, such negative health effects as respiratory infections and allergies. Some chemicals common to households (formaldehyde from plywood, for example) can become irritants at higher humidity. Ozone, also an irritant, forms more rapidly at low humidity.

50 percent (*above*). But you do not need a *humidistat* (an instrument that measures relative humidity) to test for humidity in winter: condensation on your windows will tell you enough. Cold windows essentially act as dehumidifiers; they limit the amount of moisture the air can hold. As the outside temperature drops, the windows get colder, causing more moisture from indoor air to condense. If you try to humidify your house above the level that condensation forms on the windows, you will most likely get continuous moisture on the windows, eventually resulting in soaked, rotting wood and mildew.

Humidifiers in a forced-air system are usually equipped with humidistats, which will automatically kick in when the humidity gets too low. But more often complaints come from the other extreme; the humidity's too high. Usually this occurs because many homes, especially newer ones, are much more airtight. Moist air that used to leak out is now trapped inside.

It's usually healthier to have about as much humidity in winter as possible without continually fogging up the windows. One way to control excess humidity is by installing exhaust fans in the bathrooms and kitchen that vent to the outside of the house. Always use them when showering or cooking and this will take care of two of the worst moisture-causing offenders. You can correct other persistent condensation problems by adding more ventilation, blocking sources of moisture (sealing the concrete slab or basement floor and walls), or installing energy-efficient windows (*page 142*).

Welcoming air conditioning

Once the seasons move on and the snow melts and the air warms, the last thing you want to think about is keeping warm. A bit of chill then would actually be nice.

The invention of air conditioning has made sweltering summers more bearable. It has hastened the growth of Sunbelt cities such as Atlanta, Miami, and Houston because it has made it easier for people to live and work there year-round by reducing the heat and humidity in houses and workplaces.

All air conditioners, whether window- or wall-mounted units or whole-house central air conditioning systems, work on the same principle. A fan sucks warm indoor air across a series of cool coils (containing refrigerant) and blows it back into the room. The refrigerant absorbs heat, then exhausts it outside through another system of fans and coils.

When the indoor air cools it also dehumidifies, that is, moisture condenses on the cool coils just like water collects on a glass of iced lemonade on a hot day. The water runs down a drain or, more often, drips off the air conditioner outside. Dehumidified air contributes to the cooling effect you feel.

Alternatives to air conditioning

Air conditioning feels great on those sweltering hot summer days,

so good that I wouldn't want to give it up. But your house can keep you cool in other ways, too.

If air conditioning works so well, why bother with anything else, you might ask. Alternate cooling strategies make sense for a couple of reasons. First, mechanical air conditioning is one of the most expensive ways to keep cool because it draws a lot of relatively high-priced electricity. Finding alternatives will reduce your utility bills.

And second, to make an air conditioner effective, you have to close yourself up tightly in your home so you don't waste the cool air being generated. When you shut out the summertime heat, you shut yourself in. And that's not my idea of the best way to spend a summer at home. You miss the fresh air, the smells and sounds of the yard (not including the neighbor's barking dog), and the pleasure of kicking back on a shaded deck or porch.

This is where the natural cooling features of your home can complement and lessen your reliance on air conditioning during hot weather. By improving ventilation and air movement inside and by utilizing covered porches, awnings, screens, landscaping plants, and other shading devices outside, you can conserve energy, cut your utility bills, and, perhaps equally important, enjoy your summer more without being held hostage by the heat.

Cooling with ventilation

Natural cooling relies mostly on ventilation and shading. Ventilation creates cooling breezes and flushes out hotter air, and shading blocks the heat of direct sunlight.

131

NATURAL AIR CONDITIONING WITH A CUPOLA

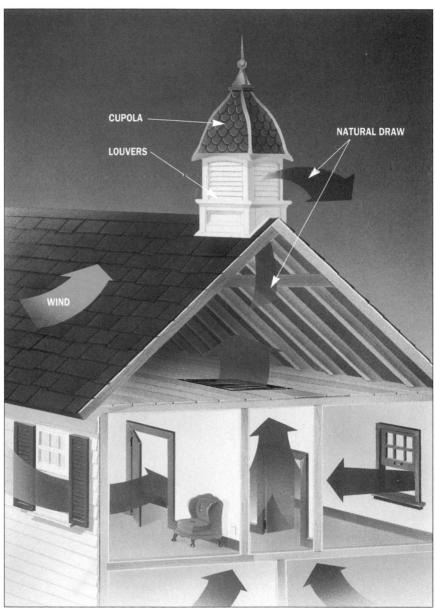

A cupola harnesses two forces to create a cooling draft in a house. Warmer air rises and escapes through the louvers, and wind rushing over the roof also pulls air inside. Both, being naturally buoyant, draw cooler air into the windows below.

It's easy to forget that a natural cooling feature from the past, the *cupola* (*facing page*), was once more than just a piece of highbrow decoration borrowed from the colonial architecture of the early United States and Canada. Though now valued for style, symbolism, and attractiveness, it, like many other building design features, also represented the high technology of its day — early air conditioning.

On one hand, the cupola was a high point in which the hottest air in the house could collect and escape outside because hot air's natural buoyancy causes it to rise. Cooler air was in turn drawn into the house through the open windows below. This *stack effect*, as it's called, becomes most effective when there's a good source of hot air to accelerate the flow, as from an attic.

The cupola was a much more effective ventilator when it caught the wind at its highest velocity as it rushed over the rooftop. The wind blowing through the cupola created an updraft throughout the house and pulled cooler air in through the windows. The draft also cooled the house down faster during the evening and night when the outside air temperature dropped. Of course, its effectiveness had a glaring weakness. Without at least a little wind, you didn't get much ventilation.

The invention of the electric fan led to the development of a device that duplicated the cupola's effect without depending on the wind—the *whole-house fan* (*right*). The fan develops a continuous draft that draws air in through open windows and doors and blows it out through the attic, which maintains a steady, cooling breeze throughout the house. Operating the fan costs less than operating the air conditioner, so it's a good cooling alternative if the outdoor temperature isn't too high.

Modern versions of the cupola

An ancestor of the cupola, if not in design, at least in principle, is the *ridge vent* (*below*). Imagine, if you will, a cupola flattened and extended all along the peak of the roof. The updraft of air created by this means extends throughout the attic area, a very effective ventilation method. But now, in this era of air conditioners and heating efficiency, ventilating this way cools only the attic because an air and vapor barrier and blanket of insulation isolates the attic from the house below.

The closest modern kin to a cupola from a performance standpoint is the open skylight. Skylights harness virtually the same natural

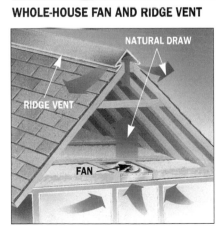

WHOLE-HOUSE FAN AND RIDGE VENT

NATURAL DRAW

RIDGE VENT

FAN

The whole-house fan draws air from the house and expels it through the attic and roof vents.

forces, especially the wind as it blows across the roof, and create the same updraft throughout the house (*right*). When shaded to keep direct sunlight from baking the upstairs rooms, they are one of the best natural ventilating devices available. Their value for cooling alone does not compensate for their initial cost, but you won't buy them for that reason anyway.

Cooling with shade

It comes as some surprise that modern insulation practices have taken away much of the impact of earlier methods of shading. The intense summer sun attacks the east side of the house in the morning, the roof most of the day, and the west wall in the evening. It is less intense on the north and south walls because it strikes them at a less direct angle. Without insulation or shading, the east and west walls and the ceiling below the attic heat up and become virtual radiators inside the house. Insulation, particularly where summer temperatures in the attic commonly reach 150 degrees in most parts of the country, radically slows the heat transfer through the walls and ceiling. Once your house is well insulated, shading with verandas and tall trees, for example, has less impact on the air conditioning bill.

Shading the windows, however, continues to make a big difference inside the house. Direct sunlight pumps a lot of heat straight through ordinary window glass. Louvered shutters, now used almost exclusively as decoration, were once commonly used to solve that problem. When closed, these shutters, with their louvers properly angled down

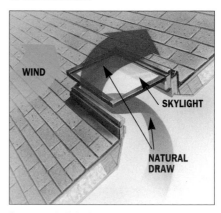

OPEN SKYLIGHT

WIND

SKYLIGHT

NATURAL DRAW

An open skylight harnesses the same natural forces as a cupola—naturally rising warm air and the wind.

and toward the outside, block the sunlight while maintaining good ventilation. They had two big disadvantages, though: they darkened the room and they blocked the view.

Perhaps when it comes to window shading, there's no perfect system. You can find fault with every alternative. Shades hung on the outside, well away from the windows, do a pretty good job, but they're not convenient to adjust and they block the view. Awnings work well, except when the sun is low, but they are more expensive and don't always fit a house's style.

Interior shades and curtains tend to block any welcome breeze. And unfortunately, they, like other interior window shading methods, block sunlight only after it already has entered the house. They reflect some heat back out again, but much remains inside.

Shades and curtains are convenient, though, especially so with horizontal blinds, which can be adjusted to the angle of the sun. Adjustable blinds allow you to see out most of the time as well as let breezes enter. As such, they're one of the better investments for summer comfort, whether you're using the air conditioner or not.

Shading options

Perhaps the biggest drawback of most of these shading methods isn't with their performance but the fact that they're manual. You have to frequently adjust them according to the schedule of the sun. Unfortunately that goes against the grain of our busy schedules and desire for convenience.

One convenient window shading system is all natural: a few broad-leaved trees. If you don't already have them, of course, they have to be considered a long-term investment. Make sure to plant them primarily on the east and west sides of the house if possible. As a bonus, broad-leaved trees conveniently drop their leaves during the cooler months, which allows sunlight to shine through just when you want help in warming the house.

Roof overhangs, awnings, and porches are also traditional window shading devices that maintain good ventilation without blocking daylight. Such devices tend to be more expensive and have to be installed as permanent parts of the house, which means that if your house does not already have them, it probably won't be worth adding them just for natural cooling alone. Unfortunately, air conditioning has allowed architects and builders to cut many of these attractive features from new house plans, and it's usually not easy to add them back on. On the other hand, if you add a porch, you're creating a shaded spot anyway, no matter how it affects the rest of the house, whether it faces the south (which is not a good location), or east, west, or north (which are good locations). The nice thing about a porch is that its shaded comfort gets you outside in warm weather.

Thinking about outdoor cooling opens up the possibility of other shading options—namely arbors and trellises. While they don't do so much to cool a well-insulated house, they're ideal for cooling the surrounding area, especially garden paths, porches, and decks.

Most natural cooling methods are not fully automatic, unlike the set-it-and-leave-it, thermostatically controlled air conditioner. Rather, you have to open and shut windows, adjust blinds, screen the porch, paint the trellis, and so on. Look at these chores as a natural part of summertime, too.

Is Your Insulation Working?

Does your house have enough?

Good insulation is the key to a comfortable house. It's the stuff that brings a smile to your face when you look outside while the cold winds blow in winter or the sun is scorching in summer. It'll cut down on cold drafts, slow air leaks, raise the humidity level in winter, and lower it in summer. There's more: it'll ease the burden on your heating and cooling system, make your house quieter, and, best of all, cut your utility bills.

Despite all these plusses, upgrading your house's insulation level probably won't rank high on your list of recreational activities, but it may be well worth your time and expense. The true payoff begins when you're warm and snug indoors while the mercury drops outdoors and snowflakes begin to drift in the wind. And it is hard to complain about a utility bill that's lower than last year's.

To make upgrading more profitable, you should be aware of how different types of insulation work, how existing insulation can be made more effective, and when adding more isn't worth the cost.

How insulation works

Heat escapes from the house in three ways: *radiation, conduction*, and *convection (facing page)*.

It's unusual to think of a house as radiating heat, but it does, much like a hot-water radiator or even the sun. It's easiest to think of radiant heat as invisible light. However, like light, radiant heat can't penetrate opaque surfaces such as walls, and therefore it contributes little to overall house heat loss.

Blocking the sun's radiant energy from *entering* a house is significant in hot weather when an air conditioner is running. Reflective films and shades on windows, light-colored exteriors, and awnings all reduce radiant heat gain (*page 134*).

The second way heat escapes, conduction, occurs when heat from one part of a solid object spreads to other parts. For instance, window frames made of aluminum quickly conduct heat to a cool exterior—sometimes so fast that in really cold weather interior moisture may condense and freeze on them. Dense materials such as metals, plastics, and concrete tend to be good heat conductors. Good heat conductors that form main components of the walls, floors, or roofs need additional low-density material—insulation—to slow heat loss. In houses, conductive heat loss tends to be high through windows, doors, concrete walls and floors, and even the wood framing inside the walls.

HOW WALLS TRANSMIT HEAT

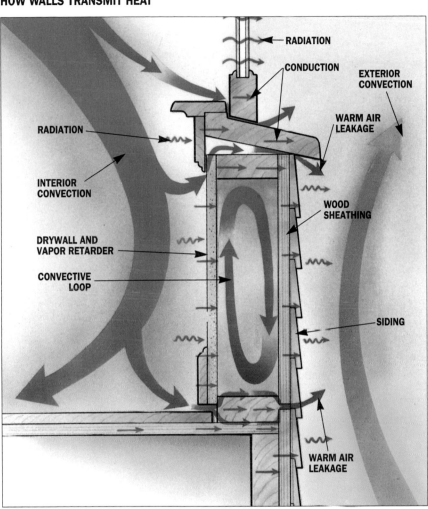

RADIATION

CONDUCTION

EXTERIOR
CONVECTION

WARM AIR
LEAKAGE

RADIATION

INTERIOR
CONVECTION

WOOD
SHEATHING

DRYWALL AND
VAPOR RETARDER

CONVECTIVE
LOOP

SIDING

WARM AIR
LEAKAGE

Walls transmit heat by conduction through solid materials, convection from circulating air currents, and radiation through windows. The convection loop reverses in summer.

The third contributor to heat loss is convection. Convection transmits heat in two ways. First, warm indoor air simply flows outdoors through gaps and cracks in the ceiling and walls. Second, the air inside the walls where there is no insulation absorbs heat from warm inner walls, loses it to the cooler outer walls, and begins to flow in a circular pattern. These steady circular currents are called *convective loops* (*above*). They develop spontaneously because the air warmed by the inner surface rises, and air cooled by the outer surface falls. If there's a large difference between these two surface temperatures, you will get stronger air movement and greater heat transmission.

You might be surprised to learn that air is an excellent insulator. It's not dense and doesn't conduct heat well. But it's an effective insulator only when it can't move in convective loops; it must be "dead" or still air. That's how most insulation works; it clogs up open cavities and stops air movement.

A more radical approach to insulation—the principle used by the Thermos™ bottle to hold hot liquids—eliminates the air completely. There is no air to convect or conduct heat, so the soup or coffee stays hot a long time. The technology needed to adapt this principle to a house wall is still a long way off.

Trapping air

There are two different methods of trapping air: with a mass of fibers in *loose-fill* and *batt* insulation, and with plastic bubbles in *rigid* insulation. Loose-fill insulation is made up of tiny pieces of material blown into a wall cavity or over an attic floor. Batt insulation is made up of blankets of varying thicknesses cut to widths to fit between studs and joists.

Fiberglass, the most popular insulation by far, uses a dense network of fine glass fibers to block convection currents. The denser the fiber pack, the greater the reduction in airflow. In fact, if it is packed tightly enough, there would be virtually no airflow at all. But there's a practical limit to this. As convection decreases, heat transfer by conduc-

HEAT LOSS THROUGH RIGID INSULATION

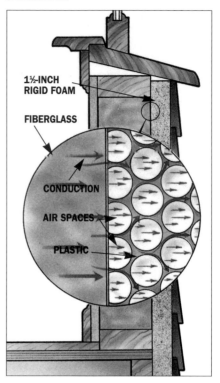

The plastic structure of foam insulation conducts heat well, but still air in bubbles does not. Replacing air with a heavier gas slows heat loss.

tion increases. As you stuff more fiberglass into a space, you displace more air with glass fiber. Glass conducts heat much better than air, so at some point the heat being conducted through the glass exceeds other gains.

Insulation manufacturers calculate that critical point and produce an insulation with an optimal density for maximum heat blockage. That's why fiber insulations should not be compressed beyond their natural *loft*, as manufacturers call it. You can't get more insulation value by stuffing more into the stud space. Fiber materials generally deliver an insulation value of about R-3 per inch of thickness. (*R-value* is a measurement of a material's resistance to the transmission of heat.)

Rigid insulation works in a similar way (*facing page*). It is designed to fill up air space, in this case by trapping the air in tiny plastic bubbles. Heft a 4x8-foot sheet of rigid insulation and you find it almost weightless. It's mostly bubbles with very little plastic to conduct heat. *Expanded polystyrene*, often called *white beadboard*, is one of three classes of rigid insulation. It performs about the same as fiberglass, about R-3 per inch. *Extruded polystyrene*, Styrofoam™ being one of the well-known brand names, performs at about R-5 per inch.

At one time extruded polystyrene was foamed with chlorinated fluorocarbons (called CFCs), which are better insulators than air. This accounts for the higher R-value. But recent evidence has linked CFCs to the destruction of the earth's ozone layer. Manufacturers replaced CFCs with hydrochlorinated fluorocarbons, called HCFCs. HCFCs have much less potential for destroying the ozone layer.

Urethane and polyisocyanurate insulation, the third type, is foamed with CFCs or HCFCs and performs in the R-6 to R-7 per inch range. It stands out because it's usually covered with aluminum foil.

Makers of foam insulation have agreed to phase out all ozone-harmful gases within the next few years.

When buying rigid insulation, you'll find that prices reflect the R-values—the higher the insulation's performance, the higher the cost. Fiberglass costs only about a quarter as much per unit of R-value, making it the economical choice when you have plenty of insulating space. But when space is tight, rigid insulation packs almost twice the R-value within the same thickness.

How much is enough?

To determine the optimal insulation level for your house, look at the bottom line: how much does it cost compared to the amount of money you will save? This cost-effective approach is often referred to as *payback*. For example, if you install $200 worth of insulation, how long will it be before the accumulated energy savings from that additional insulation total $200? A 5- to 10-year payback period makes the initial investment attractive; a 20- to 30-year payback period will not be quite so tempting for most people.

It's easy to get confused when trying to upgrade your insulation. If you double the insulation in your walls, say from R-5 to R-10, you'll cut your energy loss through the walls in half (although windows and wood studs lessen the impact).

As a result, you may save $50 a month (the payback) in the peak of the heating season. However, if you double it again, adding R-10 to make the total R-20, you'll again cut your loss in half, but your monthly payback will be only $25. You've added twice the insulation, costing twice as much, but get only half the savings. This is because the first few units of R-value block most of the transmitted heat. The subsequent units of R-value reduce the rapidly decreasing remainder.

An exact calculation of cost-efficient insulation levels is quite complicated. Building codes have simplified the calculation by requiring new houses to meet specific insulation standards based upon the local climate. You can use these guidelines for upgrading insulation as well, although if you are doing your own work, it's always worth insulating beyond the standards in the long run in order to increase the value of the house and for greater payback. The insulation recommended in this chart (*right*), adapted from a U.S. Department of Energy study, assumes you won't have to make any costly structural changes to your house. You won't want to tear off good siding in order to add foam sheathing or close off a cathedral ceiling to make an insulated attic.

To find out how much is enough, begin by calling your local building inspector and ask about the insulation requirements for new homes. To help take account of the unique variables in your home, hire a specialist called an energy auditor who will evaluate your house. This energy specialist will recommend improvements that will reduce your energy bills. Most utility companies work closely with energy auditors, so call your public utility first to find one. (The utility might even pay the auditing fee!)

Making insulation more effective
Perhaps you've already insulated your house and it isn't economical to add more. But two elements may

SUGGESTED R-VALUES FOR EXISTING HOUSES BY REGION

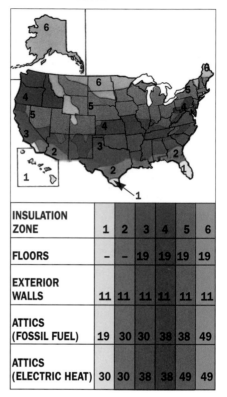

INSULATION ZONE	1	2	3	4	5	6
FLOORS	–	–	19	19	19	19
EXTERIOR WALLS	11	11	11	11	11	11
ATTICS (FOSSIL FUEL)	19	30	30	38	38	49
ATTICS (ELECTRIC HEAT)	30	30	38	38	49	49

hamper your insulation's effectiveness: air leaks and moisture.

The illustration (*facing page*) shows some typical points in a wall where air can leak out. Leaks also commonly occur around doors, window frames, chimneys, plumbing vents, foundation cracks, and any other exterior wall openings.

To prevent leakage problems, builders have developed several methods to make new houses more airtight using gaskets, caulk, and plastic. Unfortunately, they are seldom used. Once built, you have to rely on a long-lasting, flexible caulk and a can of expanding foam to plug the leaks the best you can. One good strategy is to think of the interior surface of your exterior walls and ceilings as air barriers and seal along any edges and places they're penetrated, such as electrical boxes and windows.

One caution: whenever you make your house more airtight, check the oil, gas, or wood burning devices (furnace, water heater, fireplace) for backdrafting—that is, sucking dangerous smoke or fumes back into the house. A backdrafting fireplace should be readily evident. It'll dump smoke into the house. To check the furnace and water heater, hold a smoking match near the draft hoods (usually directly on top) when they're firing. Make sure the smoke is drawn up the flue. If not, call in a heating professional to check your system.

Stopping air leaks partially resolves the second element that hampers insulation's effectiveness—moisture. Warm air leaking through a stud cavity carries a lot of moisture that condenses on cool sheathing, wetting both the sheathing and the insulation. Even worse than the loss of insulation value, however, is that wet wood in a wall cavity doesn't dry easily and may rot.

Plugging air leaks stops only part of a moisture problem. Water vapor in warm inside air can pass right through drywall and condense on the cold outer sheathing. A vapor retarder placed behind the drywall effectively slows down this water-vapor movement.

HOW INSULATION EFFECTIVENESS IS REDUCED

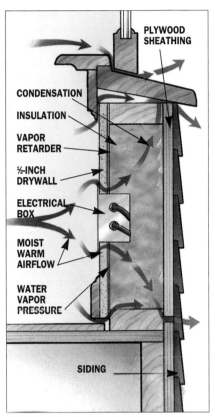

PLYWOOD SHEATHING

CONDENSATION

INSULATION

VAPOR RETARDER

½-INCH DRYWALL

ELECTRICAL BOX

MOIST WARM AIRFLOW

WATER VAPOR PRESSURE

SIDING

Air leaks allow heat to flow through the insulation. Condensation from warm, humid air wets and compresses insulation, reducing its R-value.

If your house doesn't have a plastic vapor retarder, you don't have to tear out the ceiling and walls to put one in. Simply paint your drywall with two coats of either oil- or special vapor-blocking paint, one coat of which can be a primer (*page 168*).

Insulated Glass and Energy-Saver Windows

Insulating the largest gaps in the wall

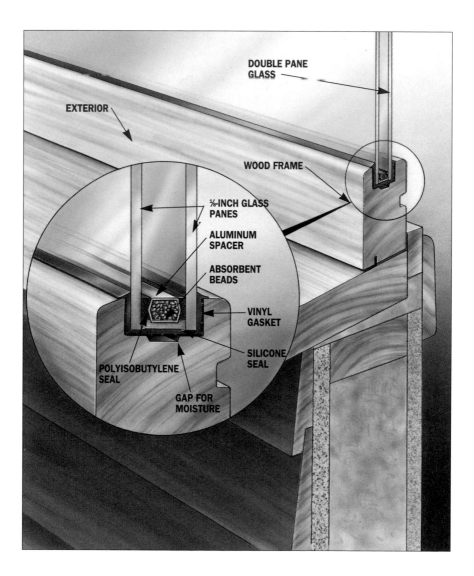

DOUBLE PANE GLASS

EXTERIOR

WOOD FRAME

⅛-INCH GLASS PANES

ALUMINUM SPACER

ABSORBENT BEADS

VINYL GASKET

SILICONE SEAL

POLYISOBUTYLENE SEAL

GAP FOR MOISTURE

S tuffing the walls and attic with insulation will take you a long way toward making your home energy efficient. But the windows, which have little insulating value, are still a chink in its armor because they allow heat to pass through them almost unchecked.

Nowadays, buyers want windows everywhere possible in their dream houses. Dim rooms are out; bright rooms are in, which means that architects and builders face a dilemma. How do they design and build window-filled walls that will comply with the high energy standards demanded today by vigilant building inspectors? And we're not talking just about cold northern regions, either, but air-conditioned southern and western regions, too.

Insulated glass has come to the rescue as a good way to keep houses comfortable and bright and to save on fuel bills as well.

What is insulated glass?

The illustration (*facing page*) shows a typical insulated window. It has two pieces of standard window glass stuck together at the edges with special adhesive. The two layers of glass trap air in between them, creating a dead air space that is usually ½ to ¾ inch thick. Glass itself never insulates well, but the trapped air does, so a sealed double-pane window

saves more on a fuel bill than does a single-pane window and saves slightly more than one with a storm window installed.

Though it was first produced during the 1950s, new research in the wake of the energy crises of the 1970s made insulated glass even better. In the sealed space between the panes, engineers spread any of several types of reflective metallic films (called *low-E coatings*) on one glass surface to reflect heat. This film can reflect heat in either direction, so it does double duty: it keeps more heat inside during cool weather and keeps more out during warm weather. Engineers also injected argon gas, which insulates better than plain air, between the panes of glass. These two improvements practically doubled the insulating ability of insulated glass.

In most regions, these low-E, argon-filled insulated windows pay off the investment in the long run. They cost about 10 percent more than regular insulated windows and about 20 percent more than single-pane windows. But usually within 10 years the savings on heating and cooling bills will make up for any price difference. Also note that, as good as they are, insulated windows aren't the only source of energy savings. Sure, they are a good choice when it comes time to buy new windows, but not when your single panes and storm windows are still in relatively good shape. You can improve the energy efficiency of your old windows in ways that are less expensive, such as by adding heavy curtains or drapes to keep heat in and shades or awnings to keep the hot sun out.

TWO-PART INSULATED GLASS SEAL

In this two-part seal, the silicone bonds the glass panes while the polyisobutylene resists moisture and corrosion. The beads in the hollow aluminum space at the bottom absorb moisture.

143

How insulated glass windows fail

But insulated glass is no bargain if the weather seals fail prematurely and you are forced to buy new windows again. Unfortunately, the bond between the sealant and glass sometimes breaks.

This failure shows up in the form of a haze that slowly creeps in. First it appears in a lower corner. You can't tell whether it's on the inside or outside until you try to rub it off. That is when you discover that the haze is spreading between the two panes of glass, where you can't reach it. Somehow the airtight seal on the edge of the glass failed, allowing air and moisture to infiltrate and permanently fog the inside surfaces and ruining the view. After several years it'll probably cloud the window so badly that the window will have to be replaced.

You'd think that the technology that produced insulated glass units could also make a seal that won't leak, but it hasn't been that easy. Seals lead a tough life. They have to be strong enough to withstand wind, rain, snow, and ice that buffet the outer glass pane and try to tear it from the inner pane. They have to be flexible enough to allow the outer pane to contract in the cold and expand in the heat. Seals can't harden or become brittle when it's cold or soften much when it's hot. They can't weaken as they age. They can't break down under the damaging ultraviolet rays of the sun or under corrosive atmospheric

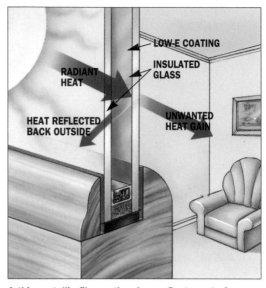

LOW-E GLASS IN SUMMER

LOW-E COATING

INSULATED GLASS

RADIANT HEAT

HEAT REFLECTED BACK OUTSIDE

UNWANTED HEAT GAIN

A thin metallic film on the glass reflects part of summer's heat back outside.

pollutants. They must remain waterproof indefinitely. And they have to endure the jarring we dish out when we slam them shut, especially when doors contain insulated windows.

In addition to this rigorous life, the seals have to remain airtight under pressure. Atmospheric pressure changes constantly, as a barometer shows every day. Insulated glass assembled at a low altitude (which means that it's under greater atmospheric pressure) will continuously bulge out at a higher altitude, say, in Denver, where atmospheric pressure is not as great.

Once the seal on an argon-filled unit breaks, the unit will lose some of its energy efficiency. And you can bet that if the gas leaks out, air will surely leak in to replace it, usually

LOW-E GLASS IN WINTER

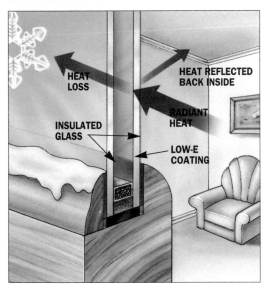

HEAT LOSS

HEAT REFLECTED BACK INSIDE

RADIANT HEAT

INSULATED GLASS

LOW-E COATING

The same film reflects part of the interior heat back inside in winter.

carrying some water vapor with it. That's how you'll discover a glass seal failure. On a cold day, some of this intruding water vapor will condense on the inner surface of the outer pane and appear as a light haze. And the haze will gradually spread as more gas leaks out and more vapor-laden air replaces it.

Because the seals lead such a harsh life, most window manufacturers who market their products nationwide opt for a double-sealant system. The inner seal resists moisture, aging, and corrosion, while the outer seal provides strength and rigidity. Some window makers use only one type of sealant, however, and these windows won't withstand as wide a range of weathering nor will they last as long.

Most manufacturers use a piece of hollow aluminum tube as a spacer between the two panes of glass. It is the part you see when looking in at the glass edge. This tube contains small beads of material that absorbs moisture to keep the window from fogging up if a small amount of water vapor manages to penetrate the seal. But water vapor infiltrating through a broken seal will soon overwhelm the capacity of this material and lead to fogging between the glass panes.

What kind of performance can we expect?

Experts say that insulated windows being made today should last 20 years. In fact, they expect most of them to last much longer than that, although they won't guarantee this. The problem is, they can't predict how much longer. That's good news for window buyers, but it's not much comfort for those whose insulated windows are already 20 years old. These people won't know whether they'll soon face a big replacement bill for their energy-efficient windows that fail. Fortunately, window companies expect only a small percentage of their insulated glass to fail early because of faulty seals from the factory or from poor installation at the job site.

An ongoing study of how well insulated glass performs, conducted by the Sealed Insulating Glass Manufacturer's Association (SIGMA), so far reports that fewer than 3 percent failed after 10 years if the unit wasn't allowed to sit in small puddles of water. Windows that did not allow water to drain from under the glass seal failed much faster.

Only an expert can tell if water can properly drain, so if you want to put insulated windows in a wet location such as in a greenhouse or near a swimming pool, buy ones with a long-term guarantee (10 years plus). The same thing goes for patio doors, because rainwater usually splashes up on them. Help protect insulated windows and doors from excess moisture by keeping them clean, their frames sealed with paint or stain, and the entire assembly protected with weatherproof caulk.

But, given a 3-percent failure rate and a house full of insulated glass windows, you can probably expect at least one or two failures within 10 years.

Replacement can be a pane

Unfortunately, glass failure poses another problem. It's virtually impossible to replace the glass in most insulated windows yourself. Manufacturers use glue, caulk, or gaskets to affix the insulated glass to the frame, and they hold it there with vinyl, aluminum, or wood stops (*facing page and below*). Often you can't figure out how to get the glass out. Sometimes the stops break when

VINYL-STOP WINDOW

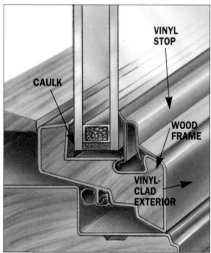

A vinyl stop snaps into the frame but is hard to pry out without breaking it.

WOOD-STOP WINDOW

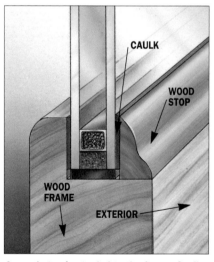

A wood stop is stapled to the frame. Caulk glues it to the glass.

you pull them off. Replacing the glass in these windows can drive window repair professionals nuts, too. Often they'll tell you that it's easier and cheaper to replace the entire sash, and usually they'll be right.

Low-E insulated glass is not cheap. A 30 x 21-inch double-pane replacement unit costs about $50. If the entire sash as a unit (glass plus wood, aluminum, or plastic frame) needs to be replaced, the cost can exceed $100. At prices like these, insulated glass must last a long time to make it a worthwhile investment for your house.

Since few home owners have the expertise to evaluate window

SOLID-FRAME WINDOW

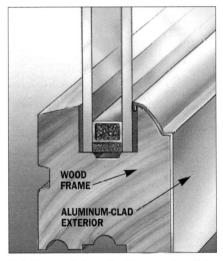

WOOD
FRAME

ALUMINUM-CLAD
EXTERIOR

Solid-frame windows don't have a stop. Take the frame apart before removing the glass.

seals, you have to look for other signs of quality. A manufacturer's membership in SIGMA is one good sign, since it is the only industry group that monitors quality among its members. But these members represent only about 100 of the more than 1,000 window manufacturers (although most of the big companies are members).

The best way to make sure you are getting your money's worth is to buy a reputable brand of window that will give you a good guarantee. Obviously, any guarantee is worthless if the company goes out of business. Before buying, check how long the company has been in business and call the Better Business Bureau where the company maintains its headquarters and ask if it has a record of complaints from consumers. Better guarantees offer free replacement glass if a seal fails within 10 years. Keep in mind that you probably cannot replace the glass yourself, so read the guarantee further to see if it covers just the new glass or the entire sash and the cost of labor, too.

Better guarantees tend to go with the higher priced windows. In part, you're paying for insurance against failure and for assurance that the company won't go out of business in the future. But no matter what precautions you take or how good the windows are, don't be surprised if one day a foggy haze appears between the panes of your windows. Chances are, you'll have to replace at least one of your windows sometime.

PROTECTING YOUR INVESTMENT

Even the best-built home will show signs of wear and look a bit shabby as it ages. Paint peels, glass breaks, concrete cracks, doors rub, floors squeak, and shingles wear out. It's all part of the normal aging process. You expect it, and perhaps, despite a little grumbling, go about household chores—performing routine repairs and maintenance.

What really hurts a house, and your pocketbook, is neglect. If you skip that routine maintenance or ignore signs of trouble, a simple problem can easily snowball into big trouble.

Perhaps the problem begins with a leaky gutter that you don't get around to fixing. The leak spills water into the wooden eaves and down the wall, causing paint to peel. Some water gets into the wall, wets the insulation, and causes the

framing to rot and weaken. The weakened frame causes the roof to sag. By then you have to call in the pros. Many a carpenter makes a good living repairing the results of neglect!

Most common problems aren't so difficult to solve once you know how and why they first occur. Wet basements are a perennial problem, although often the solution's simple enough.

Preventing Moisture Damage in the Foundation

Controlling dampness through walls and floors

Ideally, basements, crawl spaces, and concrete foundation slabs should be dry—desert quality, arid, throat parching, dusty, bone dry. There'd be no wet floors or damp walls. No fungal growth, wood rot, dank air, or smelly mildew. No peeling paint, stained wallpaper, or rusting nails. Your basement would not only make a great living space, but you would not have to worry about what other damage the moisture in the foundation was doing to your house, such as rotting the joists and flooring of the rooms above.

But often, basements are too damp to be comfortable. The solid concrete or concrete block foundations that support your house and make up the basement walls—even concrete foundation slabs that lie on top of the soil—not only get damp, they can even channel moisture into your house rather than blocking it out. Unfortunately, it seems that the foundation not only doesn't work for the house, it sometimes seems to work against it. To be honest, dampness in a basement is a vexing problem.

Stopping leaks

Strange as it may seem, it's usually easier to stop basements from leaking than it is to put an end to the other sources of dampness that often make them so uncomfortable. Most basements leak because rainwater or snow melt collects near the foundation of the house and then works its way in through cracks and small holes (*page 152*). The best solution is to channel water away from the house. Extending the bottoms of the downspouts away from the house and sloping the ground away from the foundation, about a half inch per foot, generally do the trick. It also helps to fill low areas of your yard with soil so water doesn't form puddles that eventually seep toward the foundation.

There are several additional steps you can take to control dampness and moisture in a basement, a crawl space, or on a concrete slab (*page 152*). In the case of basements and concrete slabs, it is important to seal all cracks that provide channels for water. In a crawl space, a sheet of polyethylene plastic, available at home centers or hardware stores, should cover the entire floor of the crawl space. Lap the sheet of plastic up against the inside of the foundation to control moisture through the cinder block walls.

These steps will solve most leak problems and will certainly reduce dampness. They might even stop it.

150

SOURCES OF BASEMENT DAMPNESS

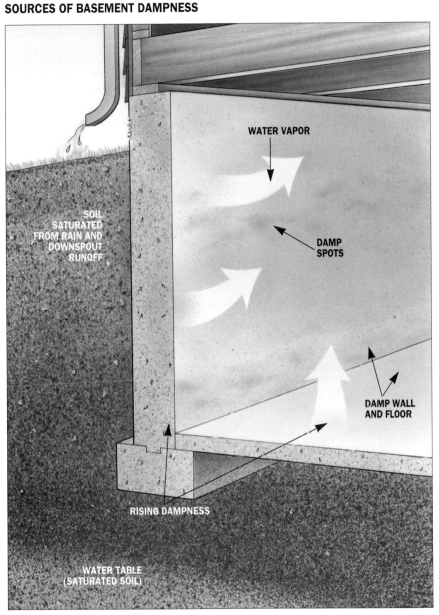

Dampness from saturated soil can seep against the basement wall. A process called *capillarity* in the concrete (*page 152*) draws the dampness through to the inside. Capillarity also draws water from saturated soil at the water table. This water can enter the footings and floor from the soil below.

But such dampness can be persistent because it enters your house in several completely different ways.

First, let's take a closer look at a concrete foundation. Remember, as solid as concrete looks, it is actually full of a great many tiny pores. Even watertight concrete is porous, so while it will not necessarily leak, that is, water will not run through it, the pores draw water in like tiny suction pumps. It is because these tiny pores interconnect with other pores in a vast network that they are able to continuously draw water onward, progressively filling up all the open spaces in the concrete.

This process, known as *capillarity*, works in all directions at once, even upward, soaking up water from any available source and drawing it toward drier areas. In a solid concrete or masonry building, capillarity can raise water within the walls as high as the second floor!

SOLUTIONS FOR A DAMP BASEMENT

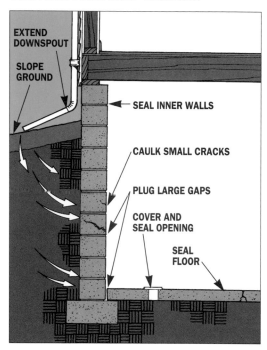

EXTEND DOWNSPOUT

SLOPE GROUND

SEAL INNER WALLS

CAULK SMALL CRACKS

PLUG LARGE GAPS

COVER AND SEAL OPENING

SEAL FLOOR

Fortunately, a concrete wall or floor can hold a lot of water without leaking because the pores retain the water. But, when water soaks all the way through a wall or floor to an inside surface, it'll wet anything it

SOLUTIONS FOR A DAMP SLAB

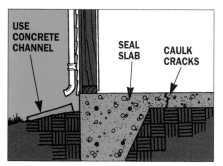

USE CONCRETE CHANNEL

SEAL SLAB

CAULK CRACKS

SOLUTIONS FOR DAMP CRAWL SPACE

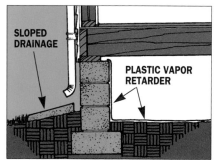

SLOPED DRAINAGE

PLASTIC VAPOR RETARDER

touches, such as wood, carpeting, and insulation. It's a major source of the moisture that causes mold, mildew, and rot in a house or basement. Moisture will also evaporate off the wet walls, saturate the air, and make everything else in the room feel damp.

Of course, for capillarity to be able to work, it has to have a good supply of water. It has three possible sources. First, water steadily works its way upward through the soil from a reservoir in the ground—called the *water table*—by capillary action, and it soaks into concrete foundations and slabs from below and the sides where they are below ground. Second, as rainwater sinks down into the soil, it seeps against the foundation and soaks in. Third, rainwater that splashes up against the sides of a foundation can soak into the concrete. You might be able to limit the splashing, but you're not going to have any luck blocking the water table or stopping the rain.

Identifying capillarity

It may take a little detective work, but it's usually not too difficult to figure out whether capillarity is at work. The clue stands out clearly on bare concrete: a powdery white line of mineral deposits that mysteriously shows up on your walls or floor.

These mineral deposits, called *efflorescence*, are a sure sign of water movement (*right*). They originally came from the ground outside or sometimes from mineral residues left in the concrete itself. Water dissolves these minerals and carries them along through the concrete, depositing them when the water finally evaporates off the inside floor

EFFLORESCENCE ON A PAINTED WALL

EFFLORESCENCE

WATER TO VAPOR TRANSITION ZONE

TIDE MARK

Efflorescence commonly appears at the highest point to which capillarity carries water. Efflorescence often occurs on exterior surfaces near ground level, as well as on interior surfaces.

or wall. While you can find the crystals anywhere you find moisture, they're always concentrated at the highest point of water penetration, leaving a telltale white line on the wall. This *tide line* can be several inches wide because the upper limit of the efflorescence rises and falls with the ebb and flow of moisture in the soil surrounding the foundation of the house.

The presence of efflorescence doesn't mean your concrete wall is deteriorating. It's harmless, and you can brush it away with a stiff-bristled brush. But expect it to return, because where minerals appear on the wall's surface, you can bet there are more just under the surface. The only way to stop efflorescence is to eliminate the water.

Unfortunately, that's not easy. The time to anticipate and stop capillarity from the outside was when the workers laid the foundation. A properly built foundation will have a damp-proof coat of asphalt, plastic, or other impervious material on the exterior to keep moisture out of the walls. It should also have good drainage alongside the walls leading to a drain pipe at the bottom of the foundation. A damp-proof layer between the foundation footing and wall, or a coarse bed of gravel under the foundation, will stop capillarity from below. Coarse gravel stops capillarity because the gaps between the individual stones are too large to draw or hold water. You usually can't tell how thoroughly workers damp-proofed your foundation unless you dig it up and inspect it. That's expensive, although perhaps worthwhile if you have serious problems with moisture.

Efflorescence will limit your success if you try to block capillarity from the inside with moisture-proof paint or some other type of coating. Capillarity usually keeps the wall that's below the tide line damp, although above that line the wall will remain dry, unless moisture from rainwater soaks through high-er up. Manufacturers simply don't formulate paints or other wall coverings to stick to wet surfaces, so no matter what coating you try, it'll fail and begin to crack and peel within a few years. Even worse, the mineral salts contained in the efflorescence that are temporarily blocked from emerging on the surface of the wall will crystallize below the surface, inside the concrete pores, and crack off the surface of the concrete causing it to flake. Sorry to say, there's not much good news when it comes to stopping capillarity once it's in the walls and floors.

More dampness: water vapor

Capillarity isn't the only source of dampness in the basement or crawl space; the second culprit is water vapor. You normally think of water vapor as the humidity in the air. Concrete contains air, too, in the same pores that cause capillarity. In fact, water can vaporize inside concrete from the same pool of water that capillarity draws up. Vapor spreads through the concrete, heading to drier air. Eventually it will filter into the basement, raising the humidity in the air and increasing the feeling of dampness in the whole basement.

Fortunately, you can paint concrete above the tide line to block water vapor movement into your basement. Well, "block" is actually too strong a word. "Retard" is better, because paint slows down the movement of the water vapor but it can't completely stop it. Of the three types of paints readily available, oil-based alkyds (*page 169*) retard vapor better than water-based latexes and concrete-based coatings.

MOISTURE FROM HIGH HUMIDITY

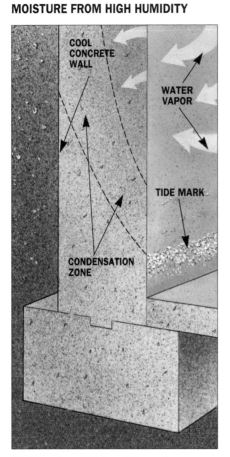

Moisture from high humidity condenses on and within cool walls. The moisture can also carry minerals to the wall surface.

Dampness from the air

The third source of dampness in a basement doesn't come from the ground or concrete. Moisture circulates throughout the house during periods of high humidity, usually in summer. The basement walls and floors are cool to the touch because they're in contact with the cooler surrounding soil. When the warm humid air strikes these cool surfaces, water condenses, just like it does on a cold glass of water. And if a wall surface is warm, water vapor can move into the wall and actually condense *inside* the concrete where it's cooler closer to the soil (*left*).

It's not always easy to determine whether the source of moisture in a basement is humidity or capillarity. An efflorescence tide line clearly shows capillarity. But condensation can be at work, too. One way you can test for condensation is to tape a sheet of aluminum foil tightly to the wall or floor and examine it over several days to see if condensation develops on its surface. Another sign of condensation is water trickling down a painted wall. Without one of these signs, you can't easily tell where the moisture is coming from—condensation or capillarity. You'll have to wait for an extended period of low humidity, say, several weeks to as long as a month. That will stop condensation and give the basement time to dry out should condensation be the problem. If the dampness continues, you'll know capillarity is at work.

If you find condensation to be the culprit in your basement, then you're in luck, because you can control the humidity that causes condensation by using a dehumidifier in the summer. Or, if your basement doesn't leak, you can cure cold walls by insulating them on the inside and then installing a vapor retarder over the insulation. It is harder to insulate cool concrete floors to stop condensation. If that is your main problem, dehumidification is probably the best defense you can take.

When Brick Fails

Rain and frost will do it in

As you've seen, water in its several forms is the primary enemy of a basement, crawl space, or concrete slab foundation. Unfortunately, it isn't any kinder to brick walls.

When I think of maintaining brick walls, I think in terms of decades and the forces that wear away mountains. Comparing a brick wall to a mountain exaggerates a bit, but some bricks fired and stacked several thousand years ago still survive today. Brick is durable, long lasting, and virtually maintenance free compared to most other types of building materials.

But mountains do eventually erode, and so do brick walls. While you won't find many problems in post-World War II brick houses, if you look at older houses, especially century-old historic ones, you'll find the same corrosive effects at work that level mountains. If you own a brick house, you won't see much change from year to year, but slowly, almost imperceptibly, cycles of heat and cold, along with rain and snow, wear down brick walls (*facing page*).

Understanding brick

Bricks are the symbol of hardness. But within the world of masonry, hardness is relative. Brick is made from clay that's molded and fired in a high-temperature kiln. Its hardness depends on the kiln temperature and firing time. Different clay compositions and the length of firing account for most variations in the color of bricks.

Whether hard or soft, bricks are able to stand up against any single weathering force. However, there are two forces that work together—water and freezing temperatures—that can break down a brick wall. Water that soaks into the brick and then freezes will begin to shatter the brick's internal structure.

To prevent this problem, brick manufacturers grade their bricks according to the weather extremes they must face. Severe weathering (SW) brick is the hardest and most dense. It absorbs the least amount of water, which makes it less vulnerable to freezing weather. Moderate weathering (MW) brick is not quite as hard and absorbs more water than SW. Negligible weathering (NW) brick is the softest and the most absorbent. Except in regions that rarely see freezing temperatures, masons should use only SW and MW bricks on exterior projects. And in all regions, without exception, masons should use SW bricks where the construction is in contact with the ground.

Mortar: the weak link

Most of the deterioration that happens in a brick wall doesn't occur to the bricks themselves; it happens

WHERE BRICK FAILS

CHIMNEY DETERIORATION

DIAGONAL CRACKS

EFFLORESCENCE

COLD WALL DAMAGE

DETERIORATED SILL CAP

ERODED JOINTS CAUSED BY LEAKY DOWNSPOUT

Bricks walls deteriorate primarily where water can penetrate the brick and then freeze. A settling or shifting foundation will also cause brick walls to crack.

in the mortar joints. At first this is puzzling. Why can't masons make the mortar as durable as the bricks? In reality, they could, but they don't for one good reason. Brick walls, like other structures, expand and contract with changes in the temperature. Of course, the actual movement is small, but bricks are extremely brittle and can't flex with wall movement. To keep the wall from cracking, the mortar must act like an elastic cushion, absorbing most of the movement. Unfortunately, to be elastic, mortars must be softer and less durable. If masons made them as hard as the brick, the entire wall would crack. And worse, the faces of the bricks would chip, a process that's known as *spalling*. This chipping ruins the appearance of a brick wall (*right*).

Mortar's elasticity also helps it maintain a strong bond with the bricks, which helps keep the wall rigid. If this bond should break, wind-driven rain will penetrate the brick veneer, soak it, and expose it to damaging freeze-and-thaw cycles.

Nevertheless, despite its elasticity, mortar is still durable. It's made by mixing cement, lime, and sand with water. Skilled masons adjust the proportions of the ingredients to make the mortar harder or softer, depending on the grade of the brick they're laying. For example, they'll use a softer mortar with softer brick. When mortar is properly mixed and smoothed to a concave or "V" shape between bricks, the joint will be virtually impervious to water penetration. As long as water stays out, a brick wall will last for decades.

Identifying the problem

When you understand the relative strengths and weaknesses of brick and mortar, it's easier to figure out why a brick wall deteriorates. There are several problem areas common to all brick structures.

Diagonal cracks along the mortar joints indicate that the supporting foundation has settled or shifted unevenly. The brick wall wasn't elastic enough to absorb the movement, so it cracked in its weakest spot, the mortar joints, often near the corners of windows or doors. If this settling continues, the cracks become larger gaps. In either case, rain can

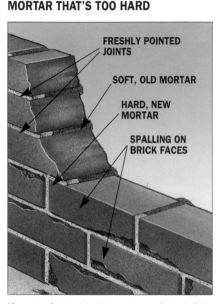

MORTAR THAT'S TOO HARD

FRESHLY POINTED JOINTS

SOFT, OLD MORTAR

HARD, NEW MORTAR

SPALLING ON BRICK FACES

If mortar is too hard, the edges of the bricks will crack and flake off, ruining the appearance of the wall. In such a situation, the joints should be repaired with mortar that's softer than the bricks.

blow in through the cracks, freeze, and quickly break down the mortar. Solve most setting problems by routing rainwater well away from the foundation of the building. Then repair larger cracks using a process called *pointing* or sometimes *tuckpointing*. This process is explained in more detail on page 160.

Eroded joints

Eroded mortar joints can often be traced directly to a leaky gutter or downspout, which lets a constant stream of water soak the brick wall and makes it vulnerable to cycles of freezing and thawing. It might leak into the inside of the house, as well. The mortar erodes and must be

ERODING SILL CAP

BRICK SILL CAP

ERODED MORTAR JOINTS

The brick sill cap absorbs water and cracks in cold weather. This allows water to penetrate and erode the brick wall below. The mason should have placed a metal flashing under the sill cap to protect the wall.

pointed. This is a sad and all too common problem with brick houses because it's the result of simple neglect. The problem could have been easily prevented by repairing the gutter or downspout as soon as the leak was first discovered.

Efflorescence

Dampness rising from the ground carries with it dissolved minerals, some from the ground and some from the wall itself. These minerals are deposited in the form of a powdery efflorescence (*page 153*) on the faces of the bricks when the moisture evaporates, just as it happens on the walls of a concrete basement or crawl space.

As on concrete, this efflorescence might look bad but it's harmless. You can scrub it away with a dry, stiff brush. But it will return unless you block the moisture source. The best solutions are to keep the soil around your foundation as dry as possible and to cover horizontal or sloping areas of the brick wall with watertight metal flashing, concrete, or a stone cap to keep moisture out.

Deteriorated sill caps

If you use brick for horizontal surfaces such as window sills and the tops of walls, be prepared to repair them, because water, ice, and snow will collect there, causing the mortar joints to deteriorate (*left*).

Ideally, sills and the top edges of walls should be capped with stone, concrete, or some other material — not brick — that rainwater can't penetrate. The brick wall below the cap should be covered with metal flashing, which is hidden in the mortar joint and is sloped to the outside to drain off any water that might get by the cap. Unfortunately, you won't find this much care taken in many old walls and sometimes not even in new brickwork.

Cold walls

Cold walls, so called because they are so far from the house that they don't get any warmth in cold weather, take a beating from all sides. Without that warmth, they undergo many more of the freeze-and-thaw cycles that will break them up. Without a water-resistant cap, called a *coping*, mortar joints in the horizontal surfaces can crack and leak, eventually causing them to erode and the bricks to crack and flake.

DETERIORATING COLD WALL

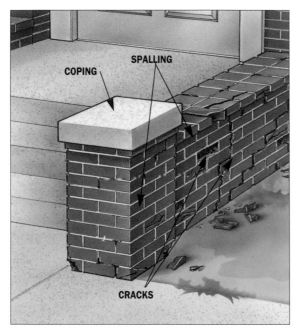

Water penetration, frost heave, and a shifting foundation can all damage a cold wall.

cold wall. Otherwise, keep the wall in good repair by replacing any cracked, chipped, or broken bricks and all loose mortar to keep it watertight. If you can, install a coping (*left*).

Chimneys

The top of a chimney faces the worst weathering problems of all (*facing page*). It faces not only all the same freeze-and-thaw cycles as a cold wall, but in addition it must endure more such cycles as the heating system of the house switches on and off. Exhaust gases from the furnace heat the chimney flue and the bricks a dozen times a day or more. If the outside temperature is low enough, the water in the bricks and mortar freezes, thaws, and refreezes each time, causing rapid deterioration of the mortar.

Unfortunately, masons often construct poorly designed *crowns* on top of brick chimneys, spreading a tapered bed of mortar over the top bricks rather than casting the entire crown in concrete or using precast concrete or stone. Over the years these mortar crowns crack, which allows water to easily penetrate the brickwork below.

Pointing brick walls

Pointing is the technical name for the process of repacking eroded mortar joints with new mortar to

A cold wall, because it's not protected from rainfall by the eaves and gutters of the house, also absorbs moisture from the ground, causing the bricks and mortar to deteriorate. And finally, unless the wall has a foundation that extends well below the frost line in the soil, or the wall itself has been carefully designed for strength, frost heave (*page 43*) will thrust it upward and crack it. These same cracks can also indicate uneven settling of the soil around it, which is usually the result of poor drainage.

A design that is well thought out takes into account all these factors and is the best protection for a

DETERIORATING CHIMNEY

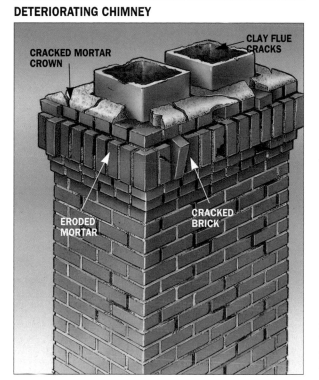

CRACKED MORTAR CROWN

CLAY FLUE CRACKS

ERODED MORTAR

CRACKED BRICK

A chimney is often the first brick area to deteriorate. Hot exhaust gases from the furnace or fireplace heat it and subject the bricks and mortar to frequent freeze-and-thaw cycles. Often, a poor cap design allows water to penetrate the brick.

keep the joints strong and watertight. The process involves chipping out the old mortar to a minimum depth of ¾ inch, brushing the joint clean, and mixing and pressing new mortar into the joints with various mason's tools to get flush, concave, or V-shaped grooves. Concave and V-shaped grooves weather better than flush joints. Joints where the mortar protrudes weather poorly and should be avoided.

Pointing is a tedious but relatively easy process. Matching the color of the new mortar to that of the old, however, can be a challenge. The new mortar doesn't often blend well with the old, which leaves the wall with a patchwork effect. Masons mix tints into mortar to try to match the old color more closely, but this is not easy to do because mortar tends to get lighter as it cures.

Making a good match of new and old mortar involves more than just finding the correct pigment, too. Next time you pass an old brick wall, take a look at its mortar joints. You'll see that the texture is sandy and rough. The softer cement crystals have worn away, leaving the harder particles of sand on the surface. Much of the mortar's color comes from the type of sand that was originally used. An experienced mason can examine this sand and will try to duplicate its color in the new mortar.

When a brick wall goes bad, it becomes an expensive headache to replace the bricks and mortar. But with a little prevention, brick walls will look great and last a lifetime.

Defeating Wood Decay

Natural and manufactured solutions

If a part of the house that is as solid and durable as a brick wall is likely to fail if it's not properly maintained, what can you then expect from an organic, less durable material like wood? For years now, home owners have been doomed to a seemingly endless cycle of periodically replacing rotted wood.

Not now. I recently read an ad from a wood products manufacturer guaranteeing its pressure-treated wood for life. This ad wasn't merely a claim, but a guarantee. Is pressure-treated wood really that good? After checking, I found that a number of manufacturers guarantee certain pressure-treated products against termites and decay for life. Pressure-treated wood does indeed appear to be a dependable product. Yet despite its common usage, pressure-treated wood continues to be a mystery to many home owners. Exactly what is it? How does it work? And, is it safe?

The problem: wood decay

Wood rots. That about sums up my frustration over crumbling foundations, mushy window sills, and falling fence posts. The source of all this destruction is fungus.

The problem isn't just one type of fungus, either. There's an entire army of fungus species that thrives in wood. These fungi eat it, mining its elements just as a plant draws nutri-ents from the soil. Fungi cause wood fiber literally to dissolve, an event that otherwise is rare in nature.

But, fortunately, fungi cannot infest wood everywhere. They need air, water, and a 50- to 90-degree temperature range to thrive. Without these conditions, they lie dormant or die (*facing page*).

Because we also need air and thrive in the same temperature range, we're left with trying to control fungi by keeping wood dry. The moisture content of air-dried wood varies with the relative humidity, so it rarely becomes damp enough to support fungal growth. Fungi live primarily on water that penetrates wood from several other sources—condensation, ground water, leaks, or rain. Foundation and outdoor wood are the prime candidates for rot when they get wet and do not get a chance to dry out.

Solutions from nature

The idea of preserving wood with chemicals began with the natural defenses of rot-resistant wood. It's long been recognized that certain species of wood, most notably redwood and cedar, decay much more slowly than others. The heartwood, the darker colored core of the tree trunk, contains chemicals that are toxic to most species of fungi. These toxins form only in the heartwood; the lighter colored sapwood toward the outside

INGREDIENTS FOR WOOD DECAY

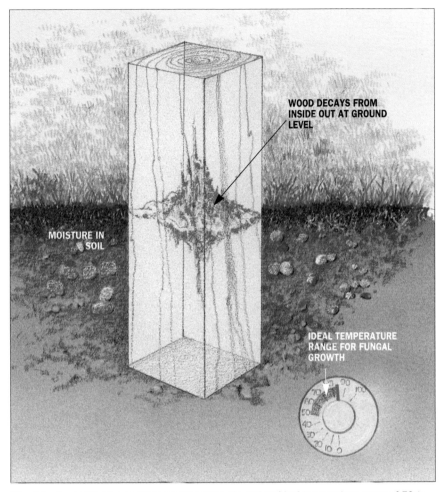

WOOD DECAYS FROM INSIDE OUT AT GROUND LEVEL

MOISTURE IN SOIL

IDEAL TEMPERATURE RANGE FOR FUNGAL GROWTH

Wood-destroying fungus requires wood, water, air, and an ideal temperature range of 50 to 90 degrees Fahrenheit. Posts eventually rot completely through at ground level.

of the tree trunk is no more resistant than any other wood.

So why do living trees decay at the center first, even decay-resistant species? It turns out that fungi can't gain a permanent foothold in living sapwood. The flowing tree sap is so wet that it eliminates all the air that the fungi need to survive. The fungi simply drown.

Not so in the drier heartwood. Fungi gain access to the inner core of a tree through broken limbs and deep scars and eventually cause rot in even decay-resistant species. The natural resistance of heartwood is limited. Most of the toxic chemicals in these species dissolve in water, so when this wood is used as lumber in places where there's a lot of moisture, its resistance decreases as the chemicals gradually leach away.

Yes, redwood and cedar posts rot. The secret to longevity for naturally resistant wood is to seal it well (painted wood siding, for example) or use it in places where, once it gets wet, it will easily dry out, such as for deck boards and railings.

The preservative solution

Many chemicals that are toxic to fungi and insects have been used during the past 50 years. The trick is not in finding toxins, but rather in making the toxins stay in the wood. Currently, there are three types of chemicals commonly used for preserving wood: pentachlorophenol (often called *penta*), creosote, and chromated copper arsenate (CCA). All three are applied commercially and under specific regulations; they are not available to home owners.

Creosote and penta are primarily used in industrial applications to protect heavy timbers such as utility poles and railroad ties. Penta is also used commercially to treat millwork, such as window sashes and sills. You may be able to detect its odor when you buy a new wood window. Otherwise, you're not likely to find these chemicals around your house.

About 90 percent of the treated lumber you can buy at home centers and lumberyards is treated with CCA or a similar chemical. You can usually distinguish it from untreated wood by its distinctively greenish color. Commercial treaters dissolve CCA in water and then force it deep into the wood under pressure, where it bonds with the individual wood fibers as the lumber dries to a stable state. After that point, the chemical won't redissolve or leach out; it protects wood indefinitely.

Quality guidelines

Pressure treatment works. In a recent study, wooden stakes treated with CCA at .29 pound of chemical per cubic foot of wood (abbreviated pcf) and driven into the ground in Mississippi showed no decay after 32 years. Untreated stakes lasted only 3½ years. (Stakes of the heartwood of naturally resistant species generally lasted up to 20 years.)

But the quality of treated wood varies. The effectiveness of the preservatives depends on how deeply they penetrate the wood and how much of the chemical the wood retains. Some species of wood don't accept pressure treatment very well, so the chemicals may be concentrated near the surface rather than penetrating the wood.

The American Wood Preservers Association (AWPA) sets its penetration standard at 85 percent of the sapwood or 2½ inches into the wood (*facing page, top*). This means that the most common lumber dimensions, 2-inch- and 4-inch-thick materials, should be almost completely penetrated. You should be able to see this if you cut through a piece of pressure-treated lumber. The distinctive greenish tint of treated wood should show throughout (although it does become lighter toward the middle). If this greenish tone appears to be concentrated toward the edges of the wood with none visible toward the middle, the treatment is

PRESSURE-TREATED PENETRATION

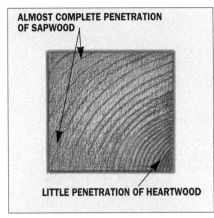

ALMOST COMPLETE PENETRATION OF SAPWOOD

LITTLE PENETRATION OF HEARTWOOD

Pressure treatment penetrates about 85 percent of the sapwood, providing good protection. It does not penetrate heartwood well, and you should avoid buying lumber with a large portion of heartwood.

inferior and the piece of lumber will decay more rapidly.

Notice that the AWPA standard specifies sapwood, the lighter colored wood that surrounds the darker heartwood core of a tree. The heartwood of many species of trees doesn't accept treatment well, and therefore it decays more rapidly. You shouldn't buy pressure-treated lumber that contains more than a half inch of heartwood.

The second quality consideration is the amount of the treating chemical retained by the wood. This measurement is most often expressed by pcf—the

more chemicals, the greater is the wood's decay resistance. Pressure-treated wood is generally rated at .25 pcf for above-ground use, .40 pcf for ground contact use, and .60 pcf for building foundations.

To know just what you're buying, look for a quality control mark that is either stamped directly on the lumber or printed on a tag that is stapled to the end (*below*). You're likely to see the AWPA mark since its standards are used by the majority of the pressure-treating facilities. A lifetime guarantee tag is also another good quality indicator to look for in pressure-treated wood.

Finally, pressure treating the lumber cannot alter some of wood's less desirable traits. Pressure-treated wood will still warp, crack, and swell. The pressure-treatment process adds water to the wood, so be sure your lumber has been dried after treatment. Once it's dry, most treated wood can be stained, painted, or treated with water repellents to keep it stable.

THE TREATER'S QUALITY MARK

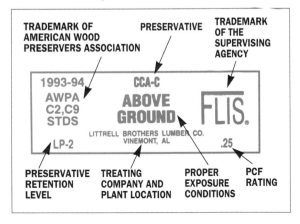

TRADEMARK OF AMERICAN WOOD PRESERVERS ASSOCIATION

PRESERVATIVE

TRADEMARK OF THE SUPERVISING AGENCY

1993-94
AWPA
C2,C9
STDS

CCA-C

ABOVE GROUND

FLIS®

LITTRELL BROTHERS LUMBER CO.
VINEMONT, AL

LP-2

.25

PRESERVATIVE RETENTION LEVEL

TREATING COMPANY AND PLANT LOCATION

PROPER EXPOSURE CONDITIONS

PCF RATING

BRUSHED-ON PRESERVATIVE

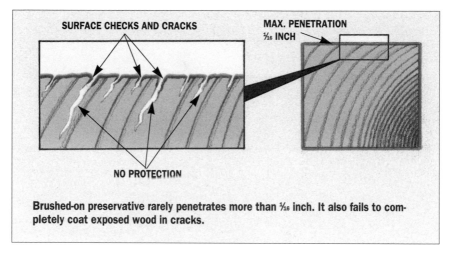

SURFACE CHECKS AND CRACKS

MAX. PENETRATION
1⁄16 INCH

NO PROTECTION

Brushed-on preservative rarely penetrates more than 1⁄16 inch. It also fails to completely coat exposed wood in cracks.

WOOD DIPPED OR SOAKED IN PRESERVATIVE

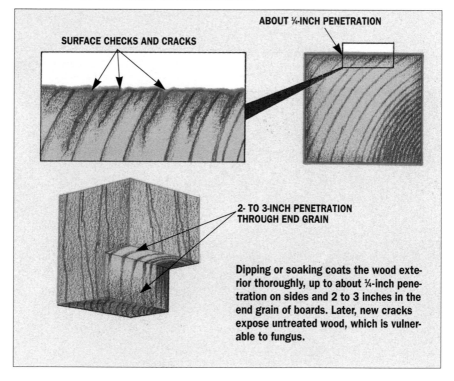

ABOUT 1⁄4-INCH PENETRATION

SURFACE CHECKS AND CRACKS

2- TO 3-INCH PENETRATION
THROUGH END GRAIN

Dipping or soaking coats the wood exterior thoroughly, up to about 1⁄4-inch penetration on sides and 2 to 3 inches in the end grain of boards. Later, new cracks expose untreated wood, which is vulnerable to fungus.

Other treatment methods

Pressure treatment is almost always superior to other treatment methods. Brushing, soaking, or dipping with preservatives available to consumers may certainly be adequate in some situations—for instance, where drainage is good or where wood gets wet only occasionally.

But these methods don't penetrate far enough for long-term resistance to decay. Fungus invades from the outside. As long as the preservative barrier remains unbroken, fungus won't get a foothold. But in the repeated wetting and drying cycles of wood, deep cracks open, exposing untreated wood deeper down, which gives fungus a place to grow. That's when deeper treatment of the wood is necessary.

Dipping and soaking do work when cutting pressure-treated lumber. It's a good idea to soak newly cut ends of pressure-treated wood to coat any untreated or partially treated wood that becomes exposed and to restore the preservative barrier.

Precautions

If you've ever cut into a freshly pressure-treated timber and felt a slight burning on your bare skin from wet sawdust, you know that the chemicals used can be harmful. Treated wood is safe when used properly, but it's wise to be aware of and respect the chemicals in it.

The Environmental Protection Agency (EPA) has mandated that consumer information pamphlets listing precautions be available wherever pressure-treated wood is sold. You should pick one up and read through it. The main thrust of the precautions is to avoid ingesting the chemicals. They're not food for fungi, and they're not good for you, either. Do not use pressure-treated wood where the preservative may become a component of food or animal feed, such as countertops, cutting boards, food containers, and pet dishes. If you use it for a picnic table top, do not place food directly on the treated wood; use dishes or place mats instead.

Use only wood that's clean and free of surface residue in locations with likely skin contact such as decks, patios, and walkways. Wash any parts of your skin that come into direct contact with pressure-treated wood. Launder contaminated clothes separately from regular wash loads.

If you are working with wood treated with creosote or penta, wear vinyl gloves. Do not use wood treated with these chemicals indoors or where there might be frequent skin contact unless the wood is sealed with at least two coats of a sealer such as urethane, epoxy, or shellac.

Avoid inhaling sawdust from pressure-treated wood. Always work outdoors and wear a dust mask when cutting it. Also, wear eye protection. Clean up dust and scrap when finished working and dispose of it by ordinary trash collection or burial. Do *not* burn it.

Unfortunately, burning excess scrap is quite common, but don't do it. The chemicals in the wood can be released in the smoke and inhaled. Ecologically, disposal is one of the most difficult aspects of treated lumber. Ironically, by treating wood so it doesn't decay, manufacturers have created waste that won't decompose, even underground, at least not for a very long time.

Choosing the Best Paint for the Job

How to solve the problem of peeling paint

It's always a satisfying feeling to make those final brush strokes, then stand back and admire a freshly completed paint job The old and worn siding on the house comes back to life, the new trim color highlights the windows and doors, and the entire house suddenly looks brand new. It is a moment to savor before you carefully clean out your brushes, rollers, and pans, recap the leftover paint and put it all away. But you know that you'll have to pull the painting supplies out again in a few years, because you know that even the best paint job won't last.

If there's one thing that is as predictable as a law of nature: paint will peel. Sometimes it falls off like confetti at a New Year's party. It also fades, chalks, blisters, and cracks. No wonder there has been a long search for alternatives to break the five-year cycle of scrapers, sandpaper, and yet another coat of paint.

But paint has proven itself to be tough to beat. It's difficult to match it for color and beauty, and it has proven to be an economical way to protect our wooden houses.

There are many reasons why paint fails, and each house affects paint differently. By focusing on how paint sticks to wood and how that bond breaks down, you should be able to diagnose some of the characteristics or troubles with it in your house and work out the most effective solutions.

What makes paint stick?

The illustration (*facing page*) shows that paint is only one of several types of exterior finishes that we loosely call "paint." It's useful to consider them all, because any one of these finishes may be the best exterior coating for your situation. It's easy to understand finishes if you keep in mind how similar they are. They all contain three basic substances: pigment, binder, and solvent.

The *pigment*, of course, is what gives the finish its color. There's no magic to it. Many small colored particles hang suspended in the paint film. They're heavier than the liquid portion of the paint, so they tend to settle to the bottom of the paint can, which is why the paint always has to be mixed before it can be used. At one time, the most common white pigment was made from lead oxide. With the growing awareness of the danger of lead poisoning, lead oxide has been banned from paint.

Pigments also affect the paint's luster after it dries (referred to as *gloss*, *semigloss*, or *flat*), extend the life of the film, and "fill" the paint so it covers more surface area. Paints

STANDARD WOOD FINISHES

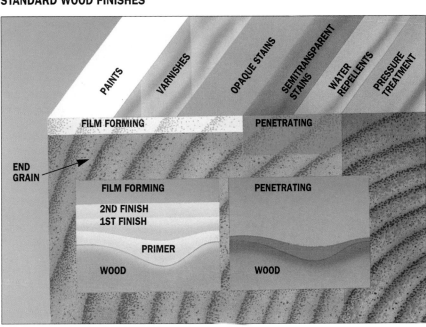

Most finishes bond to the first few layers of wood cells. Some form an elastic film as well. Only pressure treatment drives preservatives deeply into the wood.

often contain several pigments; the more expensive might use titanium dioxide for strong color (white in this case), or cheaper ones such as clay and silica (also white) to fill and extend the paint.

The *binder* makes the paint stick. It's the protective coat that glues the paint elements to each other as well as to the painted surface. There are many types of binders. Most group into two classes: *latex* and *acrylics* or *oils* and *alkyds*. Perhaps as painters we know them best by the way we clean our brushes after a painting project. Water is used to clean latex and acrylic paints, and mineral spirits such as paint thinner or turpentine are needed for oils and alkyds.

The third element, *solvent*, simply liquifies the binder so it can be spread more easily with brushes and rollers. It also helps the binder seep into the tiny irregularities and pores of the wood.

By juggling the amounts of the three elements—pigment, binder, and solvent—you can come up with the different types of finishes (*page 170*). Paints that have high concentrations of pigment, produce strong colors. But that also means the proportion of binder is reduced, so they don't stick to wood as well. Paint does adhere well to a primer, however. Primers contain little pigment and more binder, so they stick better to a wood, metal, or concrete sur-

COMPARING PAINT INGREDIENTS BY VOLUME

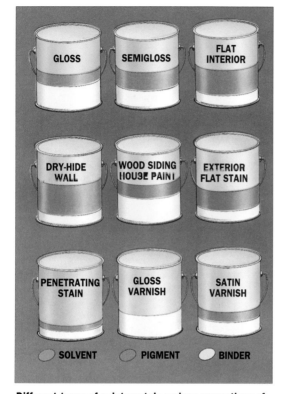

Different types of paint contain various proportions of solvent, pigment, and binder.

parent, depending upon the amount of pigment.

Finally, without the pigment and binder, the solvents alone can carry chemical water repellents and preservatives. While these products can't exactly be considered finishes, you can use them underneath other finishes to further protect the wood.

For practical purposes, finishes are divided into two groups: *film-forming* and *penetrating.* A film-forming finish, such as paint, blankets the wood surface with a membrane. A penetrating finish, such as stain, carries its binder and pigment a little deeper into the surface of the wood but doesn't form a film. Only pressure treatment drives substances deeply into the wood.

Both films and penetrating finishes have advantages, depending on their use. But the next time you scrape your siding, you'll think more about the disadvantage of a paint film because it will eventually peel; a penetrating finish will not.

Why film-forming finishes peel

Wood provides a great surface for film bonding, so it's surprising that it's also the cause of most paint failures. Wood is very sensitive to relative humidity. For example, your doors tend to swell and stick during a humid summer, even when they're well painted. Wood is not stable—it moves—expanding rapidly under

face. That's one reason to use the correct type of primer before trying to paint any bare surface.

If you completely remove pigment from paint, you'll be left with the binder, which is almost clear. This is a simple *varnish,* here used as a general term for any of the clear finishes. If you increase the amount of solvent, you're thinning the paint and forcing both the pigment and the binder to stretch further. The paint then becomes what's called a *stain,* either opaque or semitrans-

FORMING A FILM

To form a film, the solvent must first evaporate. Then the binder can harden and entrap the pigment.

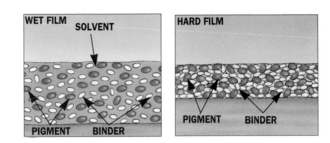

high relative humidity and contracting under low.

Surface films have to stick to the wood to which they're bonded, so they must be flexible, able to give with the expansion and contraction of the wood. Otherwise, they'll crack, which is the first step in paint failure. Surface water penetrates the crack, deteriorates the surrounding wood, and causes the bond to fail.

How moisture enters siding

If moisture causes problems, it's logical to keep it out, right? Well, that's partly right. Remember that even a well-painted door will swell. Finishes *retard* moisture movement, they don't stop it. They slow wood expansion, allowing the finish to stretch without cracking.

The fact is, finishes don't keep moisture out of wood. Water vapor in the form of humidity can pass through all finishes. It doesn't matter how hot or cold it is outdoors. Wood responds to relative humidity and will absorb water until it balances with the moisture content of the surrounding air. The wood finish helps to slow absorption considerably. Films do this best. They slow moisture much more than penetrating stains. And among films, oil and alkyd films retard moisture bet-

ter than latex and acrylic. When a finish like latex transmits moisture easily, it's said to "breathe".

But if moisture can get into the wood, the finish must also let it escape. Trapped moisture will encourage the deterioration of the wood surface, which then breaks the paint bond. For that reason, it's not always best to use a highly moisture-retarding finish on your house.

HOW MOISTURE PENETRATES SIDING

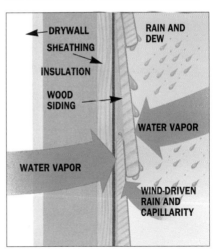

Water vapor moves through all finishes. Rain may wet the siding's back side, either by wind driving it through cracks or by capillary action.

ACRYLIC PAINT

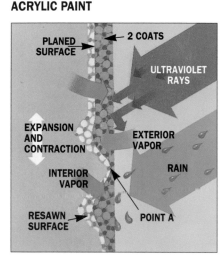

Acrylics transmit water vapor readily and block rain. Pigment absorbs harmful ultraviolet rays. A crack in the film is likely at point A.

ALKYD PAINT

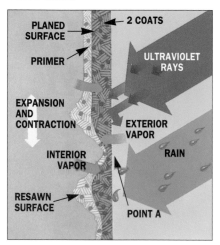

Alkyd resins bond into a tight film, which transmits much less water vapor than acrylics. Cracking over rough wood is likely at point A.

The illustration (*page 171*) reveals the many ways in which moisture can enter wood siding, all of which can lead to paint failure if the wood cannot dry. Water vapor can move through the walls from either direction and collects in the wood, especially in cooler months when interior air tends to be more moist than exterior air.

Most of the time, however, rainwater doesn't cause a problem because most types of finishes shed it well. But windblown rain can be driven into cracks and up between loose boards. Water also may be sucked up between siding boards by capillary action. Water that manages to work its way behind the siding won't dry out until the wood itself does. In such situations, finishes that breathe better will allow the wood— and the moisture lurking behind it—to dry out faster.

How common finishes perform

Acrylic paints breathe very well (*above left*). They readily allow water vapor to move in and out of wood while they block rain. Their resin binder is composed of tiny plastic beads that stick together in an elastic mat as the solvent (water) dries. Once dry, the binder does not redissolve from wetting, although you must take care not to allow the paint to get wet before it's completely dry.

Pigments play an important role in blocking the most damaging element of the sun: high-energy ultraviolet rays. The pigments absorb and reflect them. In the process, a little of the surface binder breaks down and can form a light,

VARNISH

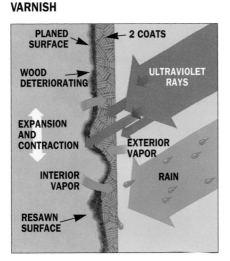

Varnishes do not block the sun's ultraviolet rays. The wood surface eventually degrades and the wood-varnish bond releases, causing peeling.

PENETRATING STAIN

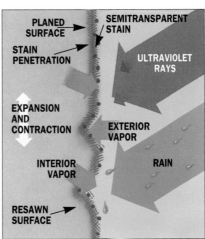

Penetrating stains weather more rapidly than film finishes but have no film to peel, so recoating is easy. They transmit water vapor readily.

powdery coat on the paint surface, called *chalking*. This is not a major problem; chalking can be washed off periodically using water and a mild detergent.

Alkyds work in a similar fashion, except they do not breathe as well (*facing page, right*). When alkyd paint is applied, the solvent (mineral spirits) evaporates, leaving a sticky film. The resin binders then slowly harden or cure, resulting in a very tight film that allows little vapor to get through. Once wood covered with an alkyd finish becomes damp, it won't easily dry out and probably will cause the paint to fail.

Clear finishes such as varnish leave wood at the mercy of the sun's damaging ultraviolet rays (*above left*). Without any pigment to block them, the rays attack the top layer of cells

in the wood, breaking them down, and breaking the bond between the wood and the varnish. Unless clear-coated objects can be shaded from direct sunlight, their finish breaks down within a few years.

For that matter, the surface of any unfinished wood left exposed to the sun for several weeks will deteriorate significantly. You'll have to resand the surface before painting to ensure a good bond between finish and wood.

Acrylics, alkyds, and varnishes work best on smoothly finished wood. Their smooth film spreads the stress evenly when the wood expands and contracts. When applied to an uneven surface like resawn or rough siding, however, notice how the film thickness varies in the illustrations for acrylic, alkyd, and var-

173

nish (*pages 172 and 173*). When the wood expands, the thick film layer, because it is much stronger, doesn't expand much, while the weaker thin layers must stretch quite a bit more. The finish cracks at those points and allows water to enter.

For this reason, film-forming finishes aren't recommended for rough-surfaced materials. Besides, these finishes are almost impossible to scrape off once peeling occurs, and scraping will destroy the texture of the siding

Here's where the semitransparent stains can be effective. They don't form a film that will break and cause peeling. Unfortunately, they erode from the wood surface fairly quickly through weathering. But you can spread more stain, perhaps every two years in the more severely weathered areas. The rough texture works to the stain's advantage; it can absorb much more of the penetrating finish than a smooth surface can. Although the stain won't last long, you can recoat it without having to scrape off a peeling film.

Choosing the best paint

So what finish should you use on your house? Well, the short answer is, it depends. Are you painting indoors or out? What are you painting? Drywall? Trim? Siding? Metal? Concrete? The illustration (*facing page*) shows some of the challenges paint faces. Fortunately, there are paints formulated for every one.

Exterior siding

Much of the discussion so far has dealt with exterior siding. Outdoor conditions make some tough demands on a paint film, so paint for-

mulators use premium resins and pigments in high-quality exterior paints. A top-quality formula will use 100-percent acrylic resins for the binder in a latex paint. Specially formulated alkyd resins in oil-based paints work almost as well, but air-quality laws in some states, which require reduced levels of solvents called volatile organic compounds, have caused these finishes to practically disappear from the shelves.

Latex and oil paints each have advantages. Oil-based alkyds brush on more smoothly than water-based acrylics, and they dry harder, but acrylics don't break down as easily under intense sunlight.

Oil-based alkyd primers have some advantages because bare wood absorbs oil-based solvents better than it absorbs water. A coat of a high-quality primer adheres well and fills the pores in bare wood. The top coat of paint bonds to the primer and forms a strong, even film. Many painters apply an oil-based primer to bare wood, then cover it with a water-based acrylic top coat for the protective film.

Exterior trim

Use the same binder-rich paints for trim as for exterior siding. Both uses must be able to withstand weathering, but many people prefer to paint their trim with a semigloss or gloss luster rather than the flat normally chosen for siding.

Porch floors

When trying to come up with a good paint for an exterior floor, paint formulators are caught between a rock and a hard place. Good exterior coatings must be flex-

CHALLENGES A PAINT MUST OVERCOME

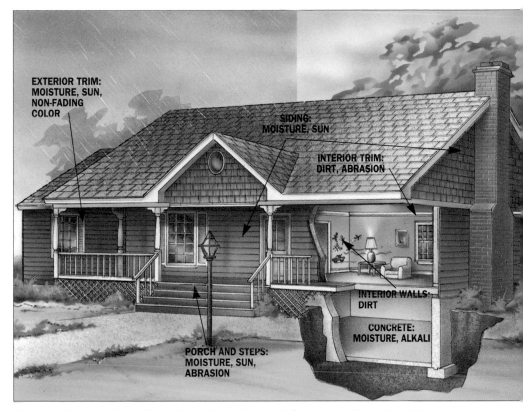

EXTERIOR TRIM: MOISTURE, SUN, NON-FADING COLOR

SIDING: MOISTURE, SUN

INTERIOR TRIM: DIRT, ABRASION

INTERIOR WALLS: DIRT

CONCRETE: MOISTURE, ALKALI

PORCH AND STEPS: MOISTURE, SUN, ABRASION

Paints are formulated according to their intended uses and the likely challenges they'll face.

ible enough to withstand changes in moisture and temperature, but on a floor they have to be hard enough to withstand the scuffing and abrasion of foot traffic. Porch and floor paints are resin-rich gloss paints sometimes made with harder resins. Acrylic resins work well. But any paint can have trouble adhering to a porch floor because water can pool on the surface for a long time, eventually soaking through and breaking the film's bond to the wood. For best results, be sure to apply an exterior primer first. Unfortunately, the finish resulting from the higher resin content can make wet painted floors slippery, so some painters add fine sand to the paint to improve traction.

Concrete

Concrete presents paint films with two challenges: moisture and alkali. Remember, concrete is porous, so moisture moving through concrete will break a paint film's bond to the surface and cause it to peel. Acrylic paints have an advantage here because they breathe and won't trap moisture as readily as the oil-based paints are likely to do.

Alkali is a corrosive substance present in all concrete, especially when newly poured. It can be neutralized, however, by washing the surfaces with a diluted solution of muriatic acid. In addition, for walls painters use a water-based concrete primer that contains a substance known as polyvinyl acetate (PVA), which is actually the standard resin used in inexpensive latex paints. PVA is too soft for concrete floors, so here painters apply two coats of a water-based acrylic or an acrylic modified with epoxy resins. Epoxy resins deteriorate under intense sunlight but perform well indoors.

Interior paints

Interior paints do not have to face the same rigors as outdoor paints do, so paint formulators can make them from lower cost binder and resin. This is why interior paints are usually priced a lot lower than exterior paints. Furthermore, most people prefer wall paints with a flat luster (*right*). A flat finish hides imperfections in the wall surface, while a glossy finish highlights every irregularity. Flat paints also contain less resin, which makes them even more economical to use.

The rough surface that makes a paint look flat, however, also catches dirt and streaks. And while most wall paints can be washed, low-cost films will eventually wash away, leaving you with a repainting job. A truly washable paint must have a

DETERMINING LUSTER

GLOSS   SMOOTH

BINDER: 65%
PIGMENT: 35%

SEMIGLOSS   SLIGHTLY ROUGH

BINDER: 50%
PIGMENT: 50%

FLAT   ROUGH

BINDER: 35%
PIGMENT: 65%

The amount of pigment in paint determines the smoothness of the film surface.

smooth surface, which usually means more resin. Paint formulators have found that they can make a smooth, washable surface without increasing the amount of resin by adding different types of pigments as fillers. These finishes are called "eggshell" paints.

Metal

When you paint metal for outdoor use, you generally run afoul of two problems: making the paint stick to the surface and stopping corrosion.

Unlike wood, which is porous, metal surfaces are smooth, even polished, so paint can't get a good grip on the surface. Paints stick better if you roughen the metal surfaces. Then you use special primers formulated to adhere to the bare metal.

The second problem is stopping corrosion of the metal, especially from water. Water causes metal surfaces to react, corrode, and flake, breaking the bond and causing paint to peel. Special primers also help stop corrosion. Oil-based and other solvent-based paints perform well on metal because they form a watertight film and adhere well.

There are a few exceptions. Do not use oil-based primer on galvanized steel. Paint galvanized gutters and downspouts only with a water-based primer designed for galvanized metal and then add an acrylic top coat. Proper prep work is critical here. Wipe all oil and grease from the surface, especially new surfaces, with a solvent such as xylol, which is available from painting stores. Solvents such as paint thinner and turpentine won't work because they leave an oily residue.

Aluminum siding already has a baked-on prime coat, so paint over it with an acrylic paint. If painting unprimed aluminum, consult a paint specialist for a primer specially formulated for aluminum.

Special problems

Some types of wood, when used outdoors, won't hold paint well. Hardwoods such oak, maple, and birch are in this category, but so is southern yellow pine. The dark grain lines in this pine species are dense and resinous. Paint will not adhere well to the grain lines where the wood will be exposed to weathering, so builders will use this wood beneath overhangs, such as eaves, where it won't get wet.

Douglas fir plywood, the most common type of plywood, doesn't hold paint well either, partly for the same reason. In addition, the surface veneer contains many tiny surface cracks that quickly fracture the paint film. An exterior stain is often a better choice than paint.

Redwood and cedar can also cause trouble. Their heartwood contains natural chemicals that help make the wood naturally resistant to rot and insects (*page 162*) but which leach through paint and leave black stains on exterior siding, decks, or fences. When painting these woods, be sure to use a primer specially formulated to block these stains.

Finally, hardboard exterior siding, which has come into wide use during the past 25 years, will quickly deteriorate if water penetrates the paint film. Hardboard is made from compressed wood fiber and resins. If it's not protected, the exposed fibers quickly soak up water, swell, and further fracture the paint film, compounding the problem. Once wet, hardboard begins to disintegrate rapidly. Watch for signs of paint failure, especially at the bottom edges of boards and at joints. Sand, then coat with an oil-based primer and repaint it immediately with a high-quality acrylic top coat.

High quality paint usually costs a bit more, but it's worth it. The real cost of a paint job is the time and effort you put into it.

Avoiding a Leaky Roof

The key signs that signal trouble ahead

Damp basements, brick walls, and painted siding all deteriorate gradually. You have time to correct the problem before damage spreads. But if your roof fails, the damage occurs quickly and it can spread to other parts of the house. You never appreciate having a leak-proof roof as much as when you don't have one. Trust me, shuffling pans and buckets around in the attic to catch dripping water on a stormy night can be a nightmare.

Fortunately for home owners, this particular nightmare doesn't occur very often. Roofs and the products we use to cover them withstand billions of raindrops, tons of snow and ice, baking and freezing temperatures, and sometimes even natural disasters such as hurricanes and tornadoes.

Eventually, though, a roof will wear out. Asphalt shingles, which cover about 80 percent of all roofs in the United States and Canada, steadily break down and fail. The remaining 20 percent are covered with either cedar shingles or shakes, tile, or metal. Many of the causes of leaky asphalt roofs apply to these types of roofs, too.

How a roof breaks down

Except during natural disasters like devastating hurricanes, which blow off not only the shingles but entire roofs, asphalt shingle roofs generally live a long and useful life. Rain, snow, ice, and cold weather hardly affect them. But regardless of your location, all asphalt shingles have a common enemy—the sun.

The first signs of trouble might be a pile of tiny colored granules that you notice under leaves and other debris as you clean out your gutters. Or while up on the roof, you might hear the shingles crack or break underfoot. Or perhaps you'll see some shingle edges curled upward or downward. All these signs indicate that your roof shingles are nearing their end and you'll probably want to replace them within the next few years (*facing page*).

By this time, the sun has done its damage. An asphalt shingle is basically a fiber mat soaked in hot asphalt and then cooled. Asphalt sheds water well, but it has no way to shed the sun's high-energy ultraviolet rays. These rays, invisible to the human eye, gradually break down the asphalt, causing the shingles to lose their flexibility, become brittle, shrink, and crack.

Manufacturers design shingles to resist this breakdown in two ways. First, they cover the asphalt with small, hard mineral granules that block the sun's ultraviolet rays (and make roofs colorful). But after a decade or so, many of these granules will have eroded off the shingle surface, leaving the asphalt more

HOW SHINGLES DETERIORATE

Ultraviolet rays and heat from the sun break down asphalt shingles, causing them to turn brittle, shrink, crack, curl, cup, and lose their protective coating of mineral granules. A layer of granules in the gutters is one sign that the shingles are beginning to break down.

exposed and vulnerable to damage. At that point, the deterioration process speeds up. Walking on a roof, especially on hot summer days, can also knock off granules, so stay off the roof as much as possible.

And second, manufacturers extend roof life by increasing the amount of asphalt they use in some grades of their shingles. These thicker grades will take longer to break down. They can last 30 to 40 years compared to the thinner shingles

that are rated to last generally only about 15 to 20 years.

In reality, how long the shingles on a roof last depends on how much sun hits the roof. Shingles in sunny Phoenix take a greater beating than those in cloudy Seattle. For that matter, the north-facing side of a roof, no matter what part of the country it's in, might last twice as long as the south-facing side because it catches less direct sunlight during summer.

179

HOW FLASHINGS FAIL

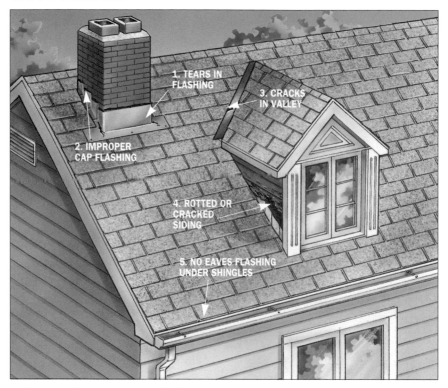

1. TEARS IN FLASHING

3. CRACKS IN VALLEY

2. IMPROPER CAP FLASHING

4. ROTTED OR CRACKED SIDING

5. NO EAVES FLASHING UNDER SHINGLES

1. Metal flashing can tear around chimneys or where it was bent during a reroofing job. Roofers sometimes drive nails through the metal too close to the corners when replacing a roof.

2. Asphalt cement, which substitutes for flashing tucked into the mortar joints in masonry chimneys, will start to leak after a few years.

3. Flashing in valleys can crack if it is stepped on.

4. Damaged siding or cracked stucco allows water to get behind the flashing and into the walls.

5. Water backed up behind ice dams can seep through the roof unless eaves flashing under the shingles stops it.

Leaks around flashing

There's no question that the shingles on a roof will eventually wear out. But this generally is not the main cause of a leaky roof. Home owners usually spot the worn roof and replace it before leaks occur.

The real culprit is usually inadequate *flashing.*

Flashing consists of sheet metal, heavy asphalt, or other flexible but waterproof materials that roofers put at vulnerable spots on the roof. These spots include such places as dormers, chimneys, plumbing vent pipes, and valleys (*facing page*).

The chimney causes the most problems. Because it's so heavy, a chimney has its own foundation, so it settles and moves independently of the house. This movement can cause flashing to stretch and tear open. Furthermore, you have to tuck chimney flashing into the mortar joints to keep water from running down behind the flashing. Unfortunately, roofers don't always do a good job, especially after the original flashing has worn out. Installing chimney flashing is a job for a professional.

Few roofers have the skills to restore this flashing, and often a home owner simply doesn't want to cough up the money for a first-class job. The cheap, quick solution is to fill any gaps with plastic roof cement. Unfortunately, this won't last long. The cement will harden and crack within a few years, and the leaks will begin soon after.

Many chimneys were constructed without an angled *saddle*, sometimes called a *cricket*. A saddle looks like a small roof added to the uphill side of a chimney. It helps direct rainwater around the chimney and keeps rain, snow, and ice from collecting there and prematurely corroding the flashing. All chimneys should have one. (Skylights should also have this special flashing on their uphill sides.)

Valley flashing, the covering that protects the junction where two roof sections meet or where a dormer meets the roof, is especially vulnerable as it ages. Unless it's metal, it becomes brittle and will crack if you step on it. Be sure to remind anyone

who climbs up onto your roof not to step in a valley.

Flashing at the junction of a roof and wall sometimes leaks because a roofer drove a nail through it when nailing down a second layer of shingles. More often, the siding itself has rotted or cracked, meaning that water can penetrate the wood or stucco siding and run down behind the flashing.

Another type of flashing, called *eaves flashing*, is a strip of asphalt roofing that runs along the eaves at the lower edge of the roof under the shingles to protect against ice dams in regions with snowfall. An ice dam occurs when water from melting snow freezes near the edge of the roof and traps other melt water behind it. This water can run back up under the shingles and will rot the wood sheathing and leak into the house unless you have eaves flashing to block it. While good roof ventilation will prevent most ice dams, eaves flashing helps prevent leaks even if ice dams occur.

But even when you know some of the causes of a leaky roof, pinpointing the exact location isn't always easy. Water can enter along the chimney, run down the underside of the roof, drip into the attic insulation near the outside wall, and finally appear only after it soaks through the drywall or plaster ceiling at a place far removed from where the leak began. Often you'll have to climb into the attic with a flashlight to trace the path of the leak back to its source.

The best fix is to install the flashing properly. Flashing is the most important part of roofing, but it easily gets shortchanged because

HOW ICE DAMS FORM

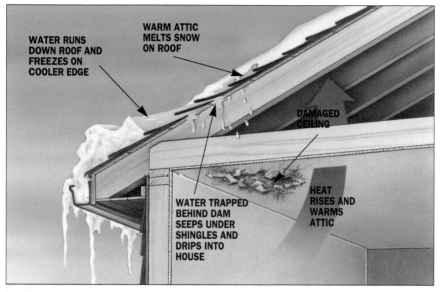

WARM ATTIC MELTS SNOW ON ROOF

WATER RUNS DOWN ROOF AND FREEZES ON COOLER EDGE

DAMAGED CEILING

WATER TRAPPED BEHIND DAM SEEPS UNDER SHINGLES AND DRIPS INTO HOUSE

HEAT RISES AND WARMS ATTIC

Ice dams form when heat escaping from below warms the roof and melts the snow on it. The water refreezes on the edge of the roof, which is colder, and forms a dam. Water trapped behind the dam can soak through the roof and damage the sheathing and eventually leak through ceiling and walls.

it's slow, tedious work that has to be done just so. Roofers, who are usually paid by how many shingles they lay, have little incentive to install the flashing carefully unless you insist and are willing to pay the price.

The importance of ventilation

You also have a certain amount of control over another factor that destroys roofs—heat. Roof temperatures in the American Southwest can hit 200 degrees Fahrenheit, and most roofs in the United States and Canada can hit the 160-degree mark or higher several times each summer. This sizzling heat breaks down the shingles by softening the asphalt and drying them out so that they become more brittle after they have cooled. Years of this abuse take their toll on asphalt roofs.

Reduce the heat buildup on your roof by making sure the attic is well ventilated, which extends the life of the roof. Vents located high near the peak of the roof and in the *soffits*, the undersides of the eaves, allow cool air to enter the soffits, flow along the underside of the roof sheathing, cool the roof, and exit as hot air through the high vents. This airflow can reduce the roof temperature as much as 20 degrees. Attic fans and ridge vents along the top of the roof, common on many houses in the South, ensure even better air flow (*page 133*).

182

DAMAGE CAUSED BY POOR VENTILATION

When an attic has poor ventilation, humid air from the house rises and condenses on the cold roof sheathing and rafters. Wet sheathing rots, and water dripping from nails wets the insulation and discolors the ceiling below. Potentially good ventilation provided by soffit vents has been blocked by insulation improperly stuffed against the roof sheathing.

Roof failure from the inside

After you go through so much trouble to have a new roof installed properly, it hardly seems fair that your roof can fail from the underside, too (*above*). You might investigate a leak and find that the shingles and flashing on the outside are perfectly sound. But in the attic, you may find a number of nails poking through the sheathing where they had been driven when an old roof was removed. At night, those nails will become cold and gather frost from the warmer humid air in the attic. When the roof heats up during the day, the frost melts and drips down onto the ceilings below.

If you are having your house reroofed, insist that the roofers pull all the old nails from previous roofing jobs, not just drive them down into the wood.

Even worse, you might find the underside of the roof sheathing covered with white frost and soaked in places. This icing is caused by warm, humid air from the house below rising up into the attic, causing the moisture to condense on the cold underside of the roof. This is what will eventually cause the roof to rot from the inside. Fortunately, good attic ventilation and closing up those warm air leaks from below should stop the problem.

183

Glossary

Italicized words are defined elsewhere in the glossary.

Aggregate: Stones of assorted sizes mixed with *cement* and sand to make *concrete*.

Ampere: Abbr. amp. A measurement of electrical current moving past a given point in one second.

Baluster: A vertical support for a railing on stairs or balcony.

Batt: An individual, blanket-like section of insulation designed to fit between the standard spaces between wall *studs*. Usually made of spun fiberglass in various thicknesses according to intended *R-value*.

Bearing wall: Any wall, interior or exterior, that supports the weight of a house.

Cement: Made from limestone, clay, and shale. The "glue" that holds together the *aggregate* and sand in *concrete*. Often called "Portland cement."

Circuit: A closed, continuous path for electrical current. The path begins at a power source and returns to that source. Appliances that use electricity tap into the circuit.

Circuit breaker: A switch that turns off current to a circuit when amperage exceeds a certain amount. Usually found in the *main service panel* of a house.

Concrete: A rock-hard building material made from a mixture of *cement*, *aggregate*, and sand.

Crawl space: The low space between the ground and the bottom floor *joists* of a house and surrounded by the foundation wall.

Dead load: The weight of the components that make up a part of a house, e.g., a roof or deck, including all boards, *sheathing*, shin-

gles, etc. (See also *live load*.)

Dormer: A section of roof projecting at a right angle from the main slope of the roof.

Drywall: Material used to finish interior walls. Made by sandwiching finely powdered gypsum between sheets of heavy-duty paper. Standard dimensions for drywall panels are 4 feet wide, 8 feet long, and $\frac{1}{4}$, $\frac{1}{2}$, or $\frac{5}{8}$ inch thick.

Ducts: Metal conduits that distribute warm or cool air in a forced-air heating and cooling system.

DWV system: The drain, waste, and vent pipes of the plumbing system.

Eaves: The part of the roof that projects over the exterior wall of the house.

Equipment ground wire: A bare wire or

wire covered with green plastic insulation that conducts stray electrical charges to the earth.

Flashing: Sheet material, usually metal or plastic, that prevents water from getting between two parts of a house—e.g., between the edge of a chimney and the shingles of a roof.

Flush door: A door with smooth faces that cover the internal *stiles* and *rails*. (See also *panel door*.)

Footing: The base for a foundation or posts. Usually made from *concrete*. It is wider than the object it supports so it distributes weight evenly over a larger area.

Gable: The triangular section of wall at the end of a roof.

Ground fault circuit interrupter: Abbr. GFCI. A safety device that detects leaks in a *circuit* and shuts off current when the current leak exceeds .005 amps.

Header: A heavy horizontal beam placed over a door or window that helps distribute weight around the opening in the wall. Headers must be used in a *bearing wall*.

Joists: Horizontal 2-inch lumber arranged in a grid that supports a floor or ceiling.

Live load: The weight of all unfixed objects on a structure, including people, plants, and furniture. Forces such as wind, snow, and water are also considered live load. (See also *dead load*.)

Low-E windows: Windows with reflective metal coatings on one surface to reflect heat away from the window.

Main service panel: A metal box where the electrical service wires enter the house and divide into various circuits that run throughout the house. The panel contains the *circuit breakers* and the main shutoff switch.

Muntins: Small vertical and horizontal strips of wood, plastic, or metal that separate individual panes of glass in a window *sash*.

Nosing: The section of a stair *tread* that extends beyond the *riser*.

On center: Abbr. o.c. The spacing between the center point of two framing members, such as wall *studs*, *joists*, and *rafters*. Standard spacing is 16 inches o.c. and 24 inches o.c.

Panel door: A door made up of individual rectangular sections divided by *stiles* and *rails*. (See also *flush door*.)

R-value: A measurement of a material's resistance to the transmission of heat. Used as a means of rating the insulation value of a material; the higher the R-value, the better the material insulates.

Rafters: A gridwork of lumber that supports the *sheathing* of a roof. The angle of the rafters determines the slope of the roof.

Rail: A horizontal piece of a door, either exposed in a panel door or hidden under the covering of a flush door. Also, the horizontal top and bottom pieces of a window *sash*. (See also *stile*.)

Riser: The vertical face at the front of a step.

Saddle: Sometimes called a cricket. An angled structure used on the uphill side of a chimney or skylight to channel water around the structure and to prevent snow and ice from building up.

Sash: A single frame of a window containing one or more panes of glass.

Sheathing: Panels of wood used to cover the exterior side of wall *studs* or *rafters*. Usually made from 4x8-foot panels of plywood or waferboard.

Siding: The finished exterior of a house. Can be wood, brick, aluminum, vinyl, stone, or stucco.

Slab: A house foundation consisting of a single layer of concrete poured directly onto the ground.

Slope: The ratio of the rise of the roof surface over a given horizontal distance.

Soffit: The underside of the *eaves*.

Soil stack: A length of the *DWV system* that extends more than one floor in a house and vents to the outside through the roof.

Sole plate: A horizontal board that serves as a base for wall *studs*. It is usually made from a 2x4.

Stile: A vertical piece of a door, either exposed in a panel door or hidden under the face of a flush door. Also, the side pieces of a window *sash*. (See also *rail*.)

Studs: Vertical members of a wall frame. They are usually made from 2x4s, although 2x6s are used in some parts of the frame.

Subfloor: The first layer of flooring, usually made from plywood or waferboard, that is attached directly to the *joists*.

Top plate: The horizontal boards that serve as top supports for wall *studs*. A top plate usually consists of two 2x4s nailed along their lengths.

Trap: A section of drain pipe designed to trap water to prevent sewer gas from entering house through pipes. Most common type is the P-trap.

Tread: The horizontal section of a step.

Vapor retarder: Also called a vapor barrier. Any sheet material used to retard the movement of moisture through a wall, floor, or roof. Usually made from plastic or heavy-duty paper.

Voltage: Abbr. volt. A measurement of electrical pressure in a circuit.

Wattage: Abbr. watt. A measurement of electrical power, i.e., the amount of "work" the electricity is performing.

Weatherstripping: Strips of material that prevent air and moisture from entering a house. Used around the edges of doors and windows or in other joints of a house. Can be made from metal, rubber, foam, or any other air- and water-tight material.

Common Building Standards

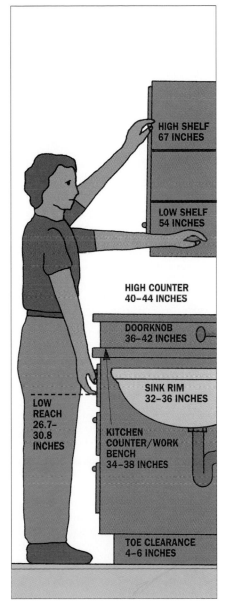

HIGH SHELF
67 INCHES

LOW SHELF
54 INCHES

HIGH COUNTER
40–44 INCHES

DOORKNOB
36–42 INCHES

SINK RIM
32–36 INCHES

LOW
REACH
26.7–
30.8
INCHES

KITCHEN
COUNTER/WORK
BENCH
34–38 INCHES

TOE CLEARANCE
4–6 INCHES

How many times have you reached for the bathroom faucet, turned a doorknob to the bedroom, or placed a box of cereal on the shelf of the kitchen cabinet? These are everyday acts that you don't have to think about because the handles and shelves are within easy reach.

It's not luck or accident that a house is built this way. Just as the rise and run of a staircase are closely regulated by building code (*page 30*) and the height of your ceiling is largely a matter of convenience and economy (*page 32*), the placement of many of the parts of your house are the result of careful study as well as trial and error.

These so-called *anthropometric* standards and measurements, several of which are shown here, are codified by the American Institute of Architects (AIA) and are based on men and women in the 50th percentile of size and height. They assume the person is standing flat footed and wearing shoes. With these standards, a person can gain additional reach by bending down or extending the shoulders and arms; stooping low is easier than stretching high.

The AIA standards are recommendations only; local codes can (and sometimes do) differ from the AIA's. These measurements make it easier for builders and architects to factor in the human element when designing a house.

Wood & Board

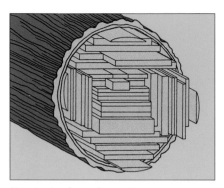

How lumber is cut from a log

Why is a 2x4 not a 2x4?

A 2x4-inch piece of lumber is not actually 2 inches by 4 inches in size—it's 1½ by 3½ inches. In fact, no piece of lumber is the size we say it is. For example, a 2x10 is actually a 1½x9¼. Why is this so?

It's all a result of how the lumber is cut from the tree. Freshly cut lumber still contains a lot of moisture. If it were not dried out, the lumber would be heavy, hard to work with, and subject to twisting and warping as well as rot.

Lumber mills dry the wood, either in the open air or in kilns, to remove most of the moisture. This drying process causes the wood to shrink somewhat, but not consistently from one type of wood to the next, or even from one batch to the next. To ensure consistent sizing and a smoother finish on the surface of the lumber, the mills "dress" or smooth the lumber, which cuts down its dimensions even more. The final result: lumber that is not the same size it was when cut from the log. Such lumber is sold by its "nominal" size, that is, the size it is when cut, but its "actual" size is consistent from one part of the country to the next. The chart shows some nominal size pieces of lumber and their actual-size equivalents.

Nominal	Actual
1x2	¾x1½
1x3	¾x2½
1x4	¾x3½
1x6	¾x5½
1x8	¾x7¼
1x10	¾x9¼
1x12	¾x11¼
2x2	1½x1½
2x4	1½x3½
2x6	1½x5½
2x8	1½x7¼
2x10	1½x9¼
2x12	1½x11¼
4x4	3½x3½
4x10	3½x9¼

How are plywood and other panel products made?

Plywood is the most common of the so-called panel products. It is made by peeling thin layers of wood, called veneers, from a rotating log with a large cutting blade, as shown in the illustration. These veneers are then glued together in layers, called plies (hence *ply*wood), with the grain direction alternated 90 degrees in each ply to give the panel strength in all directions and to lessen the chance of warping. Plywood panels always have an odd number of plies so the grain of the face and back of the panel is going in the same direction.

Plywood is usually sold in 4x8-foot panels ¼, ½, ⅝, or ¾ inch thick. Unlike boards, dimensional lumber, and beams, plywood (and all panel products) are sold only by their actual sizes.

Plywood is graded for either interior or exterior use. The major difference is the glues used between plies. Exterior-grade glues are designed to withstand water and weathering, and exterior-grade plywood is generally used for wall and roof sheathing. Interior-grade is used for subflooring and some interior walls, as well as for cabinets and furniture. Plywood is also graded for appearance, which doesn't matter much for workhorse plywood used as sheathing or flooring—strength is mostly what matters there—but appearance is important in cabinets and furniture.

Another type of panel product is called waferboard. It is made by gluing wood chips and shavings with strong synthetic resins into thin plies. Sometimes those wood shavings are cut into strands, and the strands in each ply are all oriented in generally the same direction, resulting in a product called oriented strand board, or simply OSB. In both waferboard and OSB, the general direction of the wood grain is alternated from one ply to the next, just as in plywood. Waferboard and OSB are usually sold in 4x8-foot panels ¼, ½, or ¾ inch thick; they are mostly used for wall or roof sheathing.

Particleboard and hardboard are made with fine wood chips and fibers that are glued together with synthetic resins under great pressure. They are used for such things as shelving, furniture, and sliding doors. You're probably most familiar with hardboard in the form of pegboard. Both particleboard and hardboard are generally for interior use only, as they begin to disintegrate rapidly if they get wet. (Hardboard is sometimes used as exterior siding, but it must be well protected with caulk and paint. See page 177.)

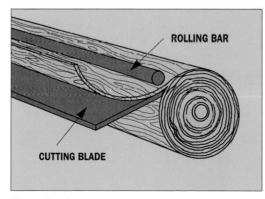

Veneer Peeling

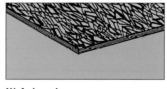

Waferboard

Plywood

Index

LIMITED EDITION
2019

BEST
LENT
EVER®

JOURNAL

WELLSPRING

North Palm Beach, Florida

i

wellspring

Design by Madeline Harris

ISBN: 978-1-63582-026-3 (softcover)

Dynamic Catholic® and Be Bold. Be Catholic.® and The Best Version of
Yourself® are registered trademarks of The Dynamic Catholic Institute.

For more information on this title or other books and CDs available
through the Dynamic Catholic Book Program,
please visit www.DynamicCatholic.com.

The Dynamic Catholic Institute
5081 Olympic Blvd • Erlanger • Kentucky • 41018
Phone: 1–859–980–7900
Email: info@DynamicCatholic.com

LIMITED EDITION

Printed in the United States of America

Make This Your
Best Lent Yet.

"Jesus came, saying, 'The time is fulfilled, and the kingdom of God is at hand; repent, and believe in the gospel.'"

– Mark 1:15

DO YOU BELIEVE?

Will this Lent be your best Lent ever?

We think so. That's why we're here. That's why we made this journal for you.

Believing can be tough, and faith can be scarce, especially when lies—convincing ones—are fed to us over the course of our lives.

We believe this Lent can be your best Lent ever because, together, we will disarm the biggest lie in the history of Christianity.

We believe this Lent can be your best Lent ever because we will walk this journey with you. We will guide you, encourage you, inspire you, and pray for you every step of the way.

This journal was designed to accompany BEST LENT EVER 2019. If you have not signed up yet, we invite you to do so at BestLentEver.com/2019. You'll receive daily videos from Matthew Kelly and the Dynamic Catholic team that will make your Lenten experience even more impactful.

We made this journal to aid you in the internal renewal and growth we hope will come over the next forty days. Lent is a wonderful season of pause. It is a time of reflection and exploration with God in which he works most mysteriously to give us exactly what we need.

To help you with this time of pause, the journal includes questions meant to provoke thought about your faith life and to provide clarity for where you want to go. You will also find daily readings from *The Biggest Lie in the History of Christianity*—the book this program is based on—and daily action steps (including Holy Moment challenges) to incorporate what you learn during your time of reflection into your life.

We know you have a lot on your plate. This journal is meant to give you just a few minutes every day to connect with God and make the absolute most out of the Lenten journey . . . we believe in the power of baby steps.

We believe God will move powerfully in your life during the next forty days as we disarm the lie together.

The question is, what do you believe?

May God bless you and your Lenten journey.

The Dynamic Catholic Team

WHERE ARE YOU GOING?

It's hard to know if you've made it when you don't know where you want to go. Now's your chance to decide what you want to accomplish this Lent.

Is it a regular prayer routine? Is it more self-discipline in a specific area of your life? Is it better communication in your marriage? Is it more peace?

Now's your chance.

Forty days allow you the time to create a new habit that will help you become the-best-version-of-yourself.

Before we get started, take a few minutes to give yourself some direction.

My personal Lenten Habit will be:

This Lent I want to improve in this way:

I will know I have achieved my goal at the end of the forty days if this is true:

I will hold myself accountable to this person:

Remember, you're not alone. We are here cheering you on, and God's grace is always at our disposal. Through prayer and reception of the sacraments, you are well on your way to accomplishing whatever it is God has placed on your heart this Lent.

"Do not be afraid to dream. Perphaps your fear is of failure. There is no shame in trying to attempt mighty things and failing. The shame is in failing to attempt those things."

– Matthew Kelly

DAY 1 | A CALL TO ACTION

Today's Focus:

God has a specific call to action for you, a sweet spot where you can do the most good and be the-best-version-of-yourself.

Personal Reflection:

Watch Matthew Kelly's video and the staff reflection from BEST LENT EVER (BestLentEver.com/Day1) and write down the one thing that most resonates with you.

_____

_____

_____

_____

_____

_____

What is your sweet spot?

_____

_____

_____

_____

_____

_____

_____

_____

My Daily Lenten Habit Tracker

☐ Completed today's **Best Lent Ever reflections**

☐ Wrote personal reflections in my **journal**

☐ Kept my **personal Lenten Habit**

Recommended Reading:

The Biggest Lie
  • This week: chapters 1 & 2
  • Today's focus: pg. 4

Today's Gospel:
  • Matthew 6:1–6, 16–18

DAY 2 | A HUNGER

Today's Focus:
God created you for a joyful, abundant life.

Personal Reflection:
Watch Matthew Kelly's video and the staff reflection from BEST LENT EVER (BestLentEver.com/Day2) and write down the one thing that most resonates with you.

_____

_____

_____

_____

_____

_____

_____

Do you really believe God wants you to be happy?
Why or why not?

_____

_____

_____

_____

_____

_____

_____

_____

"Real happiness is a sign that the human spirit is thriving."

Matthew Kelly,
The Biggest Lie in the History of Christianity

My Daily Lenten Habit Tracker

☐ Completed today's **Best Lent Ever reflections**

☐ Wrote personal reflections in my **journal**

☐ Kept my **personal Lenten Habit**

Recommended Reading:

The Biggest Lie
• This week: chapters 1 & 2
• Today's focus: pg. 8

Today's Gospel:
• Luke 9:22-25

DAY 3 | THE CRICKET BAT

Today's Focus:
The happiness that our culture promises is fleeting.

Personal Reflection:
Watch Matthew Kelly's video and the staff reflection from BEST LENT EVER (BestLentEver.com/Day3) and write down the one thing that most resonates with you.

_____

_____

_____

_____

_____

_____

_____

Having watched today's video from Matthew, what do you think is your "cricket bat"—something that you really wanted but, when you finally got it, made you feel disappointed?

_____

_____

_____

_____

_____

_____

My Daily Lenten Habit Tracker

☐ Completed today's **Best Lent Ever reflections**

☐ Wrote personal reflections in my **journal**

☐ Kept my **personal Lenten Habit**

Recommended Reading:

The Biggest Lie
• This week: chapters 1 & 2
• Today's focus: pg. 10

Today's Gospel:
• Matthew 9:14–15

DAY 4 | A RETURN TO CURIOSITY

Today's Focus:

It is important to be curious about who we are and why we are here.

Personal Reflection:

Watch Matthew Kelly's video and the staff reflection from BEST LENT EVER (BestLentEver.com/Day4) and write down the one thing that most resonates with you.

_____

_____

_____

_____

_____

_____

_____

How do you know who you are?

_____

_____

_____

_____

_____

_____

_____

_____

My Daily Lenten Habit Tracker

☐ Completed today's **Best Lent Ever reflections**

☐ Wrote personal reflections in my **journal**

☐ Kept my **personal Lenten Habit**

Recommended Reading:

The Biggest Lie
  • This week: chapters 1 & 2
  • Today's focus: pg. 13

Today's Gospel:
  • Luke 5:27–32

FIRST SUNDAY OF LENT | THE GREATEST WEAPON

Today's Focus:

Jesus combated temptations with truth.

Personal Reflection:

Watch the Sunday Gospel reflection from BEST LENT EVER (BestLentEver.com/FirstSunday) and write down the one thing that most resonates with you.

_____

_____

_____

_____

_____

_____

How do you handle temptations?

_____

_____

_____

_____

_____

_____

_____

_____

"Jesus, full of the Holy Spirit, returned from the Jordan, and was led by the Spirit for forty days in the wilderness, tempted by the devil."

Luke 4:1–2

My Daily Lenten Habit Tracker

☐ Completed today's **Best Lent Ever reflections**

☐ Wrote personal reflections in my **journal**

☐ Kept my **personal Lenten Habit**

Recommended Reading:

Today's Gospel:
• Luke 4:1-13

DAY 5 | THE GREAT PRETENDERS

Today's Focus:

Being an authentic Christian is about progress, not perfection.

Personal Reflection:

Watch Matthew Kelly's video and the staff reflection from BEST LENT EVER (BestLentEver.com/Day5) and write down the one thing that most resonates with you.

_____

_____

_____

_____

_____

_____

_____

When have you preferred pretending over living?

_____

_____

_____

_____

_____

_____

_____

_____

_____

"Authentic and perfect are not the same thing."

Matthew Kelly,
The Biggest Lie in the History of Christianity

My Daily Lenten Habit Tracker

☐ Completed today's **Best Lent Ever reflections**

☐ Wrote personal reflections in my **journal**

☐ Kept my **personal Lenten Habit**

Recommended Reading:

The Biggest Lie
- This week: chapters 3 & 4
- Today's focus: pg. 17

Today's Gospel:
- Matthew 25:31–46

DAY 6 | THIS IS THE LIE

Today's Focus:

Holiness is possible for you.

Personal Reflection:

Watch Matthew Kelly's video and the staff reflection from BEST LENT EVER (BestLentEver.com/Day6) and write down the one thing that most resonates with you.

_____

_____

_____

_____

_____

_____

What makes it hard for you to believe that holiness is possible for you?

_____

_____

_____

_____

_____

_____

_____

My Daily Lenten Habit Tracker

☐ Completed today's **Best Lent Ever reflections**

☐ Wrote personal reflections in my **journal**

☐ Kept my **personal Lenten Habit**

Recommended Reading:

The Biggest Lie
  • This week: chapters 3 & 4
  • Today's focus: pg. 32

Today's Gospel:
  • Matthew 6:7–15

DAY 7 | THE GREAT PRETENDERS

Today's Focus:
God wants to collaborate with you to create Holy Moments.

Personal Reflection:
Watch Matthew Kelly's video and the staff reflection from BEST LENT EVER (BestLentEver.com/Day7) and write down the one thing that most resonates with you.

When have you experienced a Holy Moment?

"A Holy Moment is a thing of beauty."

Matthew Kelly,
The Biggest Lie in the History of Christianity

My Daily Lenten Habit Tracker

☐ Completed today's **Best Lent Ever reflections**

☐ Wrote personal reflections in my **journal**

☐ Kept my **personal Lenten Habit**

Recommended Reading:

The Biggest Lie
 • This week: chapters 3 & 4
 • Today's focus: pg. 35

Today's Gospel:
 • Luke 11:29–32

DAY 8 | BLURRED LINES

Today's Focus:
There is a direct connection between truth and happiness.

Personal Reflection:
Watch Matthew Kelly's video and the staff reflection from BEST LENT EVER (BestLentEver.com/Day8) and write down the one thing that most resonates with you.

_____

_____

_____

_____

_____

_____

What lie separates you from God?

_____

_____

_____

_____

_____

_____

_____

_____

_____

"Truth is beautiful, and the truth about you is beautiful."

Matthew Kelly,
The Biggest Lie in the History of Christianity

My Daily Lenten Habit Tracker

☐ Completed today's **Best Lent Ever reflections**

☐ Wrote personal reflections in my **journal**

☐ Kept my **personal Lenten Habit**

☐ Collaborated with God to create a **Holy Moment**

Recommended Reading:

The Biggest Lie
• This week: chapters 3 & 4
• Today's focus: pg. 19

Today's Gospel:
• Matthew 7:7–12

DAY 9 | HE LIVED

Today's Focus:

There are lies about Christianity—we need to refute them.

Personal Reflection:

Watch Matthew Kelly's video and the staff reflection from BEST LENT EVER (BestLentEver.com/Day9) and write down the one thing that most resonates with you.

_____

_____

_____

_____

_____

_____

_____

Why do you believe in the person of Jesus? Why do you believe Jesus is who he says he is?

_____

_____

_____

_____

_____

_____

_____

> "For two thousand years, non-Christians have been spreading lies about Christians and Christianity."
>
> Matthew Kelly,
> *The Biggest Lie in the History of Christianity*

My Daily Lenten Habit Tracker

- [ ] Completed today's **Best Lent Ever reflections**
- [ ] Wrote personal reflections in my **journal**
- [ ] Kept my **personal Lenten Habit**
- [ ] Collaborated with God to create a **Holy Moment**

Recommended Reading:

The Biggest Lie
  • This week: chapters 3 & 4
  • Today's focus: pg. 21

Today's Gospel:
  • Matthew 5:20-26

DAY 10 | TRUSTFUL SURRENDER

Today's Focus:

God calls us to surrender.

Personal Reflection:

Watch Matthew Kelly's video and the staff reflection from BEST LENT EVER (BestLentEver.com/Day10) and write down the one thing that most resonates with you.

_____

_____

_____

_____

_____

_____

_____

What is preventing you from making yourself 100 percent available to God right now?

_____

_____

_____

_____

_____

_____

_____

_____

Holy Moment Invitation:

Continue to create one Holy Moment each day. Here are more suggestions:

- Pick up after someone else with a cheerful attitude.
- Give a more generous tip to your waiter or barista.
- Make a special breakfast for yourself and your family.
- Write a friend or family member an encouraging letter.
- Take some items you don't need to a donation center.

"God invites us to a total surrender and we are afraid to let go."

Matthew Kelly,
The Biggest Lie in the History of Christianity

My Daily Lenten Habit Tracker

☐ Completed today's **Best Lent Ever reflections**

☐ Wrote personal reflections in my **journal**

☐ Kept my **personal Lenten Habit**

☐ Collaborated with God to create a **Holy Moment**

Recommended Reading:

The Biggest Lie
- This week: chapters 3 & 4
- Today's focus: pg. 31

Today's Gospel:
- Matthew 5:43–48

SECOND SUNDAY | LISTEN TO HIM

Today's Focus:

God allows us to know him through Jesus.

Personal Reflection:

Watch the Sunday Gospel reflection from BEST LENT EVER (BestLentEver.com/SecondSunday) and write down the one thing that most resonates with you.

_____

_____

_____

_____

_____

_____

_____

How has knowing Jesus changed your life?

_____

_____

_____

_____

_____

_____

_____

_____

_____

My Daily Lenten Habit Tracker

☐ Completed today's **Best Lent Ever reflections**

☐ Wrote personal reflections in my **journal**

☐ Kept my **personal Lenten Habit**

☐ Collaborated with God to create a **Holy Moment**

Recommended Reading:

Today's Gospel:
• Luke 9:28–36

DAY 11 | ONE MOMENT

Today's Focus:

Holiness is possible, one moment at a time.

Personal Reflection:

Watch Matthew Kelly's video and the staff reflection from BEST LENT EVER (BestLentEver.com/Day11) and write down the one thing that most resonates with you.

_____

_____

_____

_____

_____

How do you live life one moment at a time?

_____

_____

_____

_____

_____

_____

My Daily Lenten Habit Tracker

- [ ] Completed today's **Best Lent Ever reflections**
- [ ] Wrote personal reflections in my **journal**
- [ ] Kept my **personal Lenten Habit**
- [ ] Collaborated with God to create a **Holy Moment**

Recommended Reading:

The Biggest Lie
- This week: chapters 5 & 6
- Today's focus: pg. 32

Today's Gospel:
- Luke 6:36-38

DAY 12 | LET'S BE HONEST

Today's Focus:

Being honest with God will deepen your relationship with him in a profound way.

Personal Reflection:

Watch Matthew Kelly's video and the staff reflection from BEST LENT EVER (BestLentEver.com/Day12) and write down the one thing that most resonates with you.

_____

_____

_____

_____

_____

_____

_____

What have you been lying to God about?

_____

_____

_____

_____

_____

_____

_____

_____

_____

> "The heroes, champions, and saints that we place on pedestals would be the first to admit that they did not live holy lives—they lived Holy Moments."
>
> Matthew Kelly,
> *The Biggest Lie in the History of Christianity*

My Daily Lenten Habit Tracker

☐ Completed today's **Best Lent Ever reflections**

☐ Wrote personal reflections in my **journal**

☐ Kept my **personal Lenten Habit**

☐ Collaborated with God to create a **Holy Moment**

Recommended Reading:

The Biggest Lie
  • This week: chapters 5 & 6
  • Today's focus: pg. 35

Today's Gospel:
  • Matthew 1:16, 18–21, 24A

DAY 13 | VIRTUOUS

Today's Focus:

The-best-version-of-yourself celebrates virtue and creates Holy Moments.

Personal Reflection:

Watch Matthew Kelly's video and the staff reflection from BEST LENT EVER (BestLentEver.com/Day13) and write down the one thing that most resonates with you.

_____

_____

_____

_____

_____

_____

_____

Of these three virtues, which would you like to focus on growing in?

patience

generosity

self-control

Holy Moment Invitation:

- Before bed, think of the best part of your day.
- Thank God for that moment.
- Listen to an uplifting song.
- Go somewhere to watch a sunrise or sunset.
- Stand in awe and absorb God's beauty.
- Watch an inspiring movie with family or friends.

"Our mere openness to doing the will of God is pleasing to him."

Matthew Kelly,
The Biggest Lie in the History of Christianity

My Daily Lenten Habit Tracker

- ☐ Completed today's **Best Lent Ever reflections**
- ☐ Wrote personal reflections in my **journal**
- ☐ Kept my **personal Lenten Habit**
- ☐ Collaborated with God to create a **Holy Moment**

Recommended Reading:

The Biggest Lie
- This week: chapters 5 & 6
- Today's focus: pg. 39

Today's Gospel:
- Matthew 20:17-28

DAY 14 | NECESSARY | POSSIBLE | IMPOSSIBLE

Today's Focus:

We need God's grace.

Personal Reflection:

Watch Matthew Kelly's video and the staff reflection from BEST LENT EVER (BestLentEver.com/Day14) and write down the one thing that most resonates with you.

_____

_____

_____

_____

_____

_____

When have you been aware of grace at work in your life?

_____

_____

_____

_____

_____

_____

_____

_____

My Daily Lenten Habit Tracker

☐ Completed today's **Best Lent Ever reflections**

☐ Wrote personal reflections in my **journal**

☐ Kept my **personal Lenten Habit**

☐ Collaborated with God to create a **Holy Moment**

Recommended Reading:

The Biggest Lie
• This week: chapters 5 & 6
• Today's focus: pg. 40

Today's Gospel:
• Luke 16:19–31

DAY 15 | BE THE CHANGE

Today's Focus:

The world needs changing, and it is unlikely to happen unless Christians come together to be the change.

Personal Reflection:

Watch Matthew Kelly's video and the staff reflection from BEST LENT EVER (BestLentEver.com/Day15) and write down the one thing that most resonates with you.

_____

_____

_____

_____

_____

_____

_____

What change would you most like to see in our culture?

_____

_____

_____

_____

_____

_____

_____

_____

_____

My Daily Lenten Habit Tracker

☐ Completed today's **Best Lent Ever reflections**

☐ Wrote personal reflections in my **journal**

☐ Kept my **personal Lenten Habit**

☐ Collaborated with God to create a **Holy Moment**

Recommended Reading:

The Biggest Lie
  • This week: chapters 5 & 6
  • Today's focus: pg. 41

Today's Gospel:
  • Matthew 21:33–43, 45–46

DAY 16 | BLOOM WHERE YOU'RE PLANTED

Today's Focus:

Your marriage, your children, your friends, your work . . . every area of your life needs Holy Moments.

Personal Reflection:

Watch Matthew Kelly's video and the staff reflection from BEST LENT EVER (BestLentEver.com/Day16) and write down the one thing that most resonates with you.

What area in your life needs Holy Moments the most right now?

My Daily Lenten Habit Tracker

☐ Completed today's **Best Lent Ever reflections**

☐ Wrote personal reflections in my **journal**

☐ Kept my **personal Lenten Habit**

☐ Collaborated with God to create a **Holy Moment**

Recommended Reading:

The Biggest Lie
- This week: chapters 5 & 6
- Today's focus: pg. 41

Today's Gospel:
- Luke 15:1-3, 11-32

THIRD SUNDAY | WHERE IS THE FRUIT?

Today's Focus:

Jesus calls us to repent and to change.

Personal Reflection:

Watch the Sunday Gospel reflection from BEST LENT EVER (BestLentEver.com/ThirdSunday) and write down the one thing that most resonates with you.

_____

_____

_____

_____

_____

_____

_____

What area of your life would you most like to bear fruit right now? How can you cooperate with God to achieve that?

_____

_____

_____

_____

_____

_____

_____

> "But unless you repent you will all likewise perish."
>
> Luke 13:3

My Daily Lenten Habit Tracker

- ☐ Completed today's **Best Lent Ever reflections**
- ☐ Wrote personal reflections in my **journal**
- ☐ Kept my **personal Lenten Habit**
- ☐ Collaborated with God to create a **Holy Moment**

Recommended Reading:

Today's Gospel:
- Luke 13:1–9

DAY 17 | TINY BUT MIGHTY

Today's Focus:

The majority of Holy Moments are small and anonymous.

Personal Reflection:

Watch Matthew Kelly's video and the staff reflection from BEST LENT EVER (BestLentEver.com/Day17) and write down the one thing that most resonates with you.

_____

_____

_____

_____

_____

_____

_____

What do you do that makes the world a better place?

_____

_____

_____

_____

_____

_____

_____

_____

Holy Moment Invitation:

- Cook a meal for a coworker who lost a family member, just had surgery, or is expecting a child.
- Fast from sweets or alcohol for a day.
- Pray for someone who cuts you off in traffic.
- Ask your kids where they saw God's love for them today.

"For this is the will of God, your sanctification."

1 Thessalonians 4:3

My Daily Lenten Habit Tracker

- ☐ Completed today's **Best Lent Ever reflections**
- ☐ Wrote personal reflections in my **journal**
- ☐ Kept my **personal Lenten Habit**
- ☐ Collaborated with God to create a **Holy Moment**

Recommended Reading:

The Biggest Lie
- This week: chapters 7 & 8
- Today's focus: pg. 50

Today's Gospel:
- Luke 15:1-3, 11-32

DAY 18 | THE GREAT ENCOURAGER

Today's Focus:

We are a people of possibility, and the Holy Spirit is our great encourager.

Personal Reflection:

Watch Matthew Kelly's video and the staff reflection from BEST LENT EVER (BestLentEver.com/Day18) and write down the one thing that most resonates with you.

_____
_____
_____
_____
_____
_____
_____

How can you be a person of possibility?

_____
_____
_____
_____
_____
_____
_____

> "Each Holy Moment brings with it an injection of joy. Each Holy Moment is its own reward."
>
> Matthew Kelly,
> *The Biggest Lie in the History of Christianity*

My Daily Lenten Habit Tracker

☐ Completed today's **Best Lent Ever reflections**

☐ Wrote personal reflections in my **journal**

☐ Kept my **personal Lenten Habit**

☐ Collaborated with God to create a **Holy Moment**

Recommended Reading:

The Biggest Lie
- This week: chapters 7 & 8
- Today's focus: pg. 52

Today's Gospel:
- Matthew 18:21–35

DAY 19 | THE DIFFERENCE MAKER

Today's Focus:

Unless we can differentiate ourselves, we will not transform our culture.

Personal Reflection:

Watch Matthew Kelly's video and the staff reflection from BEST LENT EVER (BestLentEver.com/Day18) and write down the one thing that most resonates with you.

_____

_____

_____

_____

_____

_____

How do you differentiate yourself from the culture?

_____

_____

_____

_____

_____

_____

_____

_____

> "The world needs to be transformed, and nobody is in a better position to do that than Christians."
>
> Matthew Kelly,
> *The Biggest Lie in the History of Christianity*

My Daily Lenten Habit Tracker

☐ Completed today's **Best Lent Ever reflections**

☐ Wrote personal reflections in my **journal**

☐ Kept my **personal Lenten Habit**

☐ Collaborated with God to create a **Holy Moment**

Recommended Reading:

The Biggest Lie
 • This week: chapters 7 & 8
 • Today's focus: pg. 55

Today's Gospel:
 • Matthew 5:17–19

DAY 20 | ONE HUNDRED PERCENT

Today's Focus:

In order to bring Christianity back to the center of the culture we need to unite behind a 100 percent issue.

Personal Reflection:

Watch Matthew Kelly's video and the staff reflection from BEST LENT EVER (BestLentEver.com/Day20) and write down the one thing that most resonates with you.

_____

_____

_____

_____

_____

_____

_____

When have you experienced the power of self-denial?

_____

_____

_____

_____

_____

_____

_____

_____

"The future of Christianity around the world depends on unity."

Matthew Kelly,
The Biggest Lie in the History of Christianity

My Daily Lenten Habit Tracker

☐ Completed today's **Best Lent Ever reflections**

☐ Wrote personal reflections in my **journal**

☐ Kept my **personal Lenten Habit**

☐ Collaborated with God to create a **Holy Moment**

Recommended Reading:

The Biggest Lie
- This week: chapters 7 & 8
- Today's focus: pg. 58

Today's Gospel:
- Luke 11:14–23

DAY 21 | THE UNDERDOG

Today's Focus:

The world has written Christianity off, but we are an Easter people—a people of possibility.

Personal Reflection:

Watch Matthew Kelly's video and the staff reflection from BEST LENT EVER (BestLentEver.com/Day21) and write down the one thing that most resonates with you.

_____

_____

_____

_____

_____

_____

When has God challenged your idea of what is possible?

_____

_____

_____

_____

_____

_____

_____

_____

"It is time for a
Christian comeback."

Matthew Kelly,
*The Biggest Lie in the
History of Christianity*

My Daily Lenten Habit Tracker

☐ Completed today's **Best Lent Ever reflections**

☐ Wrote personal reflections in my **journal**

☐ Kept my **personal Lenten Habit**

☐ Collaborated with God to create a **Holy Moment**

Recommended Reading:

The Biggest Lie
- This week: chapters 7 & 8
- Today's focus: pg. 60

Today's Gospel:
- Mark 12:28–34

DAY 22 | THE WRONG SOLUTION

Today's Focus:

We can't solve spiritual problems with worldly solutions.

Personal Reflection:

Watch Matthew Kelly's video and the staff reflection from BEST LENT EVER (BestLentEver.com/Day22) and write down the one thing that most resonates with you.

_____

_____

_____

_____

_____

_____

_____

_____

Have you ever tried to solve a spiritual problem with a worldly solution?

_____

_____

_____

_____

_____

_____

_____

_____

> "Will Christians sit idly by, or will we do everything in our power to ensure that followers of Jesus Christ are free to live his teachings for generations to come?"
>
> Matthew Kelly,
> *The Biggest Lie in the History of Christianity*

My Daily Lenten Habit Tracker

- ☐ Completed today's **Best Lent Ever reflections**
- ☐ Wrote personal reflections in my **journal**
- ☐ Kept my **personal Lenten Habit**
- ☐ Collaborated with God to create a **Holy Moment**

Recommended Reading:

The Biggest Lie
- This week: chapters 7 & 8
- Today's focus: pg. 62

Today's Gospel:
- Luke 18:9–14

FOURTH SUNDAY | THE RETURN

Today's Focus:

God runs to us—even after we wander from him.

Personal Reflection:

Watch the Sunday Gospel reflection from BEST LENT EVER (BestLentEver.com/FourthSunday) and write down the one thing that most resonates with you.

_____

_____

_____

_____

_____

_____

_____

Today, as Jesus narrates the parable of the return of the prodigal son, which character do you most relate to? Why?

_____

_____

_____

_____

_____

_____

_____

> "His father saw him and had compassion, and ran and embraced him and kissed him."
>
> Luke 15:20

My Daily Lenten Habit Tracker

- ☐ Completed today's **Best Lent Ever reflections**
- ☐ Wrote personal reflections in my **journal**
- ☐ Kept my **personal Lenten Habit**
- ☐ Collaborated with God to create a **Holy Moment**

Recommended Reading:

Today's Gospel:
- Luke 15:1–3, 11–32

DAY 23 | BEAUTIFUL CONTEXT

Today's Focus:

Our faith puts everything in context—this shows us the true value of things.

Personal Reflection:

Watch Matthew Kelly's video and the staff reflection from BEST LENT EVER (BestLentEver.com/Day23) and write down the one thing that most resonates with you.

_____

_____

_____

_____

_____

_____

_____

When has God rearranged your priorities?

_____

_____

_____

_____

_____

_____

_____

_____

Holy Moment Invitation:

- Put away your phone when you get home.
- Make a budget for the upcoming month.
- Ask a friend or family member how you can pray for them this week.
- Make an effort to truly listen to whomever speaks with you today.

"It's time for Christians to astound the world with our generosity, kindness, patience, courage, thoughtfulness and selfless care for the weak, poor, and forgotten."

Matthew Kelly,
The Biggest Lie in the History of Christianity

My Daily Lenten Habit Tracker

☐ Completed today's **Best Lent Ever reflections**

☐ Wrote personal reflections in my **journal**

☐ Kept my **personal Lenten Habit**

☐ Collaborated with God to create a **Holy Moment**

Recommended Reading:

The Biggest Lie
- This week: chapters 9 & 10
- Today's focus: pg. 68

Today's Gospel:
- John 4:43–54

DAY 24 | HOLY ATTRACTION

Today's Focus:

There is nothing more attractive than holiness.

Personal Reflection:

Watch Matthew Kelly's video and the staff reflection from BEST LENT EVER (BestLentEver.com/Day24) and write down the one thing that most resonates with you.

_____

_____

_____

_____

_____

_____

_____

When have you been attracted to holiness?

_____

_____

_____

_____

_____

_____

_____

_____

My Daily Lenten Habit Tracker

☐ Completed today's **Best Lent Ever reflections**

☐ Wrote personal reflections in my **journal**

☐ Kept my **personal Lenten Habit**

☐ Collaborated with God to create a **Holy Moment**

Recommended Reading:

The Biggest Lie
- This week: chapters 9 & 10
- Today's focus: pg. 69

Today's Gospel:
- John 5:1–16

DAY 25 | AN ABILITY TO DESIRE

Today's Focus:

The early Christians had something the people of their time needed and wanted.

Personal Reflection:

Watch Matthew Kelly's video and the staff reflection from BEST LENT EVER (BestLentEver.com/Day25) and write down the one thing that most resonates with you.

_____

_____

_____

_____

_____

_____

_____

What do you have that the people around you desperately need today?

_____

_____

_____

_____

_____

_____

_____

> "The first Christians presented a radical alternative to the people of their time."
>
> Matthew Kelly,
> *The Biggest Lie in the History of Christianity*

My Daily Lenten Habit Tracker

☐ Completed today's **Best Lent Ever reflections**

☐ Wrote personal reflections in my **journal**

☐ Kept my **personal Lenten Habit**

☐ Collaborated with God to create a **Holy Moment**

Recommended Reading:

The Biggest Lie
• This week: chapters 9 & 10
• Today's focus: pg. 70

Today's Gospel:
• John 5:17–30

DAY 26 | ATTRACTION FOR PROMOTION

Today's Focus:

Christianity has always been about attraction rather than promotion.

Personal Reflection:

Watch Matthew Kelly's video and the staff reflection from BEST LENT EVER (BestLentEver.com/Day26) and write down the one thing that most resonates with you.

_____

_____

_____

_____

_____

_____

What attracted you to Christianity?

_____

_____

_____

_____

_____

_____

_____

_____

"We need to show the people of our time what it truly means to be Christian, by living authentic Christian lives."

Matthew Kelly,
The Biggest Lie in the History of Christianity

My Daily Lenten Habit Tracker

☐ Completed today's **Best Lent Ever reflections**

☐ Wrote personal reflections in my **journal**

☐ Kept my **personal Lenten Habit**

☐ Collaborated with God to create a **Holy Moment**

Recommended Reading:

The Biggest Lie
• This week: chapters 9 & 10
• Today's focus: pg. 72

Today's Gospel:
• John 5:31–47

DAY 27 | THE GOOD DOCTOR

Today's Focus:

The way to create a new and authentic image of Christianity is to make it about others and address their human needs first.

Personal Reflection:

Watch Matthew Kelly's video and the staff reflection from BEST LENT EVER (BestLentEver.com/Day27) and write down the one thing that most resonates with you.

_____

_____

_____

_____

_____

_____

Who has been a "good doctor" in your life?

_____

_____

_____

_____

_____

_____

_____

_____

Holy Moment Invitation:

- Get up a few minutes earlier to read a good book or sit in the classroom of silence.
- Take a deep breath when you find yourself feeling overwhelmed or frustrated.
- Take a day—or even a weekend—off from social media.
- Make someone laugh.

"If we are serious about transforming the culture, we need to get out in the culture."

Matthew Kelly,
The Biggest Lie in the History of Christianity

My Daily Lenten Habit Tracker

☐ Completed today's **Best Lent Ever reflections**

☐ Wrote personal reflections in my **journal**

☐ Kept my **personal Lenten Habit**

☐ Collaborated with God to create a **Holy Moment**

Recommended Reading:

The Biggest Lie
- This week: chapters 9 & 10
- Today's focus: pg. 73

Today's Gospel:
- John 5:31–47

DAY 28 | TEN THINGS

Today's Focus:

Every one of us walks into church with important things on our minds—God wants us to bring them to him.

Personal Reflection:

Watch Matthew Kelly's video and the staff reflection from BEST LENT EVER (BestLentEver.com/Day28) and write down the one thing that most resonates with you.

_____

_____

_____

_____

_____

_____

_____

What is The Question you are grappling with the most right now?

_____

_____

_____

_____

_____

_____

_____

_____

My Daily Lenten Habit Tracker

☐ Completed today's **Best Lent Ever reflections**

☐ Wrote personal reflections in my **journal**

☐ Kept my **personal Lenten Habit**

☐ Collaborated with God to create a **Holy Moment**

Recommended Reading:

The Biggest Lie
- This week: chapters 9 & 10
- Today's focus: pg. 74-76

Today's Gospel:
- John 7:40-53

FIFTH SUNDAY | A STONE'S THROW

Today's Focus:
Jesus does not seek to condemn but to love.

Personal Reflection:
Watch the Sunday Gospel reflection from BEST LENT EVER (BestLentEver.com/FifthSunday) and write down the one thing that most resonates with you.

_____

_____

_____

_____

_____

_____

When have you felt condemned in your own life? When was a time you really felt loved?

_____

_____

_____

_____

_____

_____

> "He stood up and said to them, 'Let him who is without sin among you be the first to throw a stone at her.'"
>
> John 8:7

My Daily Lenten Habit Tracker

☐ Completed today's **Best Lent Ever reflections**

☐ Wrote personal reflections in my **journal**

☐ Kept my **personal Lenten Habit**

☐ Collaborated with God to create a **Holy Moment**

Recommended Reading:

Today's Gospel:
• John 8:1–11

DAY 29 | A HUMAN PERSON

Today's Focus:

Jesus shares our humanity. He is closer to us and more like us than we often realize.

Personal Reflection:

Watch Matthew Kelly's video and the staff reflection from BEST LENT EVER (BestLentEver.com/Day29) and write down the one thing that most resonates with you.

_____

_____

_____

_____

_____

_____

_____

When has Jesus addressed your human need?

_____

_____

_____

_____

_____

_____

_____

_____

> "Every person who crosses the threshold into church on Sunday is looking for answers and carrying a burden of some kind."
>
> Matthew Kelly,
> *The Biggest Lie in the History of Christianity*

My Daily Lenten Habit Tracker

☐ Completed today's **Best Lent Ever reflections**

☐ Wrote personal reflections in my **journal**

☐ Kept my **personal Lenten Habit**

☐ Collaborated with God to create a **Holy Moment**

Recommended Reading:

The Biggest Lie
  • This week: chapters 11 & 12
  • Today's focus: pg. 77

Today's Gospel:
  • John 8:12–20

DAY 30 | REPUTATION

Today's Focus:

Christianity does not have a good reputation today for helping others—it's up to us to change that.

Personal Reflection:

Watch Matthew Kelly's video and the staff reflection from BEST LENT EVER (BestLentEver.com/Day30) and write down the one thing that most resonates with you.

_____

_____

_____

_____

_____

_____

Have you ever witnessed a miracle?

_____

_____

_____

_____

_____

_____

_____

> "Encouragement is one of the primary responsibilities of the Church and every Christian community."
>
> Matthew Kelly,
> *The Biggest Lie in the History of Christianity*

My Daily Lenten Habit Tracker

☐ Completed today's **Best Lent Ever reflections**

☐ Wrote personal reflections in my **journal**

☐ Kept my **personal Lenten Habit**

☐ Collaborated with God to create a **Holy Moment**

Recommended Reading:

The Biggest Lie
• This week: chapters 11 & 12
• Today's focus: pg. 78

Today's Gospel:
• John 8:21–30

DAY 31 | SERVING POWERFULLY

Today's Focus:

God wants us to serve the people of our own time and place and to serve them powerfully.

Personal Reflection:

Watch Matthew Kelly's video and the staff reflection from BEST LENT EVER (BestLentEver.com/Day31) and write down the one thing that resonates with you the most.

_____

_____

_____

_____

_____

_____

_____

When have you chosen to get involved with someone else's "mess"?

_____

_____

_____

_____

_____

Holy Moment Invitation:

- Say "I love you" when you don't feel like it.
- Say a decade of the rosary.
- Offer someone your seat in a crowded room.
- Turn off the music to say a prayer after driving past a car accident.

> "There is no contest between what authentic Christian communities have to offer and what this distorted and morally bankrupt modern secular culture has to offer people."
>
> Matthew Kelly,
> *The Biggest Lie in the History of Christianity*

My Daily Lenten Habit Tracker

☐ Completed today's **Best Lent Ever reflections**

☐ Wrote personal reflections in my **journal**

☐ Kept my **personal Lenten Habit**

☐ Collaborated with God to create a **Holy Moment**

Recommended Reading:

The Biggest Lie
- This week: chapters 11 & 12
- Today's focus: pg. 79

Today's Gospel:
- John 8:31–42

DAY 32 | A MOMENT OF FORGIVENESS

Today's Focus:

Forgiveness is one of the most difficult and powerful Holy Moments.

Personal Reflection:

Watch Matthew Kelly's video and the staff reflection from BEST LENT EVER (BestLentEver.com/Day32) and write down the one thing that most resonates with you.

_____

_____

_____

_____

_____

_____

Whom do you need to forgive?

_____

_____

_____

_____

_____

_____

_____

_____

My Daily Lenten Habit Tracker

☐ Completed today's **Best Lent Ever reflections**

☐ Wrote personal reflections in my **journal**

☐ Kept my **personal Lenten Habit**

☐ Collaborated with God to create a **Holy Moment**

Recommended Reading:

The Biggest Lie
• This week: chapters 11 & 12
• Today's focus: pg. 83

Today's Gospel:
• John 8:51-59

DAY 33 | A WAKE-UP CALL

Today's Focus:

It is easy for us to sleepwalk through life and miss things. The Gospel is our wake-up call.

Personal Reflection:

Watch Matthew Kelly's video and the staff reflection from BEST LENT EVER (BestLentEver.com/Day33) and write down the one thing that most resonates with you.

_____

_____

_____

_____

_____

_____

_____

When have you received a wake-up call in your life?

_____

_____

_____

_____

_____

_____

_____

_____

> "Sometimes we are just sleepwalking through life, completely unaware of the extraordinary people, moments, and possibilities that surround us."
>
> Matthew Kelly,
> *The Biggest Lie in the History of Christianity*

My Daily Lenten Habit Tracker

- ☐ Completed today's **Best Lent Ever reflections**
- ☐ Wrote personal reflections in my **journal**
- ☐ Kept my **personal Lenten Habit**
- ☐ Collaborated with God to create a **Holy Moment**

Recommended Reading:

The Biggest Lie
- This week: chapters 11 & 12
- Today's focus: pg. 84

Today's Gospel:
- John 10:31-42

DAY 34 | NO EXCUSES

Today's Focus:

We often are discouraged or tempted to make excuses and justifications as to why we can't live the faith.

Personal Reflection:

Watch Matthew Kelly's video and the staff reflection from BEST LENT EVER (BestLentEver.com/Day34) and write down the one thing that most resonates with you.

_____

_____

_____

_____

_____

What is your favorite excuse?

_____

_____

_____

_____

_____

_____

_____

My Daily Lenten Habit Tracker

☐ Completed today's **Best Lent Ever reflections**

☐ Wrote personal reflections in my **journal**

☐ Kept my **personal Lenten Habit**

☐ Collaborated with God to create a **Holy Moment**

Recommended Reading:

The Biggest Lie
- This week: chapters 11 & 12
- Today's focus: pg. 89

Today's Gospel:
- John 11:45–56

PALM SUNDAY | WHEN DARKNESS REIGNS

Today's Focus:

The Passion of Jesus was the world's darkest moment.

Personal Reflection:

Watch the Sunday Gospel reflection from BEST LENT EVER (BestLentEver.com/PalmSunday) and write down the one thing that most resonates with you.

_____

_____

_____

_____

_____

_____

When have you felt darkness overwhelm you in life? What got you through those times?

_____

_____

_____

_____

_____

_____

_____

> "Then Jesus, crying with a loud voice, said, 'Father, into thy hands I commit my spirit!' And having said this he breathed his last."
>
> Luke 23:46

My Daily Lenten Habit Tracker

- ☐ Completed today's **Best Lent Ever reflections**
- ☐ Wrote personal reflections in my **journal**
- ☐ Kept my **personal Lenten Habit**
- ☐ Collaborated with God to create a **Holy Moment**

Recommended Reading:

Today's Gospel:
  • Luke 22:14–23:56

DAY 35 | TWELVE HOLY MEN

Today's Focus:
As Christians we are called to discipleship.

Personal Reflection:
Watch Matthew Kelly's video and the staff reflection from BEST LENT EVER (BestLentEver.com/Day35) and write down the one thing that most resonates with you.

_____

_____

_____

_____

_____

_____

_____

When have you seen spiritual multiplication at work in your own life?

_____

_____

_____

_____

_____

_____

Holy Moment Invitation:

In preparation for Easter, consider some of these Holy Moment ideas:

- Attend daily Mass.
- Go to Confession.
- Watch The Passion of the Christ.
- Fast on Good Friday.

"We have one collective mission: to go out and transform the world by making disciples of every nation."

Matthew Kelly,
The Biggest Lie in the History of Christianity

My Daily Lenten Habit Tracker

☐ Completed today's **Best Lent Ever reflections**

☐ Wrote personal reflections in my **journal**

☐ Kept my **personal Lenten Habit**

☐ Collaborated with God to create a **Holy Moment**

Recommended Reading:

The Biggest Lie
- This week: chapters 13, 14, & 15
- Today's focus: pg. 92-95

Today's Gospel:
- John 12:1-11

DAY 36 | DIRTY LITTLE SECRET

Today's Focus:

Our dirty little secret is that we don't want our lives to be transformed.

Personal Reflection:

Watch Matthew Kelly's video and the staff reflection from BEST LENT EVER (BestLentEver.com/Day36) and write down the one thing that most resonates with you.

_____

_____

_____

_____

_____

_____

_____

How do you resist God's invitation to transform your life?

_____

_____

_____

_____

_____

_____

_____

My Daily Lenten Habit Tracker

☐ Completed today's **Best Lent Ever reflections**

☐ Wrote personal reflections in my **journal**

☐ Kept my **personal Lenten Habit**

☐ Collaborated with God to create a **Holy Moment**

Recommended Reading:

The Biggest Lie
- This week: chapters 13, 14, & 15
- Today's focus: pg. 97-99

Today's Gospel:
- John 13:21-33, 36-38

DAY 37 | GOD'S CRITERIA

Today's Focus:

God uses the type of people who make themselves available to him.

Personal Reflection:

Watch Matthew Kelly's video and the staff reflection from BEST LENT EVER (BestLentEver.com/Day37) and write down the one thing that most resonates with you.

_____

_____

_____

_____

_____

_____

_____

When has God's way taken you by surprise?

_____

_____

_____

_____

_____

_____

_____

_____

> "Availability is what God looks for in the résumé of our hearts."
>
> Matthew Kelly,
> *The Biggest Lie in the History of Christianity*

My Daily Lenten Habit Tracker

- ☐ Completed today's **Best Lent Ever reflections**
- ☐ Wrote personal reflections in my **journal**
- ☐ Kept my **personal Lenten Habit**
- ☐ Collaborated with God to create a **Holy Moment**

Recommended Reading:

The Biggest Lie
- This week: chapters 13, 14, & 15
- Today's focus: pg. 101

Today's Gospel:
- Matthew 26:14–25

HOLY THURSDAY | THE BIGGEST MISTAKE

Today's Focus:

There will be obstacles to the transformation God wants for you. The biggest mistake we can make is relying on ourselves.

Personal Reflection:

Watch Matthew Kelly's video and the staff reflection from BEST LENT EVER (BestLentEver.com/HolyThursday) and write down the one thing that most resonates with you.

_____

_____

_____

_____

_____

_____

_____

When have you relied too much on yourself instead of others or God?

_____

_____

_____

_____

_____

_____

_____

_____

> "God has a mighty, awesome, wonderful transformation in mind for you."
>
> Matthew Kelly,
> *The Biggest Lie in the History of Christianity*

My Daily Lenten Habit Tracker

☐ Completed today's **Best Lent Ever reflections**

☐ Wrote personal reflections in my **journal**

☐ Kept my **personal Lenten Habit**

☐ Collaborated with God to create a **Holy Moment**

Recommended Reading:

The Biggest Lie
- This week: chapters 13, 14, & 15
- Today's focus: pg. 103

Today's Gospel:
- Luke 4:16–21

GOOD FRIDAY | HEARTS ON FIRE

Today's Focus:

People won't do anything until they are inspired, but once they are inspired there is almost nothing they won't do.

Personal Reflection:

Watch Matthew Kelly's video and the staff reflection from BEST LENT EVER (BestLentEver.com/GoodFriday) and write down the one thing that most resonates with you.

_____

_____

_____

_____

_____

_____

_____

What inspires you?

_____

_____

_____

_____

_____

_____

_____

_____

> "God has a mighty, awesome, wonderful transformation in mind for you."
>
> Matthew Kelly,
> *The Biggest Lie in the History of Christianity*

My Daily Lenten Habit Tracker

- ☐ Completed today's **Best Lent Ever reflections**
- ☐ Wrote personal reflections in my **journal**
- ☐ Kept my **personal Lenten Habit**
- ☐ Collaborated with God to create a **Holy Moment**

Recommended Reading:

The Biggest Lie
- This week: chapters 13, 14, & 15
- Today's focus: pg. 107

Today's Gospel:
- John 18:1–19:42

HOLY SATURDAY | GOD SAID

Today's Focus:

God never stops speaking to us, but often we stop listening.

Personal Reflection:

Watch Matthew Kelly's video and the staff reflection from BEST LENT EVER (BestLentEver.com/HolySaturday) and write down the one thing that most resonates with you.

_____

_____

_____

_____

_____

_____

What is one thing God has helped you discover this Lent?

_____

_____

_____

_____

_____

_____

_____

"If we can drag ourselves away from the crazy, noisy, busy world and step into the classroom of silence, God will speak to us in this place and this time."

Matthew Kelly,
The Biggest Lie in the History of Christianity

My Daily Lenten Habit Tracker

☐ Completed today's **Best Lent Ever reflections**

☐ Wrote personal reflections in my **journal**

☐ Kept my **personal Lenten Habit**

☐ Collaborated with God to create a **Holy Moment**

Recommended Reading:

The Biggest Lie
- This week: chapters 13, 14, & 15
- Today's focus: pg. 108

Today's Gospel:
- Luke 24:1-12

EASTER SUNDAY | VICTORIOUS

Today's Focus:

If you take part in the movement of creating Holy Moments, something incredible will happen.

Personal Reflection:

Watch today's Easter video (BestLentEver.com/Easter) and write down the one thing that most resonates with you.

_____

_____

_____

_____

_____

_____

_____

How can your life be changed by the news that Jesus brings life out of death?

_____

_____

_____

_____

_____

_____

_____

My Daily Lenten Habit Tracker

☐ Completed today's **Best Lent Ever reflections**

☐ Wrote personal reflections in my **journal**

☐ Kept my **personal Lenten Habit**

☐ Collaborated with God to create a **Holy Moment**

Recommended Reading:

Today's Gospel:
  • John 20:1–9

CONCLUSION

Happy, happy Easter! We hope this journey to the Resurrection has been life-giving and resulted in a personal resurrection for you, too.

The good news is this is just the beginning. There are innumerable Holy Moments awaiting you. You have a mission—becoming the-best-version-of-yourself. We hope you accept it, and we hope you'll let us continue to walk with you in this wondrous journey.

God bless,

The Dynamic Catholic Team

For more world-class resources on the Catholic faith and becoming the-best-version-of-yourself, visit DynamicCatholic.com/Resources.

How many people do you know who could benefit from reading this book?

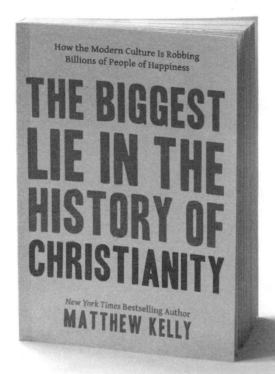

Visit **DynamicCatholic.com** and request **SIX** copies for just $18.

NOTES

NOTES

NOTES

NOTES

NOTES

NOTES

NOTES

NOTES

NOTES

NOTES

NOTES

NOTES

NOTES

NOTES

HAVE YOU EVER WONDERED HOW THE CATHOLIC FAITH COULD HELP YOU LIVE BETTER?

How it could help you find more *joy* at work, *manage* your personal finances, *improve* your marriage, or make you a *better* parent?

THERE IS GENIUS IN CATHOLICISM.

When *Catholicism* is lived as it is intended to be, it elevates every part of our lives. It may sound simple, but they say *genius is taking something complex and making it simple.*

Dynamic Catholic started with a dream: to help ordinary people discover the *genius of Catholicism.*

Wherever you are in your journey, we want to meet you there and walk with you, *step by step*, helping you to discover God and become *the-best-version-of-yourself.*

To find more helpful resources, visit us online at DynamicCatholic.com.

 **Dynamic Catholic**

FEED YOUR SOUL.